Renew online at
www.librarieswest.org.uk
or by phoning any Bristol library

Bristol Libraries

THE SCOURGE OF SOHO

DICK KIRBY
has also written

Rough Justice – Memoirs of a
Flying Squad Detective

'… the continuing increase in violent crime will make many readers yearn for yesteryear and officers of Dick Kirby's calibre'. POLICE MAGAZINE

The Real Sweeney

'Its no-nonsense portrayal of life in the police will give readers a memorable literary experience'. SUFFOLK JOURNAL

You're Nicked!

'In *You're Nicked!* he describes his hair-raising adventures … with an equal measure of black humour and humanity'. NEWHAM RECORDER

Villains

'This is magic. The artfulness of these anti-heroes has you pining for the bad old days'. DAILY SPORT

The Guv'nors

'They were heroes at times when heroes were desperately needed'. AMERICAN POLICE BEAT

The Sweeney

'It's a rollercoaster ride; detectives took crime by the scruff of its neck and wouldn't let go'. EAST ANGLIAN DAILY TIMES

Scotland Yard's Ghost Squad

'… the fascinating true story of a talented squad of gang-busting detectives who were there when special deeds were essential. Dick Kirby … knows how to bring his coppers to life on the page'. JOSEPH WAMBAUGH, AUTHOR OF THE CHOIRBOYS

The Brave Blue Line

"Through a series of gripping, individual stories … the author highlights the incredible courage often shown by officers on the front line'. *DAILY EXPRESS*

Death on the Beat

'… another book by the redoubtable Dick Kirby … Nobody reading this book can fail to be sobered and impressed by the courage and humanity of the men and women working to keep our streets safe for us'. HISTORY BY THE YARD WEBSITE.

THE SCOURGE OF SOHO

THE CONTROVERSIAL CAREER OF SAS HERO DETECTIVE SERGEANT HARRY CHALLENOR MM

DICK KIRBY

PEN & SWORD
TRUE CRIME

First published in Great Britain in 2013 by
Pen & Sword True Crime
an imprint of
Pen & Sword Books Ltd
47 Church Street
Barnsley
South Yorkshire
S70 2AS

Copyright © Dick Kirby 2013

HBK ISBN 978 1 78159 350 9
TPB ISBN 978 1 78346 401 2

Typeset in Ehrhardt by
Mac Style, Driffield, East Yorkshire
Printed and bound in the UK by CPI Group (UK) Ltd,
Croydon, CR0 4YY

Pen & Sword Books Ltd incorporates the Imprints of Pen
& Sword Aviation, Pen & Sword Family History, Pen &
Sword Maritime, Pen & Sword Military, Pen & Sword
Discovery, Pen & Sword Politics, Pen & Sword Atlas,
Pen & Sword Archaeology, Wharncliffe Local History,
Wharncliffe True Crime, Wharncliffe Transport, Pen &
Sword Select, Pen & Sword Military Classics, Leo Cooper,
The Praetorian Press, Claymore Press, Remember When,
Seaforth Publishing and Frontline Publishing.

For a complete list of Pen & Sword titles please contact
PEN & SWORD BOOKS LIMITED
47 Church Street, Barnsley, South Yorkshire, S70 2AS,
England
E-mail: enquiries@pen-and-sword.co.uk
Website: www.pen-and-sword.co.uk

Contents

This book is dedicated to
the memory of Doris May Challenor –
and to Ann, who like Doris
waited, wondered and worried

Acknowledgements

If Brigadier Henry Wilson of Pen & Sword Books had not provided his backing and Alan Moss of History by the Yard had not given his wholehearted assistance, it is fair to say that this book would never have been written. My friend Gordon Cawthorne very kindly wrote a splendid foreword for the book as well as diplomatically pointing out some very annoying typos. Had he not done so, that task would have fallen to George Chamier, my eagle-eyed editor; my profound thanks to them all.

In addition, Paul Dew of the Met Collection gave unstintingly of his time, and I was assisted by: the National Archives; Paul Millen FFSSoc; Sioban Clark from the Metropolitan Women Police Association; Bob Fenton QGM, secretary to the Ex-CID Officers' Association; Suzanne and Steve Cowper in the minefield of computer-land; Robert Kirby; Susi Rogol, editor of the *London Police Pensioner* magazine; Professor Dick Hobbs of the London School of Economics; 'Chunky' Philp; Steve Purl; Karen Harpur; Major Hugo White of the Duke of Cornwall's Light Infantry Museum and Sir William Mahon Bt LVO.

My thanks to Ron Cork, Don Gibson, Peter Jay, Russell King, John Legge, Alan Moss, Arthur Porter, the late Des Prendergast, Thomas Proudfoot, Beverley Rexstrew, Carol Stokes, the late John Vaughan and Tony Woodland for providing photographs. Every effort has been made to trace copyright holders and publishers, and I apologise for any inadvertent omissions.

Norman Birch, Frederick Burgum, Ron Cork, David Dixon, Raymond 'Dick' Docking, David Eager, Peter Elston, Fred Faragher, Rekha Gangadeen, Don Gibson, John Grey, Cecil Francis 'Frank' Gutsell, Maurice Harding, Janet Janes, Peter Jay, Russell King, John Legge, Doug Lynn, the late Len Moore, Ken Neville-Davies, the late Terry O'Connell QPM, David Parkinson, John Parrott, Frank Pillinger, Arthur Porter BEM, the late Des Prendergast, David Pritchard, Thomas Proudfoot, Gordon Pugh, Leonard 'Nipper' Read QPM, Coral Rexstrew, Maureen Ridout, Frank Rushworth, John Simmonds, Jim Smith BEM, John Troon, Ken Walker, Derek Webster, David Woodland and Laurie Young were amongst those who contributed to this book, as did a number of others who for one reason or another wished to remain anonymous. My thanks go to them all.

There were a number of people who might have assisted in the compilation of this book but who, for whatever reasons, did not. Bereft of their assistance, I have endeavoured to ensure that the book is as accurate as possible and acknowledge that any faults or imperfections are mine alone.

My thanks go to my family, Sue and Steve Cowper and their children, Emma, Jessica and Harry; Barbara and Rich Jerreat and their children, Samuel and Annie Grace and Mark and Robert Kirby, for their enduring love and support; and most of all to my wife Ann, who over the space of fifty years has been my mainstay.

Dick Kirby
Suffolk, 2013

Foreword

Dick Kirby's remarkable book about Harry Challenor MM will appeal not only to ex-policemen like me but also to members of the general public. It covers the life of this extraordinary man and also describes in detail the Soho of his days (and nights) as a detective there amid an atmosphere of criminality, violence and corruption which existed in the early 1960s throughout London's West End.

Challenor entered the fray determined to clear up the mess he found, and he managed to do just that and to frighten the criminal underworld into submission. This successful campaign came to an abrupt end on one fatal day in July 1963; he was brought down by grave mistakes he made during the visit by Queen Frederika of Greece. These included the planting of pieces of brick upon left-wing activists, who had mounted a hostile and potentially violent disturbance outside Claridge's where the Queen of Greece was staying. The aftermath, which included the imprisonment of three of Harry's aids to CID and the eventual abolition of the whole aids-to-CID system, resulted in Harry's suspension from duty and confinement in a mental hospital as being of unsound mind.

The author's diligent and painstaking research discloses the character of this driven man, dedicated to eradicating crime whenever and wherever he found it. Already a decorated war hero, he comes across as a very physically fit and forthright man, whose boisterous behaviour was often misunderstood but served him well when dealing with criminals. As Robert Fabian (of the Yard) once remarked to me when asked to explain his phenomenal successes in detection: "Treat your criminal rough, my boy. He's never heard of the Queensberry Rules." The past is, indeed, another country. We now have the National Council for Civil Liberties – 'Liberty', to give it its correct up-to-date title – to guard the criminal against any infringement of the multifarious regulations which have sprung up since the 1960s.

Was Harry Challenor mad? When I met him towards the end of his life, he said, "I'm mad, you know." Though evidently a shadow of what he once was, he appeared normal to me. But this was after spells in mental institutions, the death of his wife and, possibly, years of medication – often referred to as a chemical cosh – for his supposed mental state. One knighted doctor declared him normal after two examinations soon after his suspension. The term Post-Traumatic Stress Disorder had not yet been coined, but is a possible explanation for some of his later behaviour when a serving police officer. The self-inflicted stress of working horrendously long hours and walking home fifteen miles was nonetheless real.

The words of Sir Richard Mayne, written in 1829 when a first Metropolitan Police Commissioner, come to mind:

> The primary object of an efficient police is the prevention of crime; next, that of detection and punishment of offenders if crime has been committed.

They have never been improved upon. Harry Challenor certainly exemplified these objectives in everything he achieved. Effective? Most certainly. Mad? One wonders.

Ex-Detective Superintendent Gordon Cawthorne MBE

Author's Note

Since allegations of police corruption and malpractice feature large in this book, it is only sensible for me to tackle the subject head-on and explain the issue of complaints against the police and their investigation.

When I first joined the Metropolitan Police, almost half a century ago, an old police adage used to be drummed into me and my contemporaries: 'If you don't get complaints, you ain't doing your job properly.' Well, that homily wasn't strictly true, of course, but some officers took it to heart and spent the next thirty years of their service dodging the column and sedulously avoiding any form of confrontation with proactive police work. Eventually, after three decades which they had devoted to bone-idleness, devoid of both commendations and accusations, they retired with their mortgages paid off and an index-linked pension which, really, they had obtained by means of false pretences.

But for those of us who genuinely wanted to serve the community, to go out and arrest the thieves and tearaways of the area which we policed, there was a price to pay – complaints. My first came early in my service; within six months of joining I was in the dock, accused of assault occasioning actual bodily harm, which carried a maximum jail sentence of five years' imprisonment. I had arrested a violent former prison escapee who had assaulted a fellow constable, and during the course of his arrest the prisoner's thumb had been broken. This he attributed to me and claimed that I had acted unlawfully. Fortunately, the whole of the arrest had been witnessed by a member of the public, who informed the court that I had used no more force than was necessary, and the case against me was thrown out. This complaint was, however, the first of many.

Malicious allegations of assault, planting evidence and verballing (attributing incriminating statements to suspects) were rife during my service, never more so than when I was a member of the Flying Squad. Armed robbers, knowing full well that if they were convicted they stood a very good chance indeed of receiving a prison sentence running into double figures, would go all out with their fanciful assertions; sometimes these struck a chord with a credulous jury and they were acquitted, sometimes not. Some robbers pleaded guilty – not many – but among the remainder who contested the charges, I cannot remember a single case where damaging allegations were not made.

Some of these accusations were confined to the courtroom; others made an official complaint to New Scotland Yard, upon which an investigating officer would be appointed, usually of detective chief inspector rank, together with a detective sergeant as his 'bag carrier'. In the vast majority of the internal investigations made in respect of my conduct, I was treated with scrupulous fairness. I was sat down, cautioned and then interviewed, with the questions and answers being meticulously recorded by the investigating officer's sergeant. After that, the file containing the statements of all the witnesses and complainants, together with a covering report, would be sent to the Director of Public Prosecutions to see if there was a basis upon which to prefer criminal charges, and if not, to determine whether there had been any breaches of the police disciplinary code. The majority of investigating officers viewed this job as distasteful, but carried out investigations that were exhaustingly thorough (if they were not, the investigating officer would be investigated himself). At the end of the day (and this could take months, sometimes years) the accused officer would either be punished or exculpated; if the latter, he could get back to his crime-busting duties. And if anybody believes that internal police investigations are whitewashes, I'm here to tell them that the idea is laughable.

One of the few occasions that I received shabby treatment was when I was accused of planting ammunition on an armed robber and then committing perjury in court when I gave evidence about him. The officer appointed to investigate the matter was someone I had known for years, a person of consummate spitefulness whom I held in utter contempt, and I made no attempt to disguise my feelings of disdain. This, I now realize, was a mistake. I believe he knew all along that I was wholly innocent of the charges, but he revisited the witnesses in the case time and again in an effort to get them to change their original testimony. It took four years before I was completely exonerated.

Malevolent allegations of impropriety were made against police officers for a variety of reasons: revenge, spite, to get a bothersome police officer moved to another area (very common, that one!) and to make allegations so potentially damaging that the officer would be suspended and any trial in which the accuser featured would have to be abandoned. And yet, these allegations were a one-way street. In all my service, I never heard of anyone being punished for making a malicious complaint. Let me give you an example.

Another officer and I (both in uniform) were patrolling the streets during the 1960s when we stopped and arrested a couple of youngsters who had committed an offence of sacrilege – in other words, stealing items from a church. It was a straightforward case: the lads admitted their guilt, the ecclesiastical property was recovered intact, they went to court, pleaded guilty and were fined; and that, really, was that – except that it wasn't.

About a year later, I was informed that an allegation had been made by the youths that a few weeks previously, the other arresting officer and I – both of us in uniform – had stopped them once more in Ilford High Road and, for some unexplained reason, had threatened and assaulted them. By now, I had been posted to another division and was an aid to CID (in those days we were referred to as Temporary Detective Constables), so I would not have been in uniform in any event; but I checked my CID diary to determine exactly what I had been doing on the date and time in question. In fact, I had been detailed with another aid to CID to keep observation in a shop premises, miles away from Ilford High Road, which had been experiencing a number of thefts; the other aid and the shopkeeper both confirmed this.

The other arresting officer was also interviewed; he too had been posted to another division and was still in uniform, so he did not have the benefit of a diary to track his movements. However, by a remarkable coincidence, the date of the alleged incident had been his birthday, and on that day he had been quite ill and confined to bed at his home, which was also a considerable distance away from Ilford High Road. The records were checked and revealed that he had indeed been placed on the sick list at the time in question, and his confinement was authenticated by the officer's wife, his GP and a concerned neighbour, who had come in to commiserate with him since his illness had precluded any normal birthday celebrations.

And yet, nothing happened to those youths, who quite clearly had conspired together – as far as I could see, for no reason whatsoever – to pervert the course of public justice by alleging that we had committed a criminal offence of assault against them.

I'm afraid I've gone on far too long with this dissertation, but the reason I have done so is because what happened to me also happened to thousands of other police officers. In this book you will read of many allegations of police impropriety. Sadly, a small minority of them were true; but certainly not all of them. All I ask is for you to examine these assertions carefully, look at the people who made the complaints against Harry Challenor and ask yourself: were they really true – or was there a hidden agenda?

Prologue

I was beginning to regret my day down at Kingswood Grange in November 1995.

I had met Harry Challenor briefly at the Special Forces Club, and when his friend from the Special Air Service, Russell King, who visited him on a monthly basis at his care home in Lower Kingswood, Surrey, had to go off overseas, he asked me if I would care to visit Challenor. I jumped at the chance; as a former police officer I had for many years heard astonishing tales about this legendary figure in police circles and I had read his memoirs, *Tanky Challenor – SAS and the Met* (Leo Cooper, 1990).

The day had started off well enough; we met in his room – it was neat and tastefully decorated – and he seemed genuinely pleased to see me and kindly signed my copy of his book. As he did so, I gave him the once-over. Challenor was an inch or so taller than me and strongly built. Although my companion was over twenty years my senior, he still looked tough enough to be able to punch holes right through me. His hands were unusually large; as one of his aids to CID, 'Nobby' Birch, later told me, "You couldn't see his knuckles." In his face I could see authority, determination and decisiveness: good attributes for a CID officer, even for a man who had ceased to be one over three decades previously. There was a certain hardness, a wariness about him, and something else in his physiognomy. What was it? Ruthlessness? Yes, ruthlessness, that was right; and a little later on I would personally experience some of it.

We chatted about inconsequential topics – I thought it prudent to steer well clear of 'The Brick Case'! – but I soon discovered that he found it immensely difficult to fully comprehend matters; this was understandable when he mentioned the veritable cocktail of tablets which he had to take on a daily basis. So I had to gently disabuse him of the notion that we had served together in the SAS; and when I told him that I too had been a member of the Flying Squad, he affected to remember me, and it was with exceptional difficulty that I endeavoured to humorously explain to him that as he was joining the Flying Squad, I was leaving school.

I spoke about his contemporaries during his time on the Flying Squad – the legendary Tommy Butler of Great Train Robbery fame, in particular – but although he purported to recall Butler and some of the other Squad luminaries I mentioned, I did wonder if his recollection of those names was genuine. I disclosed how the Metropolitan Police had changed since his time, and since mine as well. For no apparent reason this produced the comment, "I've never done anything that I was ever ashamed of!" When I mentioned the introduction of ethnic minorities into the police – and not in a disparaging way, either – it caused an immediate and a rather over-the-top reaction. "I haven't a racist bone in my body!" he snapped; perhaps he was thinking of the allegations about his behaviour made over thirty years previously by one Sydney Harold Dacosta Padmore, of whom more later.

But then he relaxed. His good humour was restored when he lovingly mentioned his grandchildren, and when one of the carers enquired as to his preferences for dinner that evening, his deference and charm to her would not have disgraced a courtier or a diplomat.

I asked him if he would permit me to write an article about him in the *London Police Pensioner* magazine, the quarterly periodical for retired London police officers, but that drew a categorical refusal; he asked me to promise not to write anything about him until after his death – which of course I agreed to. Perhaps it was because five years previously he had had published his memoirs, which contained the account of his life which he wanted the public to know about and accept as being correct.

As he drifted in and out of reality, I invited him for a drink at the local pub; not one of my better decisions! At times he was bluff and hearty, addressing the publican as "Me old darling", but by now the day had drawn on and conversation was getting more and more difficult. There were longer and longer silences as I desperately tried to formulate questions which I hoped he would find interesting but which he would answer in monosyllables. And now the unwise concoction of anti-depressants and bitter which he had been consuming had worked its dangerous magic. Leaning towards me in the pub, he held his empty pint glass an inch away from my face and said quietly, "You know, Dick, you ask far too many fucking questions."

He had tired of my discourse, quite possibly saw me as an interrogator and therefore the enemy; hence the terse accusation to me, glass in hand. In this rather fraught situation a number of matters quite clearly flashed into my mind.

First, despite the assurances in his book that he would never need to see the interior of a psychiatric hospital again, it would be right to assume that I was far from convinced. When I read the book, I could sense the madness coming off the pages at me; now that I had spent some time in his company, I was in no doubt whatsoever that the man sitting opposite me could suddenly be transformed from a genial senior citizen into a rather dangerous individual.

Next, I was aged fifty-two at the time and I was in a physically fit, hard condition and still possessed of fast reflexes. However – and lastly – although I had some notion of unarmed combat, I had no doubt that if I had made any move to disarm Harry Challenor – even if I made the slightest movement – that glass was so close that it was going to go straight into my face.

So I simply sat there, said and did nothing and waited in the hope that the moment would pass. And after what seemed an eternity it did, and the glass was lowered.

That was how I came to spend the longest day of my life, with Harry Challenor. As he lumbered away in the twilight towards the residential home, I admit I expelled a sigh of relief. I might have to drive home around a quarter of the M25, but at least I would do so with my manly beauty unscathed and also my pockets devoid of building materials.

And that, for the time being, was the end of the matter; I never saw him again. Then Harry died and I duly filed a piece about him in the *London Police Pensioner*; there was a mixed reaction to it. Although I had written the article in what I hoped was an even-handed way, some former police officers castigated me for trying to turn him into a hero, others because they felt I had demonised him. One berated me in a public toilet, not the most wholesome surroundings for such a denunciation.

In fact, I had not tried to portray him in either light, nor have I done so now. In writing this book I have followed the dictum, often voiced by John Stevens,[1] my old Guv'nor in Northern Ireland: "We'll go where the evidence takes us."

Harry Challenor had been a brave and a resourceful soldier in the Special Air Service, and when he joined the Metropolitan Police he used his SAS tactics to bring the war right into the enemy's camp. The gangsters, pimps and racketeers of Soho simply did not know what had hit them. No longer did club owners have a summons served on them by a trembling uniform officer for some infringement of the licensing laws resulting in a £2 fine, which would invariably be quashed on appeal; now Challenor would order them out of their club, instruct them to padlock the front door,

---

1. Now Lord Stevens of Kirkwhelpington

then drop the key down a drain and tell them to "clear off". And they were the fortunate ones. Other members of the underworld sometimes found themselves in possession of a bewildering display of hardware of which they often disclaimed ownership. Magistrates and judges adored Challenor. Senior officers loved him – he was cleaning up Soho and they basked in the reflected glory. His colleagues admired him and his subordinates worshipped him.

And then came 'The Brick Case', and, almost overnight, circumstances changed. The National Council for Civil Liberties alleged that a number of innocent people had been convicted as a result of Harry Challenor's activities, and these allegations were taken up by the media. The commendations stopped arriving, the floodgates opened and the complaints started pouring in. Questions were raised in the House, a number of people had their convictions overturned or had no evidence offered against them and others were freed from prison. Two police investigations and one public enquiry were launched, the Home Secretary and the Commissioner of the Metropolitan Police were vilified, the Prime Minister resigned, several police officers were sent to prison and Challenor was sucked down into a maelstrom of insanity.

When it was all over, when the dust had settled, there were some transfers and some resignations. There were those who had perhaps hoped for promotion; it was not forthcoming. The system of having aids to CID was, after forty successful years, abolished.

The name of Harry Challenor was on everybody's lips. It was understandable; after all, he had been the Scourge of Soho.

This is what happened.

CHAPTER 1

'Dark Satanic Mills': Staffordshire, 1922

In the years which followed the end of the First World War, England – the winners – should have been enjoying a victorious peace in a land which the rascally little Liberal Prime Minister, David Lloyd George, had described as being 'a fit country for heroes to live in'.

In fact, England was little better off than her vanquished foe Germany, whose economy was in chaos. Trading had virtually ceased during the war, and now the allied nations owed the United States of America vast sums of money which had been borrowed during the hostilities. In consequence, crime in England went through the roof (aided and abetted by the Police Strikes of 1918 and 1919), while the pandemic known as 'Spanish flu' swept across the globe. It commenced in 1918 and would not be contained until two years later, during which time it claimed 100 million lives (or almost three times the number of fatalities during the war); another half a billion people were infected by the virus but survived. Added to all that, during 1922–3 almost three million men in Britain – about one quarter of the working population – were out of work; and worse was to follow.

But in 1922, on the other side of the Atlantic, Americans must have been considerably cheered up by listening to Al Jolson's number one hit, *April Showers*, and were certainly thrilled to see Douglas Fairbanks Sr athletically shinning up the chain of the drawbridge which was supposed to protect the inhabitants of Nottingham Castle from the attentions of scallywags such as Robin Hood, in Allan Dwan's film – even if his objective was nothing more sinister than virtuously saving Lady Marion Fitzwalter (aka Enid Bennett) from a fate worse than death.

However, Hollywood and its glamorous inhabitants were far removed – in fact, 5,327 miles away – from Caledonia Street, Bradley, near Wolverhampton, Staffordshire, a thoroughfare that stretches between Wellington Road, the A41 trunk road, and Mountford Lane. Since 1894 this dismal area had been part of the Coseley Urban District Council as a suburb of nearby Bilston; the north of the village was encircled by the Wednesbury Oak Loop of the Birmingham Canal Navigation, and to the south a separate canal, the Bradley Branch, terminated at Wednesbury Oak. With Bilston (population 27,565 in the 1920s) to the north and Sedgeley (population 17,200) to the west, it was an area devoted to coal mining and to ironworks which manufactured rivets, chains, nails and safes.

This was the dreary corner of England which on Thursday 16 March 1922 saw the birth at 3 Caledonia Street of a boy. He was baptised Harold Gordon Challenor; to his family he was known as 'Pete', his army contemporaries referred to him as 'Tanky', his wartime Italian friends called him 'Pietro', but to his police colleagues (and the majority of people) he was known simply as 'Harry'. He was the second of five children; his sister Doris had been born two years previously, and six years after Harry's arrival his brother Tommy was born, followed by his remaining siblings, Hazel and Richard.

It might have sparked a modicum of interest amongst the residents of Caledonia Street if they had known that prior to, during and after Harry's birth, the wife of a certain Percy Thompson was conspiring with her lover to murder her husband, slowly poisoning him by adding broken glass to meals. But perhaps not … and in any event, Ilford in Essex, where this was happening, was so far south that most of Caledonia Street would never have heard of it. It was not until the unfortunate Mr Thompson died on 4 October that year that what became known as the Thompson and Bywaters case hit the headlines, one of the most controversial trials of the twentieth century.

It is also a fair assumption that, on the day of Harry's birth, it would have registered not the slightest interest in the denizens of the area that Sultan Fuad I had been crowned King of Egypt. There were far more pressing matters to address, such as the getting of food, accommodation and employment.

At least for the time being, this cheerless area provided employment for many of its inhabitants, and the rented Challenor family home was a typical 'two up two down' terraced house of that period, with a lavatory in the back garden. Harry's father, Thomas Henry Challenor, had been a soldier with the Staffordshire Regiment during the First World War (as had a relative, George Challenor, who had been a prisoner of war and who lived at 5 Caledonia Street). So there was a roof over the heads of the Challenor family, and there was food – not necessarily particularly nutritious or plentiful – on the table. But Tom, a heavily built and enormously strong man, who at the time of Harry's birth was working in the local steelworks, was a drunken brute, prone to thrash his son for the slightest reason – or for no reason at all.

Meanwhile, Messrs Jolson and Fairbanks, together with 121,767,000 other Americans, needed to look to their finances, because the Wall Street Crash of 1929 was upon them. With the resultant worldwide economic depression of the 1930s, Tom Challenor, like many men in the area, lost his job; and deprived of the money to fund his drinking, his bouts of temper intensified and Harry's beatings increased and grew worse.

* * *

St Lawrence's Hospital was set in 154 acres on the Surrey Downs and funded by the Metropolitan Asylums Board; it had opened on 9 October 1870. Initially described as 'The Metropolitan District Asylum for Chronic Imbeciles' and later as 'The Caterham Lunatic Asylum for Safe Lunatics and Imbeciles', by 1920 the place was known as the Caterham Mental Hospital. Since its inception, a great deal of money had been spent to enlarge the hospital and improve standards, and by 1930, when the London County Council took over administrative control, electric lighting had replaced gas, and the hospital boasted a recreational hall with a stage, a swimming pool, a laundry and sufficient beds for 2,109 patients. In addition, a large house named Chaldon Mead had been purchased as a hostel for male patients, and the hospital had acquired a new superintendent. He had been the battalion medical officer of the Staffordshire Regiment, and when Tom Challenor heard this piece of news, it was to his former wartime officer that he applied – and was accepted – for the position of nurse.

Tom Challenor set off alone on the 120-mile walk to his new employment, leaving his wife and young family to fend for themselves. His wife Ellen (née Barnes) brought in a pittance working as a charlady, waiting for the call from her husband to come and join him. Instead, she received the unwelcome news that he had formed a relationship with another woman, and together with Harry and his elder sister, Mrs Challenor set off to Caterham to furiously confront and successfully eject her rival. Harry's remaining siblings were then summoned, Blake's 'dark satanic mills' were left behind (as was Harry's childhood friend Bert Williams, who was born six weeks prior to Harry and would go on to become the Wolves and England goalkeeper), and the semblance of a family life resumed.

With a regular weekly wage, Tom Challenor celebrated once too often; on his way home from the local pub he stole a bicycle and the following day was arrested and fined; his employer then transferred him to Caterham's sister hospital, Leavesden Mental

Hospital. The family set off again, this time travelling north-east to arrive in Garston, near Watford, just south of Abbots Langley, where the hospital was situated. Leavesden had opened a week prior to Caterham for patients suffering from tuberculosis, but when the London County Council took over the running of the hospital, it was decided that most of the 2,209 beds should be allocated to patients suffering from mental infirmity. This hospital, too, had been well funded, and improvements had been made; the steam-driven generators had been replaced with electricity in 1931, and in the same year the Leavesden Residential School had closed and its site had been purchased as an annexe to the hospital.

Harry had done well at school; he was school captain at games and physical training and had played football for Watford Schools XI. In addition, he was quite bright academically, collecting an award for writing an essay and winning a scholarship to Watford Grammar School. But the dreams of an enhanced education and the possibility of playing for Watford Football Club were brutally dashed when Tom Challenor harshly informed his son that having reached the age of fourteen, he was going out to work, and his first employment thus began while he was still a schoolboy; finishing school at four o'clock, Harry worked as a 'lather-boy' in a local barber's shop for a weekly wage of 2s 6d (12½p) – coincidentally, the exact sum that Scotland Yard's Informants Fund was paying at that time for each piece of information received.

He was fortunate to obtain an apprenticeship in the machine shop at Scammell Lorries, Tolpits Lane, Watford, in 1936. In common with many large companies of that time, they had their own sports club, and Harry boxed for the company and was a winger for their football team. Strangely – because apprenticeships were then at a premium – after six months at Scammells Harry resigned and took a job at Leavesden Hospital as a nurse, whilst his father was still similarly employed there. Given the picture painted of Tom Challenor, it is difficult to imagine him dealing with the inmates of the hospital with the judicious mixture of firmness and compassion which their frail mental condition required; and although Harry later claimed that he himself used only 'gentle persuasion' on the inmates, this may not necessarily have been the case. Harry would later say that the reason he took employment at the hospital was because single nurses had their own quarters there; but since relations with his father were still hostile, it nevertheless seems an inexplicable career move. Perhaps Tom Challenor had realized that he would have been ill advised to try to chastise his son on the hospital wards, both from the point of view of keeping his employment and if he wanted to retain his own teeth, since seventeen-year-old Harry was now a proficient boxer.

The die was beginning to be cast for young Harry Challenor. He was not unintelligent, he was beginning to develop a taste for beer, he was extremely strong, a fine athlete and rather aggressive. He possessed a profound contempt for his father, who had prophesised that his eldest son would end up 'inside', but who would never lay a hand on him again.

As the war clouds gathered over Europe, neither had the slightest idea that Harry Challenor would emerge from the coming hostilities as a decorated hero in an élite unit, or that he would become London's most contentious police officer of all time.

CHAPTER 2

Who Dares Wins

At the outbreak of war in September 1939 Harry Challenor was aged seventeen and a half and aggressively keen to volunteer for the armed services. But on his eighteenth birthday he was rejected, first by the Royal Navy, then by the Royal Air Force. Waiting for his call-up papers to arrive, he left the hospital and drifted from one job to another before he secured employment as a labourer at the site of the De Havilland aircraft company. Working long hours there, his large wage packet permitted him to indulge his fondness for drink and womanising. It was while he was working at an airfield near Liverpool that his call-up papers finally arrived.

On 30 April 1942 Private 7406037 Challenor discovered to his horror that instead of being posted to the fighting regiment he had dreamt of, he was posted, due to his medical experience at Leavesden Hospital, to the Royal Army Medical Corps. It appeared that the man who had wanted nothing better than to lead bayonet charges at battalions of German crack troops would be consigned to emptying bedpans. Although he beseeched the adjutant to be transferred to the infantry, it was firmly pointed out to him that his past experience made him invaluable – as indeed it did – to the RAMC.

Posted to Algiers in North Africa, Challenor was held in reserve, on attachment to the First Army. Nothing was happening, and he sat and fumed at the inactivity. In all probability, he had never heard of the Small-Scale Raiding Force.

* * *

Whilst France was still fighting the invading German forces, and following the ferrying by a miscellany of vessels of 388,000 beleaguered troops off the shores of Dunkirk between 27 May and 4 June 1940, the newly appointed Prime Minister, Winston Churchill, wrote a minute dated 6 June 1940: 'I look to the Chiefs of Staff to propose me measures for a vigorous, enterprising and ceaseless offensive against the whole German occupied coastline.'

The result was the Commandos – initially called 'Leopards' – and they were trained to fight as raiders, in groups or if necessary alone, carrying out aggressive and clandestine operations against the enemy. Training was initially carried out in the North of England, training that taught the soldiers self-reliance. Physical fitness was paramount; the men were trained to cover seven miles per hour with full kit and rifle, and as well as learning rock climbing they were also taught close-quarters combat.

The former Assistant Commissioner of the Shanghai Municipal Police Force, William Ewart Fairburn, and Eric Anthony Sykes, the officer in charge of the Shanghai Sniper Unit, arrived at the Commando Depot to instruct unconventional troops in unconventional warfare. Their instructors could not have been better. Both men had been involved in over two hundred close-combat confrontations in the back alleys of Shanghai with some of that city's toughest inhabitants.

They trained the Commandos in the use of a variety of firearms, including pistol shooting, although a favourite weapon was the 9mm Sten gun, Mark II. Firing up to 550 rounds per minute from a 32-round magazine, the Sten was cheap to manufacture and considered very reliable; it would continue firing even after it had been dropped in water.

The short, portly, avuncular Captain Sykes instructed the Commandos in the art of silent killing, using cheesewire such as a grocer might employ; this thin, strong wire, held at each end by a wooden toggle, was to be applied with devastating effect to the necks of German sentries. Coshes were also used for the purpose of disabling the enemy; an early version was a sock filled with sand. However, the introduction of a more ambitious model coincided with puzzled London Transport officials bemoaning the sudden and inexplicable loss of large numbers of the spring-designed straps for their standing passengers.

Tall, thin Captain Fairburn also taught unarmed combat. This was hand-to-hand combat of a sort few of the recruits had encountered before. There was instruction in manual strangulation, as well as in kneeing one's opponent in the testicles (plus endeavouring to pull them off). In addition, inserting one's fore and middle fingers into an antagonist's nostrils in an attempt to rip his nose off was taught, as well as slipping one's thumbs inside an opponent's mouth, with the same rupturing intent in mind. Wrist and arm locks were also taught, in case a prisoner was required to accompany a Commando back to his lines for the purpose of interrogation. Instruction in these holds was necessary, since had the unfortunate prisoner's nose been separated from his face or his mouth ripped open, answering questions would have presented certain difficulties.

Living off the land – in other words, stealing from crofts and farmhouses – was a necessity. In addition, Commandos were often dismissed at six o'clock in the evening with orders for them to rendezvous at a location 100 miles distant at six o'clock the following morning; how they did it was up to them. Many excelled at this type of challenge and left a trail of discarded bicycles, motorcycles, cars and, on one auspicious occasion, a furniture lorry, in their wake.

The first raid by one hundred officers and men from 3 Commando and 11 Independent Company took place barely one month after Churchill had issued his decisive order. Codenamed 'Operation Ambassador', its mission was to capture prisoners on the German-occupied Channel Island of Guernsey and obtain as much intelligence from the islanders as possible. It was a complete and utter cock-up.

The equipment which was delivered to the Commandos was a fraction of what was actually required, and in addition, the original plan was completely changed half an hour prior to departure. As the speedboats ferrying the Commandos to shore left their destroyer, it was discovered that their compasses had not been adjusted. It was a miracle that three of the speedboats actually reached Guernsey; one missed the island completely and was believed to have ended up on the shore of the neighbouring Channel Island of Sark. The Commandos raided the German barracks, which turned out to be unoccupied, so no prisoners were taken. The islanders declined to impart any information whatsoever, either because they were too frightened or because they refused to believe that the Commandos were British, thinking instead that this was some cunning trick of the Germans. Having been thwarted in respect of both their appointed assignments, the Commandos decided to vacate the island. This appeared to be an eminently sensible decision. It was an ignominious end to a badly thought-out plan but at least, the personnel reasoned, nothing else could go wrong. However, it is an irrefutable fact under the provisions of Sod's Law, that when things start to go amiss, they continue to do so before reaching a final gaffe of catastrophic proportions.

As soon as the Commandos reached the beach, it was immediately discovered that a heavy swell had smashed one of the speedboats and had dragged the other two vessels fifty feet from the shore. As the commanding officer rushed down the concrete steps he slipped, went arse over bollocks and dropped his revolver. Since for some unaccountable reason he had cocked the weapon, it went off as it hit the ground. This not unnaturally alerted the Germans, who opened fire. Thereupon, the Commandos had to swim for it; all, that is, except for the three men who, upon acceptance to the unit had untruthfully stated that they could swim, and who had to be left behind. One was handed a torch and was told to flash it in the direction of the submarine which would come to pick them up the following night. To nobody's surprise, the Admiralty was hugely disinclined to dispatch one of His Majesty's submarines into enemy territory to retrieve three soldiers who had been disingenuous regarding their aquatic capabilities, and the stranded Commandos were all caught. They were joined in their captivity by a secret agent who had not been told of the last minute change of plan and who had been waiting fruitlessly for the raiding party at the landing point in the original plan.

Meanwhile, the Germans enthusiastically machine-gunned the swimming Commandos, but fortunately their aim turned out to be as defective as the British commitment to this operation. After an exhausting swim, during which time the few weapons which they possessed sank to the sea bed, the Commandos eventually reached their speedboats, one of which promptly broke down. The crew of the remaining boat actually started an argument as to who should do what, and after they eventually set off, towing the disabled speedboat, it was discovered that the destroyer which had brought them had left. It was only by a gracious dispensation of providence (plus covering support from the RAF) that the destroyer returned to pick them up and they were able to return to England. Probably the unkindest cut of the entire, wretched expedition occurred when the Commandos' commanding officer, who had been obliged to discard his clothing during the swim to the speedboats, accepted the offer of the destroyer captain's jacket. Gratefully snuggling his shivering body inside the warm jacket, he was rather less than impressed when the captain casually informed him that he was suffering from scabies. Incredibly, there were some officers on the operation who thought that, 'they hadn't done too badly.' Presumably, the same officers were rather miffed at not being awarded Military Crosses.

Quite properly, Churchill growled, "Let there be no further silly fiascos like that perpetuated at Guernsey!"

There weren't. From such an undistinguished beginning, and during five years of warfare, the Commandos collected eight Victoria Crosses, plus 471 other awards for bravery.

★ ★ ★

Several of the commando units diversified; emerging from the Royal Marine Commandos came the Landing Craft Obstruction Clearance Units, the Combined Operations Assault Pilotage Parties, the Sea Reconnaissance Unit, the RM Boom Patrol Detachment, the RM Detachment 385, the Small Operations

Group, the RN Beach Commandos and the Combined Operations Scout Units. Among the Army Commandos, one of them – 62 Commando – became known as the Small-Scale Raiding Force (SSRF). The group, which included the Dane, Major Anders Lassen VC, MC and two bars (and whose reports read, 'Landed. Killed Germans. Fucked off.'), Major Geoffrey Appleyard DSO, MC and bar, MA and Captain Philip Pinckney, carried out some daring raids in enemy-occupied territory.

Another élite unit, the Special Air Service (SAS) had been formed in November 1941 by Lieutenant Colonel David Stirling DSO, OBE to strike at the enemy in North Africa, using hit-and-run tactics to carry out devastating attacks on enemy-held airfields from their camp at Kabrit; but in January 1943 Stirling was taken prisoner. Stirling's brother Bill had been promoted to lieutenant colonel in September 1942 and had been given command of 62 Commando, which was sent to Algeria at the end of that year; but following the 'Operation Torch' landings, no one could find a use for the unit. However, Bill Stirling was given permission from Allied Forces HQ in Algiers to form a second SAS Regiment for service with the First Army.[2] In addition, the SAS had developed the Special Boat Section (SBS), under the command of Major the Earl Jellicoe KBE, DSO, MC, PC; they acquired 121 Free Greek troops, who were formed into the Greek Sacred Squadron commanded by Colonel Christodoulos Tzigantes DSO; and 1 SAS was renamed the Special Raiding Squadron, with Lieutenant Colonel Blair 'Paddy' Mayne, who would go on to be awarded four Distinguished Service Orders, as its commanding officer.

Initially, the SAS personnel were issued with rather provocative white berets (which sometimes led to misunderstandings in bars in Cairo), and their cap badge was a winged dagger, bearing the motto, 'Who Dares Wins'. It was the SAS which became the inspiration for all modern day Special Forces units, worldwide.

With 62 Commando being in the process of being wound up, two of its officers – one was the Prime Minister's son, Major Randolph Churchill MBE – arrived in Algiers asking for volunteers for a fresh clandestine unit. Some of the members of the now defunct 62 Commando (which included Lassen) were assimilated into the Special Boat Squadron, but Appleyard and Pinckney, plus several former members of 3 and 4 Commando, were selected for training with a view to service in the new unit, as were one or two

---

2. Asked what the letters 'SAS' stood for, David Stirling famously replied, "Stirling and Stirling, naturally!"

others – including Harry Challenor. However, some of the men selected were without battle experience, and others had not even received Commando training. Harry Challenor, tough as he was, was deficient on both fronts.

Bill Stirling set up a commando camp at Philippeville, close to the beach and surrounded by a forest of cork trees. His brother David had sent Sergeant Dave Kershaw to help set up the training programme, which would be just as taxing as the course at Kabrit had been. To separate the wheat from the chaff, all recruits had initially to run up a 600-foot high mountain (known as a *jebel)* in full pack and back again in under sixty minutes – those who could not were RTU'd (Returned to Unit). There were long route marches in small groups carrying sixty-pound packs, as well as night infiltration exercises; everything was geared to encourage self-reliance. There was rigorous physical training every day, practice with small arms (in which close-quarter shooting was the order of the day), lessons in silent killing (armed and unarmed) and demolition work. Parachute training was held in Morocco. The men learned to land by sea using West African dories and to infiltrate overland, both on foot and by jeep – although initial raids using jeeps in Tunisia were not the success which was hoped for, because of the hilly terrain. The whole camp was buzzing with activity, the rattle of small-arms fire, the sound of explosions. Major Vladimir Peniakoff DSO, MC (the originator of 'Popski's Private Army') arrived in the camp to take part in the forthcoming raids, and Major Jellicoe's men planned a parachute raid on enemy-occupied aerodromes in Sardinia. The drawback of the camp, however, was the presence of malarial mosquitoes, as Challenor would soon discover to his cost

The fact that Harry Challenor declined to take his anti-malarial tablets was so stupefyingly idiotic that it defied belief. He had been, firstly, a nurse, then a member of the Royal Army Medical Corps, and therefore he must have been aware of the debilitating and life-threatening consequences of malaria – yet he did nothing to prevent it. And his actions – or lack of them – not only threatened his own health, they also later endangered the lives of extremely brave people in an enemy-occupied country who attempted to help him. And when they did try to assist him, his health was further put in jeopardy by their own ignorance. It is difficult – admittedly with hindsight – to imagine a more ridiculous set of circumstances.

In any case, Harry Challenor passed the course with flying colours. Opinions vary as to whether or not stocks of the coveted green Commando beret had arrived, or whether having received one he lost it, but whatever the reason, Challenor, bereft of suitable headwear, donned a black Tank Corps beret and was dubbed

'Tanky' thereafter. However, he was still classed as a medical orderly, although in his own words, "I was the most aggressive medical orderly the Commandos ever had". It was not too long before with a mixture of wit and guile he succeeded in handing over his medical duties to another orderly. There was more training, and some raids were carried out, including Operation Marigold.

On the night of 30 May 1943 three Special Boat Section personnel under the command of Captain Roger Courtney were transported together with eight SAS soldiers to the coast of Sardinia by the submarine *Safari;* the purpose of the operation was to storm the German garrison and kill all of its occupants save one, who was to be brought back for interrogation purposes. The SAS team was under the command of Captain Patrick Dudgeon MC, who because of his size was known as 'Toomai the Elephant Boy', after the Kipling story. Dudgeon had been in the assault on the Channel Island of Sark and became part of SSRF legend when in order to silence a German sentry he hit him over the head with his revolver. Unfortunately, it was the barrel instead of the revolver's butt which landed on the sentry's head, and since Dudgeon had his finger on the trigger he had blown the top of his adversary's head off.

The first part of the operation went well; Captain Courtney and his men paddled ashore in a folbot (folding kayak) and left a notebook to be later retrieved by a secret agent on the island. However, the SAS group had experienced difficulties in inflating their dinghies and were running late; they reached the island undetected, but once ashore, as they were scrambling up a low cliff, one of their party, Private Hughes, dropped his rifle. This was sufficient to alert the enemy, who opened fire; one man was captured, but the rest of the SAS were fortunate to escape unscathed and more fortunate still to discover that the submarine had waited for them.

This abortive exercise was followed by still more training; but by now, Harry Challenor was a fully-badged member of 2 SAS.

* * *

In September 1943 Bill Stirling decided to launch a plan, codenamed Operation Speedwell, to destroy Axis railways in enemy-held Italy in the areas between Bologna and Pistoia, Bologna and Prato, Florence and Arezzo, Genoa and La Spezia. The teams from 2 SAS were to be parachuted into the area of Pontremoli, just north of the beginning of the long spine of the Apennines mountain range, which bisects most of Italy down to Rome. The apex of this triangle was Bologna to the north of the Apennines, with Florence – on the opposite side of the mountain range – fifty miles to the south. To complete the triangle and roughly between the two cities, but situated on the west coast of Italy, was La Spezia.

It was a bold, daring plan, and if Bill Stirling had had his way, the raid would have required two squadrons – at least 150 personnel – to carry it out successfully. But he was overruled. The Army Group permitted just two aircraft to drop four officers and nine men from 'A' Squadron into the area.

On top of their uniforms the group wore US Army overalls; these had been used by members of 6 Commando the previous year during the North African landings. Since the area was under the control of the Vichy French, it was thought that the sight of British uniforms might inflame an already tricky situation. However, on this occasion they gave the SAS personnel an edge because at a distance they resembled Wehrmacht uniforms. In addition, the SAS were permitted to draw on a selection of weaponry not normally associated with the British Army; in Challenor's case this was a captured German Schmeisser machine-pistol, which used 9mm ammunition. This made sense; not only was the weapon reliable and accurate, but further supplies of ammunition could be acquired from the enemy. This was absolutely necessary; it was a clandestine operation where re-supply was impossible – there was no liaison with underground organisations in Italy, since at that early stage of the country's liberation, none existed.

As well as his Schmeisser, Challenor was equipped with a Fairbairn-Sykes fighting knife. Named after the two Shanghai police officers who had instructed the troops in the arts of silent killing, 250,000 of the knives (at a cost of 13s 6d each) had been manufactured by the Wilkinson Sword Company of Pall Mall. The stiletto blade, measuring six and seven-eighths inches (170mm) had two edges and a very sharp point, with a roughened handle (to provide a firm grip in the event of wet weather or nervousness) and a cross-guard (to prevent the user's fingers slipping down on to the blade). It was the ideal tool for dispatching German sentries, and Challenor ensured his was honed to razor-sharpness.

The Allied invasion of mainland Italy commenced on 3 September, and four days later the SAS team took off in two Albermarles from Kairouan airfield in North Africa and were dropped in two 'sticks' from a height of 7,000 feet, north of La Spezia, near Castiglione. The first stick was led by Captain Philip Pinckney, accompanied by Lieutenant Tony Greville-Bell and five other ranks. Pinckney's task was to attack the rail lines south of Bologna before returning to the Allied lines. The second stick comprised Captain Dudgeon,

Lieutenant Thomas Wedderburn and four others, who included Harry Challenor. They landed in the Magra valley, near Pontremoli.

Pinckney – his back was in plaster as a result of a previous injury – became separated from the others in his team; they received no answer to their pre-arranged signal, and as the nearby villagers were becoming inquisitive they left after ninety minutes without Pinckney. Greville-Bell was badly injured on landing, severely damaging his back and breaking two ribs; he split his party into two, retaining Sergeant Daniels and Corporal Tomasso, and on 14 September they derailed two trains in tunnels, followed by two more in open countryside. Sergeant Robinson, in charge of the second party comprised of Lance-Sergeant Stokes and Parachutist Curtis, similarly blew up a train in a tunnel, also on 14 September. As the weeks went by, they moved across country, evading the Germans until they arrived in Rimini on the east coast before they reached the 8th Army lines. Greville-Bell was awarded the DSO and Sergeant Daniels, the Military Medal. It was later discovered that Captain Pinckney had been captured and shot.

Captain Dudgeon decided to split his group into three teams: himself and Gunner Bernard Brunt; Sergeant William Foster and Corporal James Shorthall; and Lieutenant Wedderburn and Lance Corporal Challenor. Dudgeon was due to attack the railway lines between Genoa and La Spezia. He and Gunner Brunt killed a number of Germans and stole their truck to reach their target, but were captured and shot by firing squad at Cisa Pass on 3 October 1943. The second team, Foster and Shorthall, headed for a different part of this railway line but they too were caught and executed on 30 September 1943 at Ponsano Magra.

But Lieutenant Wedderburn and Challenor blew up two trains on the La Spezia-Bologna line – one on the 'up' line, another on the 'down' – in a tunnel, having set charges at both ends of it. They reached the planned rendezvous point as previously agreed, but none of the others arrived. After waiting three days and having learnt of the Italians' surrender to the Allies, they set off and with the help of a friendly farmer found another tunnel, where on 18 September they blew up a train on the La Spezia-Pontremoli line. Their mission completed – as well as having used up all their 808 plastic explosives – the two men set off south, travelling by day and staying close to the Apennines mountain range to cover over 300 miles towards the Allied lines.

By regular army standards it was a strange pairing: Wedderburn – short and stocky, with thick glasses, and known as 'Tojo' – the pre-war law student from Edinburgh, and Challenor, a very rough diamond indeed. But not to the SAS – after all, David Stirling had said, "All ranks in the SAS are of 'one company' in which a sense of class is both alien and ludicrous."

The weeks turned into months on this long and dangerous trek, and all the while – and unknown to the two men – other SAS operations were being promulgated in Italy. Operation Jonquil commenced at Ancona on 26 September, and Operation Candytuft one month later at Pescara. There followed more operations between Ancona and Pescara on Italy's east coast: Saxifrage on 14 December, with Sleepy Lad four days later and Begonia on 2 October. Operation Maple-Driftwood was launched south of Rimini on 7 January 1944, Pomegranate, inland between Florence and Terni five days later and two weeks after that, Baobab, close to Rimini.

Although Challenor's grasp of the Italian language was improving daily, food and shelter were at a premium for both men. They were fortunate to meet friendly Italians who fed them, gave them shelter and also provided warning of German troops, with whom they had some uncomfortably close encounters. But the balmy days of September when they had first landed in Italy had long gone; they were now in the depths of a bitter winter, and Wedderburn was suffering a great deal with his feet, while Challenor went down with malaria, further complicated by jaundice. Wedderburn and Challenor had travelled well over 200 miles in the most hazardous and exposed conditions. The Allied lines were now only eighty miles away at Cassino, but the atrocious weather and their bad health prevented any further advance. For three weeks they were hidden and well cared for by a friendly Italian family named Eliseio in Coppito, a village near the town of L'Aquila. This was an enormous risk to the family (who were already sheltering three escaped British prisoners of war); had the men been discovered by the Germans, the whole family would have been summarily executed. So on Christmas Day, with increased German activity in the area, the two men separated; Harry Challenor remained in the mountains and Wedderburn sought refuge at a house in the valley. On 27 December 1943 Wedderburn was captured; the woman in whose house he had been sheltering was shot. Wedderburn later escaped from a train taking him to a camp in Germany; recaptured, he was badly beaten up and then escaped again, only to be captured, once more ill treated and spend the rest of the war as a prisoner.

It was impossible for Challenor remain where he was; the Germans would have guessed that where there was one British serviceman on the run, there were probably more. To have stayed would have endangered the whole of the Eliseio family, so, still suffering from malaria, he set off towards the town of Popoli, en route to the Allied lines.

Challenor was caught, dressed in a civilian suit, as he entered a German-occupied village. Taken to SS Headquarters at Popoli, he was beaten up, interrogated and beaten up again. Transferred to a prisoner-of-war camp at L'Aquila for execution, he escaped, dressed as a washerwoman. He made his way back to the Eliseio family, who cared for him once more after his health broke and he came down with malaria and pneumonia. The Eliseio family were assisted by an engineer and his wife from L'Aquila. Shivering uncontrollably, his temperature soaring, his body lice-ridden, Challenor was injected with quinine by the Eliseio family. This was acquired at great personal risk to themselves, but with their ignorance of medical matters, and doubtless working on the assumption that the more quinine Challenor received, the quicker he would recover, he was seriously overdosed; this would lead to health problems for him in later life.

By now Challenor was close to death, and he did not recover sufficiently to continue his escape until 1 April 1944, when he crossed the Gran Sasso mountain range. Seven months previously, when he and Wedderburn had performed their sabotage operations, another daring raid had been carried out at Grand Sasso. German Special Forces, headed by Obersturmbannführer Otto Skorzeny, swooped out of the clouds from a height of 12,000 feet, crash-landed their gliders almost at the front door of the Hotel Campo Imperatore and rescued Germany's deposed ally, Benito Mussolini. But now the snow was knee-high, and as Challenor trudged on he managed to find shelter in a house already occupied by four South African pilots.

He rested there, then set off again and had almost reached the British lines when at Guardiagrele he was captured once more. This time he escaped in his bare feet, ran for three kilometres and reached the Allied lines on 7 April 1944. He had been behind enemy lines for over seven months. Out of the original personnel of thirteen who had comprised Operation Speedwell, only seven returned. As a result of combined SAS operations, fourteen trains were derailed.

It was clear that the SAS troops had not been used to their best advantage; quite apart from their lack of numbers, they had been poorly supplied and there had been no escape plan other than to suggest they make for the Allied lines. Bill Stirling was in no doubt that had he been listened to, and had substantial numbers of SAS operatives been committed to Operation Speedwell, German supply and reinforcement by rail would have been severely disrupted, as would telephone communications, power supplies and road transport. Stirling was furious at what he perceived to be the misuse of the SAS (he was not alone in his views) and he later resigned his command.

Challenor recovered his fitness, but by the time he arrived in Casablanca he discovered that 2 SAS had returned home to Prestwick after operations in France. Using a modicum of low cunning, he obtained a seat on a Liberator destined for Cornwall; in all probability he used a similar trick to that regularly used by another SAS officer, who would approach a clerk in the courier's office at an airport and murmur, "Frogspawn, you know, Frogspawn – Top Secret!" In this fashion he would be given a seat on whatever flight he desired. Shortly after his arrival, Challenor was once again laid low with a bout of malaria, but whilst he was on leave he met Doris May Broome, a twenty-three-year-old coil winder in an ammunition factory and – a common bond – the daughter of an iron foundry worker. Later described by one of Harry's police contemporaries as 'a wonderful woman', she and Harry were married, after a whirlwind courtship, at Epsom Registry Office on 1 August 1944. It was just as well; eighteen days later, Challenor landed at Rennes, part of a sixty-man team with twenty jeeps under the command of Major Roy Farran DSO and bar, MC and two bars, heading 'C' Squadron of 2 SAS. They were about to embark on Operation Wallace.

* * *

Following the D-Day landings, the SAS – consisting of British, French and Belgian members of the regiment – had been dropped into France. Now the Americans had broken through at Avranches, and the SAS, using hit-and-run tactics, were in a position to attack the Germans who were withdrawing from the advancing Americans. Farran's group intended to link up with the personnel of Operation Hardy under the command of Major Grant Hibbert, who had been parachuted into the Fôret de Châtillon, north of Dijon, on 27 July and had already established a base. Hibbert had acquired a secure supply dump and had been ordered not to attempt offensive action at that stage, but to provide intelligence of enemy activities. He was well equipped, with nine officers and forty-seven other ranks, plus twelve jeeps; but as well as intelligence gathering, some members of the group had been unable to resist disobeying orders. They had ambushed German convoys and had blown up a stretch of railway line between Dijon and Langres.

Farran had covered fifty miles – one quarter of the journey – in a day and now, on 22 August, he split his party into three groups: eight under him, five under the very excitable Frenchman, Captain Ramon Lee (aka Couraud) and the remainder under the command of Lieutenant David Leigh; the last group included Challenor, who was the driver/gunner of a jeep which had been specially modified. The driver had access to a single Vickers-K machine gun, and the front passenger – Lieutenant Hugh Gurney – had a twin Vickers machine gun. Another Vickers was mounted at the rear, manned by Parachutist Bob 'Will' Fyffe, who was also the wireless operator. In fact, the Vickers had originally been designed as an RAF observer's gun, and because there was no slipstream to cool them on the jeeps they did have a tendency to overheat and jam; however, the SAS loaded the magazines with a mixture of tracer, armour-piercing and explosive bullets, and the resultant effect on enemy vehicles was devastating.

Farran told them to bypass the enemy until they had met up with the men from Operation Hardy. The first group under Captain Lee disobeyed orders and engaged the enemy in the village of Mailly-le-Château. With the loss of one jeep Lee got through, but the next group, led by Farran, were ambushed. He was furious with Ramon Lee for his reckless behaviour and reduced his command to just two jeeps. Farran and his party detoured to the south and managed to rendezvous with Lee's group in Forêt de St Jean. The next day, this group again encountered the enemy; Lee escaped but the jeeps were destroyed. Lee was unable to warn Farran, who encountered the same party of Germans but managed to escape. Travelling 200 miles in just four days, he fought his way through; Challenor was engaged in several ferocious fire-fights which resulted in the death of a number of his comrades (including Lieutenant Leigh), and Challenor suffered another attack of malaria. Challenor's group was shipped back to England, having been told they would be later parachuted back to join Major Farran. With just seven jeeps left, Farran had engaged the enemy, resulting in thirty-five German casualties, then driven into the Hardy base camp at Plateau de Langres, near Châtillon. With the resources of the Hardy personnel, Farran now had a combined force of a truck, ten jeeps and sixty men, and in the next few weeks they carried out successful ambushes and caused great damage to the enemy.

Challenor – who according to Farran had 'gone astray' with Gurney, Fyffe and Ramon Lee – was dropped into France on 6 September and once more was involved in fierce fighting, sometimes at very close quarters; on one occasion with Lieutenant Gurney, despite orders to the contrary, they killed some high-ranking

German officers travelling in a staff car. The scene of the action was very close to the SAS base camp; it had the effect of German troops converging on the area, and Farran was furious. After blowing up a lorry filled with explosives, Challenor was wounded in the face but was more fortunate than Lieutenant Gurney, who turned back to help him and was killed. Challenor suffered further bouts of malaria, but the operation ended on 17 September with the arrival of the US 7th Army. During the SAS' time behind enemy lines, the RAF had carried out thirty-six sorties and had supplied the men of Operation Wallace with 484 supply panniers and twelve new jeeps. In just one month 500 Germans had been killed or seriously incapacitated, and twenty-three cars, thirty-six other vehicles and 100,000 gallons of petrol had been destroyed. In addition, a train had been attacked by the SAS at point-blank range, forcing it to come to a halt after its boiler was punctured. The French driver escaped unharmed; the German guards were not so fortunate. On the debit side, the SAS had lost seven men (one of whom was killed in a parachuting accident), seven wounded, two captured (one of whom escaped) and sixteen jeeps. The extraordinarily hot-headed Captain Ramon Lee disobeyed orders once too often, faced a court martial and was dismissed from the service.

After leave in a newly-liberated Paris (officially it was out of bounds to British troops, an order which Farran blithely ignored), Challenor returned home and was delighted to discover that he had been awarded the Military Medal in recognition of his exploits in Italy. The citation – which had been recommended by Lieutenant Colonel Brian Franks DSO, MC (the new Commanding Officer of 2 SAS) and sanctioned by Brigadier R. W. McLeod (later General Sir Roderick McLeod GBE, KCB) read:

This N.C.O. was dropped by parachute near Borgo val di Taro, north of Spezia on 7th September 1943. The total detachment consisted of two officers and four other ranks. After the landing the detachment split, Lance Corporal Challenor accompanying one officer. This small detachment succeeded in derailing two trains on the Spezia-Parma line on night of 14th September at a point north of Pontremoli. Again on night 18th September a third train was derailed south of Villafranca. Having no further explosives the detachment started to return to our lines. During this time the enemy were continually searching for escaped prisoners of war and on 27th December the officer was captured. Lance Corporal Challenor continued southwards alone; he was captured north of Chieti, but succeeded in escaping later from Aquila prisoner of war camp. He continued south and on 5th April 1944 was again captured while attempting to pass through the enemy lines; on 7th April he again escaped and reached our lines. Throughout the seven months spent behind the enemy lines, the N.C.O. displayed the highest courage and determination.

★ ★ ★

The Squadron was brought up to strength, and following more specialised training, Challenor was back in Europe, this time pushing into Germany tasked with destroying 88mm gun emplacements; after he was involved in some bitter street and hand-to-hand fighting, the war in Europe ended. With David Stirling released from Colditz, immediate plans were made for the SAS to be shipped to the Far East, but the detonation of two atomic bombs on Japan put paid to that; instead, Challenor, after a short period of leave in England, was sent to Norway, where in Stavanger captured U-boat crews and Gestapo officers were introduced to a physical fitness routine instigated by Corporal Challenor which inevitably ended in an exhibition of fisticuffs, a display in which the presence of a boxing ring was found not to be strictly necessary.

Both regiments of the British SAS were disbanded in 1945; after his return to England from Norway, Challenor was promoted to sergeant and transferred to the 17th Parachute Battalion, where he boxed for the battalion; shortly afterwards he was promoted once again, to company quarter master sergeant, and posted to Palestine. He spent a month on a plumbing rehabilitation course in Cairo before he was honourably discharged on 17 February 1947 with his character assessed as 'Exemplary'. However, what was not recorded was that during his army service several disturbing traits had emerged.

That Harry Challenor had always been a cheerful extrovert there was no doubt; however, he was also an exhibitionist, a teller of seriously unfunny jokes and given to outbursts of laughter which drew attention to his presence and, in the case of enemy engagements, was likely to endanger his comrades as well as himself. In addition, he often took action without thinking of the possible consequences. On one such occasion, when he was first captured in Italy, he roared with laughter when his German captors scattered during an Allied bombing raid; he was then severely beaten up for his pains. Another incident, by his own account, occurred when he thought it hugely amusing to fire at a group of his own men returning from a training exercise. During the exchange of fire which followed, in Challenor's words, his 'boyish sense of devilry' resulted in one of the group being shot in the arm. Challenor facetiously mocked a fellow paratrooper when supposedly checking his static line before his first jump, behaviour which so unnerved the man that he requested to be returned to his parent unit. He refused to believe that his initial (and then persistently recurring) bouts of malaria were caused by his refusal to take anti-malarial tablets and thought the proper treatment was to drink the local spirits.

Drinking on operations was seriously frowned upon; during a raid on Benghazi, David Stirling had caught Randolph Churchill drinking rum. "Captain Churchill, we never drink on operations," Stirling icily remarked and tossed the bottle out of the jeep. It was a dictum blithely disregarded by Harry. Challenor's extraordinary outbursts – usually bellowed at the top of his voice and normally under the influence of drink – were often aired in the presence of the enemy. En route to the Allied lines following Operation Speedwell, he encountered a group of German soldiers who had attended a Christmas church service. Staggeringly drunk, he roared, "God didn't hear you bastards!" But since the enemy were possibly similarly inebriated, they probably did not hear Challenor either. Following Operation Wallace and in a wood surrounded by 600 SS troops, four armoured cars, six troop carriers and twenty staff cars, Challenor, driving his jeep, thought it appropriate to bellow, "Whoah! Welcome back to bloody France!" His sentiments would not have been appreciated by the French Boy Scouts, who at enormous risk to themselves had bravely volunteered to inform Roy Farran of this clear and present danger; four of them were later shot. Then hearing a bird singing, Challenor shouted, "Spring – the time for bloody love!"

It was in 1942 that Hitler issued his infamous *Kommandobefehl*, in which he stated that all allied troops on 'so-called commando missions in Europe who were captured were to be slaughtered to the last man', adding, 'It does not make any difference if they are dropped by parachute.' It arose after the SSRF raid on Sark; a number of German personnel had been killed, including a sentry who had been knifed to death by Lassen, but in the *Guernsey Evening Star* it had been reported by the occupying Germans that prisoners from the raid had been shackled with handcuffs and manacles and had had their mouths stuffed with mud. The report was untrue, but it mattered not; it was sufficient for Hitler to issue the directive. All Special Forces personnel and parachutists were aware of this order. It therefore makes it all the more odd that when Challenor was first captured, wearing a civilian suit provided by one of his

Italian rescuers, he informed the Gestapo not only that he was a member of the SAS, but that he had been engaged in a sabotage operation in which a train had been derailed. Unsurprisingly, he was sentenced to be shot, which prompted his first escape. It was when he was on the run, dressed as a woman, that he repeated his homily of, "God didn't hear you bastards!" at the top of his voice; a passing peasant obviously thought (with considerable justification) that the very tall and well built woman to whom he had offered a lift on his cart was quite unwell.

And right at the end of his post-war service, his 'sense of fun' prompted him to throw a large stone through the window of the Brigade Sergeant Major's hut. Perhaps this was a portent of things to come.

Taken individually, these occurrences might not have caused too many comments; taken collectively – and of course, at the time, they were not – they would have represented a very real cause for concern. Challenor had a vitriolic hatred of the Germans and delighted in killing them; as a member of an élite unit, this was what he had been tasked to do and he had done so bravely and conscientiously. But now the war was over and it was time to switch off; for many men, especially those who had been involved in dangerous and clandestine warfare, this was extremely difficult. Men like Blair 'Paddy' Mayne, who found it challenging to revert to his peacetime occupation of solicitor, and who drank heavily, became involved in brawls and died in a car crash. Or Brigadier Michael 'Mad Mike' Calvert DSO and bar, who commanded the SAS at the end of the war and resurrected it five years later, but like Mayne drank heavily and was later cashiered.

Harry Challenor, and who like both Mayne and Calvert was a talented boxer and a heavy drinker, had additionally started to display some of the symptoms of mental illness. But this was a time when for an Englishman to admit any such ailment was regarded as a sign of weakness. To do so would have prompted the response, "Pull yourself together!" or that old chestnut, "Snap out of it!" So even had he felt inclined to do so, Harry Challenor did not turn to anyone for help, and therefore returning to a normal lifestyle was pretty nigh impossible for him.

And when help was made available, it would be too late. Far too late.

CHAPTER 3

The Metropolitan Police – a School of Hard Knocks

On his return to England Challenor was reunited with Doris, who had been living with her parents in a requisitioned house in Cheam. Doris' father, William James Broome, got his son-in-law a job working as an iron moulder at Pullen Foundries Ltd, Beddington Lane, Croydon, and after several years there Challenor moved to another steel foundry, this time in Staines, Middlesex. It was certainly hard if intellectually undemanding work; he regularly played football, and although the disturbing symptoms which had reached boiling point by the end of the war were abating, Challenor was restlessly seeking new horizons.

Then, right out of the blue, he received a letter from his old SAS squadron commander Roy Farran, who in addition to his British decorations had ended the war with the American Legion of Merit and the French *Croix de Guerre*. In March 1947 Farran, who had already served in Palestine, was instructing cadets at Sandhurst when he was ordered to return to Palestine to teach the Palestine Police the arts of clandestine warfare, in order to combat the outrages committed by competing Arabs and Jews in the last months of the British Mandate. Farran set to work with a will; organising 'Q' Cars filled with tommy guns, ammunition, food and petrol and manned by Jewish-looking personnel, he took the war right into the heart of the Jewish paramilitaries – the Irgun Zvai Leumi, the Stern Gang (aka the Lehi) and the Haganah. He now invited his former corporal to join him.

This, thought Challenor, was the answer to his prayers; when he served in Palestine he had hated the terrorist gangs who were, almost with impunity, shooting British service personnel, and he had tried some ad hoc tactics of his own against them, without success. However, Doris obviously disapproved of the proposition, and after thanking Farran for his offer, Challenor declined. It was probably just as well. Farran believed that he had been given carte blanche to deal with the terrorists, but it appeared he had been misinformed. Following some dangerous and daring exploits, Farran was arrested and charged with the murder of a Jewish terrorist. It appears that the charge was based on the thinnest of evidence, but a supine British Government felt that a culprit was

required, and since Farran had been vocal in his denunciation of
the gutless government policy towards the Jews, he was a suitable
candidate. Although the case was thrown out and he was repatriated
to England, Farran's troubles did not end there. His acquittal had
not found favour with the Stern Gang, the smallest and most
radical of the three paramilitary groups, whose murderous reach
stretched beyond the Middle East. They sent a parcel bomb to the
Farran family home in Codsall, Staffordshire. It was addressed to
'Mr R. Farran' and, opened by Farran's brother Rex, it exploded,
killing him instantly.

But when Doris noticed a newspaper advertisement for recruits
to the Metropolitan Police, she encouraged her husband to answer
it. Applicants who had seen service with the armed forces and
were sportsmen were snapped up by the Met, and Challenor, with
his Military Medal plus his prowess at football and boxing, was
certainly no exception. During his medical examination Challenor
mentioned his malaria and the wartime wound to his eye, but made
no mention of the hernia which had precluded his entry into the
Royal Navy at the commencement of hostilities, since this was a
bar to acceptance into the police (in fact, it was not until December
1959 that a successful operation to repair the hernia was carried
out). He certainly made no mention of his strange behaviour
during the war; in any case, he passed the physical with flying
colours. He also passed his entrance examination with 408 marks
out of a possible 650, and on 24 September 1951 was allocated
warrant number 137161. As Police Constable 95 'TS' he was one
of eighteen men and three women accepted into Peel House, one
of the two Metropolitan Police training establishments, situated at
105 Regency Street, London SW1. This grim, six-storey building
was to be his home for the next fourteen weeks.

In fact, the course should have been thirteen weeks, and
therefore it is likely that Challenor was 'back-squadded' – in other
words, obliged to spend an extra week in the next class in line. This
happened when a candidate failed one of the periodic examinations
during the course or (far more likely in Challenor's case) because
of misbehaviour during the classes.

Len Moore (a tough veteran of the Regional Crime Squad, who
six years later was awarded the Queen's Commendation for Brave
Conduct for attempting to arrest three criminals in a stolen car)
was in the class after Challenor's, and because the two of them
were the only ones in both classes to wear wartime medal ribbons
on their tunics, they often reminisced about service life. Talking
to me sixty years later, Moore remembered Harry Challenor as
being, "An extrovert – a nice bloke, really". But one afternoon,

Challenor's class was leaving the gymnasium just as Moore's was about to enter it. "Harry said, 'Hello Len, let's show 'em how it's done'," Moore told me, "and we began to spar. Suddenly, he launched a haymaker which connected with my chin. I laughed it off, but I told him, 'Pack it in'. Really, Harry was just showing off."

Showing off or not, Challenor's boxing expertise was good enough for him to win three bouts in a row. Eventually he did well academically, too; he passed the final examination at Peel House very creditably – 111 marks out of a possible 120 – and his report read:

> A very hardworking recruit, aged 29 years, exceptionally willing, keen and hardworking. Seeks diligently after knowledge and at times needs someone to keep the brake on for his excess of energy.

As Challenor entered the Metropolitan Police, it was in some ways the end of an era. The Commissioner of the Metropolitan Police was the largely ineffective Sir Harold Scott GCVO, KCB, KBE, who in uniform or out of it looked the pasty-faced civil servant he always had been; and Basil Dearden's 1949 film, *The Blue Lamp*, had enshrined Police Constable George Dixon in the hearts and minds of the British public. Although the world was changing, and post-war rationing and the memories of wartime were beginning to disappear, the police were still high in the general public's estimation. However, the kindly, avuncular George Dixon, skilfully resurrected for a long-running television series, was as alike to Harry Challenor as the man in the moon.

* * *

Ever since its inception in 1829, the Metropolitan Police has had its share of 'characters' – men who for one reason or another have captured the attention both of the police and the public. Men like Detective Sergeant Frederick Porter Wensley, who in 1911 arrested a deeply unpleasant individual named Steinie Morrison (aka Morris Stein), who had served sentences of penal servitude and hard labour totalling twelve years and had been flogged. Morrison had murdered a receiver of stolen property, and when Wensley arrested him in an East End café with the words, "Stein, I want you!" Morrison's response was to reply, "Don't go putting anything in my pockets!" He later stated that Wensley had said, "Stein, I want you for murder!" This was regarded as a suspect's classic slip-up and was denied by Wensley and his men. A certain Police Constable George

Greaves appeared for the defence, saying that Wensley had indeed uttered those words; at the Old Bailey, Morrison was convicted, and Greaves was discredited and was transferred to Ruislip, Middlesex, just as far from his East End home as it was possible to send him. But Wensley prospered; he was presented with a £25 bursary for his work at the siege of Sidney Street, awarded the first King's Police Medal, appointed MBE (later advanced to OBE), was commended on hundreds of occasions, promoted to Chief Constable of the CID and created the Flying Squad.

One of the first men that Wensley acquired for the Flying Squad was Ted Greeno, a very tough ex-sailor with an encyclopaedic knowledge of gangsters and pickpockets. His way of dispersing the racetrack gangs was to stroll on to the track, confront forty of the worst tearaways and tell them to 'clear off'. Anyone who demurred was sent sprawling by a right-hander from Greeno, whilst the rest of the gang fled; in fact, he would fight anybody who challenged his authority. This included a gang of safebreakers whom Greeno thrashed into a coma; only later was it established that their jackets contained sticks of gelignite and detonators – it was fortunate that Greeno's mauling had not resulted in the immediate blowing-up of all those present. Following a win at the races, Greeno lavished £25 or £50 on informants who provided him with the most up-to-date information; he collected eighty-eight commissioner's commendations, was appointed MBE and retired with the rank of detective chief superintendent.

Bert Wickstead, known as 'The Gangbuster', was awarded the Queen's Police Medal and rose to the rank of commander. Built like a tank, he was renowned for his ruthlessness in dealing with gangsters; when he dealt with two opposing criminal factions, they would be separately told, "Come over to my side or end up in the dock." There was often an unseemly rush to do so; one East End hard man was brought into the police station and, upon being told that Wickstead intended to interview him, had to be bodily carried, sobbing, up the stairs to the CID office. Wickstead had that effect on criminals; charismatic in the witness box at the Old Bailey, he was an ace manipulator of the Press.

So in the Metropolitan Police, there were characters and there were characters – and then there would be Harry Challenor.

He stood alone.

* * *

On 7 January 1952 Challenor was posted as Police Constable 616 'W' to Mitcham police station, part of the Metropolitan Police's

'W' Division in south London, which at that time was situated at 58 Lower Green East. The Domesday Book of 1086 records the area as being known as Michelham, and the 250 people then living there gradually increased over the years until at the time of Harry's arrival the population had swollen to 67,269 in 20,000 houses. The area had been under local Conservative control for three years; this would continue for another twenty-one years, although Harry Challenor's behaviour could not be described as remotely conservative.

Challenor made his presence felt immediately. Doug Lynn had been at Mitcham for several months prior to his arrival. "He was a powerfully built man who was quite a good amateur boxer, not very sociable as I remember," ninety-one-year-old Lynn recalled. "My impression of him was that he was a 'loner' who was not too interested in mixing with the rest of the lads." As with all probationary constables, Challenor was given an older officer to teach him 'learning beats', it was a chore which was usually thoroughly disliked by the older police constables. They had their own way of working their beat and their own 'watering holes', which they were not inclined to share or divulge to newcomers. Challenor effectively dealt with this, as Lynn remembers. "It was the talk of the station that while he was learning beats, he apparently gave his mentor the slip and was next seen in the charge room with a prisoner!"

Maureen Ridout (then Maureen Norsworthy) was the only woman CID officer to cover ten stations in the area, and recalling Challenor when she was eighty-seven years of age, she told me, "Although he was always polite to me and always seemingly full of life, he always seemed to be getting into trouble; not serious, because he was so happy-go-lucky."

An example of Challenor's carefree attitude was his habit of addressing anybody, irrespective of rank, as "My old darling/my old dear/my old beauty", and this was recalled by Arthur Porter, who had arrived at Mitcham six months before him. "On his arrival, he was accepted as a bit of a character," recalled Porter, "always appeared to be cheerful and never appeared to worry about things."

One of the things that did concern Harry Challenor was that the public should have respect for the law, so when a street bookmaker near Rose Hill, off Bishopsford Road, gave Challenor a 'V' sign as he cycled by in full uniform, it was like a red rag to a bull. It was at that time a curious anomaly that the law permitted a gentleman to place a bet, quite properly, on the telephone with his bookmaker, but deemed it an offence for an ordinary working man to put a bet on with a street-corner bookie, both punter and bookie being in contravention of the law. It was a ridiculous situation, and it would not be rectified until the Betting and Gaming Act came into force in 1960. Meanwhile, breaches of the law were dealt with by the local inspectors of divisions, who appointed officers to be detailed to work in plain clothes to make arrests. Unfortunately, some officers took this to be a golden opportunity to work hand-in-glove with the bookies; they would arrest a series of 'mugs' or stooges, men with no convictions, to be offered up as street bookies and, thanks to their clean record, to be fined a paltry amount at the Magistrates' Court. The fine was then paid by the real bookie, who was also able to provide a bonus to the erring officers' weekly wage of £7 13s 4d.

What happened next in the V-sign incident is recalled by Thomas Proudfoot, then a police constable at Mitcham: "Harold cycled home to Sutton, changed into old clothes, got past the look-out and arrested the bookie. At the station, he stood back and waited for the congratulations; instead he got the biggest bollocking of his career. He was threatened with disciplinary action for leaving his beat and going off his sub-division without authority, and of course, the special plain-clothes squad which dealt with bookies and runners were not happy with him." Nevertheless, it is highly likely that good behaviour was established on Challenor's beat.

"He was the scourge of the yob element," recalled one of his Mitcham contemporaries. Challenor exercised his authority by arresting them for 'insulting behaviour', which was formally catered for under the provisions of Section 54(13) of the Metropolitan Police Act 1839, a 'catch-all' piece of legislation for a variety of anti-social offences.

Although he cleared the ground of the local tearaways, matters were nevertheless seldom quiet on PC 616 'W' Challenor's beat. During one night duty, Arthur Porter remembered that, "We had a few War Reserves and on one occasion, [Harry] frightened the life out of one of them by suggesting that if he threw a brick through a shop window, the PC could nick the next person coming along for shopbreaking." This undoubtedly was an early example of Challenor's dubious humour.

As he strode round Mitcham, Challenor displayed his hardiness. "He very seldom wore a greatcoat," recalled Thomas Proudfoot, "and said he enjoyed the 'champagne air' of Mitcham Common; perhaps it reminded him of his days on the run in Italy." Possibly the fragrance which Challenor took pleasure in was the large amount of lavender which grew on the 460 acres of the Common; or perhaps he was already formulating plans for his future career within the police force.

He made no secret of the fact that entry into the CID was certainly his intention; with just over thirteen months' service at Mitcham (and with his probationary period as a uniformed constable having another eleven months to run), he submitted his hand-written application to become an aid to CID and was accepted. He had already passed his intermediate examination with a mark of 85 per cent, and two months after being accepted as an aid to CID he passed his final examination with 93 per cent.

The 'aids system' had been in place for thirty years; at the time, it was the only way (and in the view of the vast majority of veteran CID officers, the *best* way) to be accepted into the Criminal Investigation Department. In Victorian times and right up until the 1920s, applicants for the CID were known as 'Winter Patrols' – uniformed constables who donned plain clothes in the run-up to Christmas to keep observations and to stop, search and carry out arrests on criminals who raided stores, factories, vans and railway rolling stock. Later, they became known as aids to CID and worked in pairs; their partners were known as 'bucks', and only if they brought in a sufficiency of arrests (or 'bodies', as they were referred to) and presented their evidence creditably at court, would they be considered for full acceptance into the CID – in Victorian and Edwardian times as a 'permanent patrol' and in later years as a detective constable.

Challenor spent three years as an aid to CID; during his first seven months he carried out 105 arrests for crime. Mitcham – certainly in the 1950s – could hardly be described as a hotbed of crime, and to accomplish an average of fifteen arrests per month was quite exceptional. Nevertheless, there were some officers who were uncomfortable working with Harry; a large number of his arrests were for 'sus' ('Being a suspected person loitering with intent to commit a felony'), for which the penalty was 'a carpet' – to the uninitiated, three months' imprisonment – and it was felt that Challenor's zeal sometimes substituted for what he had actually witnessed. Some of the prisoners were homeless people who quite literally brought it upon themselves. Fred Burgum, eighty-three years of age when he spoke to me, was also an aid at the time, and he recalled hearing that some of Challenor's customers asked him, especially in the cold weather, "Harold, get us inside for a bit."

But it should not be thought that these comments are derogatory in respect of Challenor's work; he was a good aid to CID, he had a 'nose' for the villains, he cultivated and ran informants and he brought in a number of very fine arrests. His first commissioner's commendation was awarded on 12 July 1955 for 'initiative in a case of forgery', and he was also commended in the same case by the

Bench at St Albans Magistrates' Court. How this came about is not clear; a sergeant and a station sergeant were also commended, and they were both from 'A' Division (where the Houses of Parliament are situated), a long way from St Albans in Hertfordshire.

His next was five weeks later, this time for 'initiative and ability in arresting two troublesome housebreakers' in company with Police Constable 444 'W' Nash. The arrest had taken place on neighbouring 'V' Division, which suggests that once more the two officers must have followed the suspects for a considerable distance before their actions justified the prisoners' detention. Another commendation, again after five weeks, for 'ability and initiative in arresting a known criminal for being in possession of an offensive weapon and a firearm' was carried out in the company of a CID officer, Detective Constable Reed. Less than three months later he was again commended by the commissioner for 'alertness and ability in effecting the arrest of a persistent housebreaker', this time alone. In total, Challenor would be awarded a total of eighteen commendations.

One such award was forthcoming in the following circumstances, as recounted by Arthur Porter. "I remember one evening I was with my buck (Police Constable Bill Duff) at Mitcham and Harry was on the 'Q' Car, but [he was] in the station CID office when there was a call saying there was man with a gun in the St Helier Arms pub, which was situated in the middle of a council estate at Carshalton. On our arrival at the pub, it was agreed that my buck and I went into the pub first. It was a little bit like a Wild West film. Everyone in the pub was seated in one corner and the guy with the gun was standing at the bar, looking at the barman. As soon as we walked in, the group sitting indicated the guy at the bar. We went to the bar and stood either side of the suspect. Then Harry came in and tapped him on the shoulder, as soon as he turned to face Harry, we grabbed his arms. Harry then found the gun in a holster, made from army webbing. I think the Luger pistol was unloaded … it turned out that the guy was a soldier on leave from Germany and acquired the weapon there."

Arthur and Bill were aids at Tooting police station and returned there, leaving Challenor to charge the soldier. He was the only person to receive a commendation; Arthur and Bill were not even mentioned as being witnesses on the charge sheet. In those days it really was the survival of the fittest! However, perhaps the balance would be redressed fourteen years later when Arthur Porter was awarded a very well deserved British Empire Medal for gallantry, for his part in arresting an armed prison escapee.

The court to which Challenor would have taken his prisoner was South Western Magistrates' Court; in fact, Daventry House, a large building at 217 Balham High Road, SW17, was used as both the Juvenile and the Magistrates' Court, because the old court had been destroyed by a German bomb. The prisoners were kept in cells in the basement, and the police officers would congregate in a makeshift jailer's office. The back rooms of the house had been knocked through, thereby enlarging the main room, which was used as a court and where there was a roaring fire in cold weather.

This room was where the stipendiary magistrate, Glenn Crask, sat; he had a reputation for irascibility, but not when Challenor gave evidence. On one of these occasions, Peter Elston, then an aid to CID stationed at Balham, saw Challenor for the first time. "He was of average height, well built and well dressed. He always seemed to be in a happy mood and would address everyone as 'my old darling' or words like that. I watched him give evidence," Elston, now eighty-five and living in Canada, told me. "He stood straight as a ramrod and spoke with a clear voice telling the court how he had seen the prisoner go from car to car, apparently trying to steal from them. His presence and evidence was so good, he had to be believed. The magistrate loved him and often told him so, in court. This added to the list of commendations that Harold was collecting. The other aids in the Division could not keep up with him. Harold was the star."

That was the opinion of another aid to CID, Ken Rexstrew, who was based at Tooting police station. Mrs Coral Rexstrew recounted to me how her late husband told her, 'I've met a chap, we went out on night-duty patrol together and he told me his life story'. It was the beginning of a friendship which would endure for over fifty years.

In his memoirs, Harry Challenor projects himself as being hard but fair, giving a suspect the benefit of the doubt when caught in highly suspicious circumstances, gently arresting an escapee from Rampton Mental Hospital, acting compassionately (and not retaliating) when a deaf suspect punched him in the mouth. With regard to this last case, a different interpretation was put on it by Fred Burgum, who recalled that Challenor decided to treat the suspect, who had been found in possession of a large amount of impedimenta with which to break into Barclay's Bank at Tooting, to some rather firm handling. "I don't want none of that!" roared the suspect and promptly flattened Challenor, who prudently kept whatever had happened to cause his 'fat lip' to himself, the following morning at court. So – Challenor, benevolent? No, not really. In the days when aids to CID were extremely keen to arrest anybody for just about anything, Harry Challenor was *feral*.

So these encounters listed in his memoirs do tend to stretch the reader's credulity, but none more so than when Challenor recalled how he decided to repeat his wartime 'escaping washerwoman' escapade and, dressed as a woman, met an informant in a pub so that the informant could point out various criminals to him. The very thought of Challenor in drag, with borrowed high heels pushing his height of almost five feet eleven inches to well over six feet, utterly beggars belief.

But there is little doubt that Challenor's aiding days were effective ones; he put in long hours of work, his correspondence was admired by his senior officers, as was his presentation of court cases. His detective superintendent strongly endorsed his permanent appointment to the CID, and on 9 January 1956 Challenor was appointed detective constable and sent on the Junior CID course. When the Detective Training School at Hendon was opened in 1935, the then commissioner, the illiterate and inarticulate Lord Trenchard GCB, OM, GCVO, DSO, was disliked by the rank and file in general but openly derided by the CID in particular. He got his revenge by ensuring that the CID candidates were schooled in the arts of investigation in two wooden huts of World War One vintage, and this would remain the case until 1961. It made little difference to Challenor; he achieved high marks and he had realized his dream.

Harry Challenor was now a fully fledged detective and he was on his way.

CHAPTER 4

Graduating with Honours

D etective Constable Challenor was posted to Croydon police station, an imposing three-storey building situated on Fell Road, where it had stood for over sixty years. It was the Divisional station of 'Z' Division, the southernmost in the Metropolitan Police area and part of 4 District. 'Z' Division had become the twenty-second division of the Metropolitan Police in 1921, formed to separate Croydon, which had previously been part of 'W' Division. Croydon had suffered badly from the Luftwaffe's bombing during the Second World War – Inspector Arthur Townsend had been decorated for his gallantry in rescuing two children from a bombed, burning house in 1941, and War Reserve Constable Leonard Henry Freake and Police Constable John Fotheringham had received the King's Commendation for Brave Conduct – but following the end of hostilities, new stores and businesses opened and soon the town became congested. Challenor's arrival coincided with the passing of the Croydon Corporation Act, and this, coupled with government incentives for office relocations from the capital's centre, led to new offices and roads being built.

At the time of Challenor's arrival at Croydon, the Metropolitan Police was enjoying some tremendous leadership. Not, unfortunately right at the top; the lacklustre Commissioner Sir Harold Scott had resigned in 1953, and his place had been taken by his deputy, Sir John Nott-Bower KCVO, KPM. Although his King's Police Medal had been awarded in 1931 for conspicuous gallantry in arresting a gunman who had shot him in the arm, Sir John was not regarded as a strong leader; he was referred to as 'a nice man when what was needed was a bit of a bastard'. However, the new deputy commissioner was Sir Ronald Howe KBE, CVO, MC, who had joined the Metropolitan Police as a deputy assistant commissioner in 1932 and knew CID work inside out; much like Deputy Commander (Crime) William Rawlings OBE, MC, a member of the Metropolitan Police since 1919. And for a year prior to Challenor's arrival, 4 District's CID had been under the control of the legendary Detective Chief Superintendent Jack Capstick, who had been awarded a total of forty commissioner's commendations for his work with the Flying Squad and the ultra-secret post-war Ghost Squad. Capstick's affectionate nickname among the underworld was 'Charley Artful', in direct contrast to that of Croydon's newest DC – 'That Bastard Challenor'.

Harry Challenor was in illustrious company at Croydon; Detective Sergeant Fred Fairfax was there who two years previously had been the first Metropolitan Police officer to be awarded the George Cross, following a gunfight on the roof of a warehouse in what became known as the 'Craig and Bentley case'. It was for this incident that two police constables were awarded George Medals, a third won the British Empire Medal for Gallantry, and an officer who was murdered received a King's Police and Fire Services Medal, awarded posthumously for gallantry. Woman Police Constable Kathleen Parrott and Woman Police Sergeant Ethel Bush were there, the first two Metropolitan Police women officers to be awarded the George Medal, two months previously, for their daring decoy work. Detective Constable Bernard Robson was also there, notable for a different reason, since fifteen years later he was to fall foul of *The Times* enquiry and be sentenced to a total of seven years' imprisonment.

The Detective Superintendent was Harold 'Daddy' Marshall, who suffered from an ulcer. During the Friday night staff 'debriefings', when a bottle of Scotch would be produced, he would say to the youngest member of the staff, "Laddie, go and fetch a pint of milk." Producing two glasses from his locker, he would fill the first with the milk and swallow it with a grimace, proclaiming, "That's for my ulcer." Scotch would then be poured into the second glass and this too would be consumed, followed by the words, "And that's for me!"

That was how the much-loved 'Daddy' Marshall was remembered by David Woodland, then an aid to CID. He also recalled Challenor. "As you know," he told me, "Harry was a larger than life character, liked a drink as we all did in those days and didn't give shit for anybody. He was not impressed with rank and invariably treated everybody from the detective superintendent downwards with the same easy-going manner. He was as hard as nails and generally well liked although somewhat erratic or possibly eccentric, and for that reason, my vague recollection is that there were some who preferred to remain in calmer waters and not work with him".

But this did not apply to everybody. Within three months of arriving at the station, Challenor was awarded another commissioner's commendation, in company with two aids, Police Constables 135 'Z' James Robert Cruse and 251 'Z' Ronald Street, for 'ability and determination in arresting a gang of active shopbreakers'. (Eighteen months later, the same two aids would play a decisive role in the investigation of the murder of four-year-old Edwina Marguerita Taylor.)

However, usually working solo probably suited Challenor, because whatever kudos was going could be reserved for him alone. The late Ted Tosney was also a detective constable at Croydon, and Challenor confided in him that he intended to 'get promotion' and that the best way of achieving this was by making a large number of arrests. In addition, said Tosney, Challenor would telephone the local newspaper and tell them that if they were at a certain location at a certain time, they would be able to witness him making an arrest. This would bring him to the attention of his senior officers, but his coverage in the Press was not everybody's cup of tea. This was borne out by David Parkinson, who later knew him at West End Central and who said that Challenor was not particularly well liked at Croydon, especially by the uniform branch.

Well liked or not, Harry Challenor was highly respected. "He was always well dressed, even dapper, dark suit, polished shoes," recalled David Woodland. "As a young aid, knowing something of his wartime exploits (not from himself but through others) it would be true to say that I was in awe of his reputation as a thief-taker. He was known as a competent, confident officer in the witness box, in short, 'a safe pair of hands'." A number of complaints had been made about Challenor's conduct, but as one of his contemporaries was heard to say, "Harry was a prosecutor of 'tasty' people." And a car-load of such 'tasty people' was a group of local tearaways whom Challenor arrested for being in possession of a miscellany of offensive weapons.

As a detective constable, Challenor continued his crime-busting escapades while on 'Q' Car duties. He was ideally suited to this type of work. The 'Q' Car crews were given carte blanche to patrol the division – and often beyond the divisional boundaries – in the big, powerful, nondescript cars of the period: Morrises, Humber Super Snipes, Wolseley 6/80s and Austin A95s. Fitted with two-way radios for contact with Scotland Yard's Information Room, the three-man crew – a Class I or II driver in plain clothes, an aid to CID and Challenor – were in their element, going anywhere at any time to arrest villains. Using hit-and-run tactics to carry out arrests, 'Q' Cars were dubbed by the press 'the Commandos of the CID', and the comparison was not far-fetched.

Three such 'Q' Car arrests were made due to one of Challenor's informants, euphemistically referred to as 'a lady of easy virtue', who provided him with a great deal of useful information. On this occasion she was responsible for bringing about the apprehension of three young men for conspiracy to commit burglary. David

Woodland recalled hearing that Reggie Seaton, the Chairman of the County of London Sessions, was furious when the jury acquitted one of the gang. He called Challenor back into the witness box and for the benefit of the jury demanded to know who, in his opinion was the gang's ringleader. Challenor, recognising a feed-line when he heard one, quickly replied, "The one the jury let off, sir!"

He was extremely active in catching villains, he passed the examination for detective sergeant (second class) on 26 January 1957 and his home life was improved when he and Doris adopted a boy, Andrew, who was born in 1957 and who settled in to the family home at Hallmead Road, Sutton, Surrey. "Ken and I used to meet Harry and Doris at Sutton swimming baths when the children were young," Coral Rexstrew told me. "Harry, who was a magnificent swimmer, used to carry the children on his back. He was a very kind man, who adored children."

In addition, Challenor passed the Standard Car Course at Hendon Driving School on 7 February 1958; it would have presented few problems to him. His behaviour was still effervescent; Len Moore recalled him chasing the girls around the office: "I think they liked it!" commented Moore.

As the case concerning the arrested bookmaker had proved, Challenor did not suffer personal slights lightly; this also applied to affronts to other police officers. A police constable at Mitcham was on night-duty patrol in London Road, Morden, when the wireless car pulled up and asked him if he had seen a large, left-hand-drive American car; this vehicle had driven off at speed at the approach of the police car in a nearby factory estate. The officer, who had seen nothing, continued on his patrol but suddenly became aware of such a vehicle crawling along the kerb just behind him. The driver wound the window down and then pointed a pistol at the officer. Before the officer could react, the driver revealed himself to be an extremely cocky aid to CID – the wireless car returned and there was a very heated confrontation which almost developed into a fight, thanks to the aid's ridiculous and provocative behaviour. He later resigned from the police and became deeply involved with a well known gang from the nearby St Helier Estate.

Enter Challenor. He received information that during the course of an early evening, this gang was going to break open a safe at a company on an industrial estate; in fact, it was said that the rogue aid was the informant and that the door at the far end of the warehouse was going to be left open, so that when Challenor & Co burst in, the former aid would be able to escape.

The gang duly arrived at the road leading to the premises. The only other persons in the thoroughfare were a learner with a competent driver in a battered old car bearing 'L' plates, and as the car lurched and skipped backwards and forwards, practising three-point turns, it failed to sound any alarm bells with the gang. This was unfortunate, because the competent driver was Harry Challenor and the aspiring apprentice was another detective constable. With the gang inside the warehouse, Challenor led the raid; the former aid ran through the warehouse to escape through the far door, only to discover that it was securely locked. How could this have happened? Nobody knew. But of course, the erstwhile aid had been well and truly caught in the act with the other criminals and unfortunately for him he was sent to prison, just like his associates. Whoever had been responsible for the door being well and truly secured, it was felt that justice had been done for the Morden incident.

It was during the period 1958/9 that concerns were voiced by senior officers regarding the CID's caseload; during these years, a further 150 officers were appointed to the CID. Not that hard work appeared to faze Harry Challenor; with Detective Inspector Jimmy Still endeavouring to supervise him, Challenor's star was in the ascendant; his annual qualification reports revealed that he was 'a magnificent worker', was 'excellent' and 'very hard working' and that he continued 'to forge ahead'.

Harry Challenor had certainly 'forged ahead'; the Flying Squad was beckoning.

★ ★ ★

In his memoirs, Challenor firmly stated that the Flying Squad did not cut corners, nor were they a law unto themselves; that being the case, it is difficult to say which Flying Squad Challenor was posted to, because it seems tolerably certain that it was not the one which had been in existence at the Yard since 1919.

Created to combat the enormous rise in crime following the end of the First World War, initially known as 'The Mobile Patrol Experiment' and staffed with just twelve officers noted for their thief-taking and informant-running abilities, the Flying Squad – or 'Sweeney' – had gained momentum and became world-famous for their physical toughness and acute knowledge of the underworld. By the time Challenor was posted to the Squad on 5 August 1958 as a detective constable, it possessed a hundred officers in eight separate squads, each under the supervision of a detective inspector. Each squad was made up of detective sergeants (both first- and second-class) and detective constables, and they were allocated Class I drivers for the very fast Squad vehicles. Their brief was to

gather information about professional villains, then hit them hard
and fast, preferably catching them in the act of committing a crime.
Armed robbers, lorry hi-jackers, warehousebreakers and smash-
and-grabbers were the Squad's prey; and once criminals knew that
the Squad was after them, many would surrender rather than risk a
confrontation, with all of the attendant risks that that entailed. So the
Flying Squad personnel were physically and mentally tough, they ran
informants, they knew the villains and the areas of London which
they frequented and they were tireless and sometimes unscrupulous
in their quest to arrest and convict them. Harry Challenor was in
that mould – and for him to deny that corners were cut or that the
Squad did not have their own set of rules is fatuous in the extreme. It
was because the Sweeney were ruthless in their pursuit of criminals
that knowledge that the Flying Squad was on their case caused the
gangsters and thieves of London considerable discomfort.

The head of the Squad at the time of Challenor's arrival was
Detective Chief Superintendent Bert Sparks – at six feet one and a
half inches, he was known as 'The Iron Man', and at fifty-one years
of age this three-year appointment would crown a glittering career,
during which he had been awarded twenty-four commissioner's
commendations. He was enormously respected, and as the tide
of crime rose – indictable offences in England and Wales had
numbered 626,509 in 1958 and would continue to rise by the
end of his tenure in 1961 to 806,900 – Sparks hit the criminals
head-on. With the Metropolitan Police woefully under strength
at 16,661 officers (in 1931 the personnel had numbered 20,000),
Sparks needed considerable assistance; he got it.

Two first-class sergeants at that time were Ian Forbes and Bob
Huntley; both served several tours on the Flying Squad, and the
former would rise to the rank of Deputy Assistant Commissioner
and be awarded the Queen's Police Medal. Huntley would go on
to become Commander of the Bomb Squad and be awarded both
the British Empire Medal for gallantry in disarming a gunman and
the Queen's Police Medal for distinguished service.

Also present was Alec Eist, who had arrived on the Squad
exactly three months prior to Challenor as a detective constable,
been promoted to detective sergeant (second-class) and stayed.
Eist's probity was highly questionable; his informants put up stolen
lorry-loads of various commodities, and the persons who were
arrested driving those lorries were not necessarily the thieves. Not
that Eist carried out the arrests; he had a dread of going to court
but was punctilious in his preparation of the informants' reports.
He would thoughtfully accompany an informant to the loss
adjusters to ensure that the 10 per cent reward was duly paid over,

although it was sometimes questionable if the fee in its entirety was handed to the snout. However, he had an acute knowledge of the underworld and, like Huntley, was awarded a British Empire Medal for gallantry in disarming an armed suspect.

Alf Durell was a second-class sergeant who served for eleven years on the Squad. He had an impressive knowledge of forthcoming robberies and lorry hi-jackings, particularly in the area of South London where he had spent his formative years. He had boxed as a middleweight under the ring name of 'Darkie' Durell (due to his swarthy complexion), as a vicious armed robber, who had mercilessly attacked a seventy-year-old night watchman with a pickaxe handle, discovered to his cost. Durell, who was thought by some to be a little 'too close' to the criminal fraternity, had nevertheless been commended on twenty-eight occasions. Harry Challenor was in good company.

The Commander of the CID – and as such, in overall command of the Flying Squad – was George Hatherill CBE, a six-feet-six colossus of a man who spoke six languages fluently. He reported, within a month of Challenor's arrival, that the new man 'had made his presence felt by his initiative and drive'.

It appeared that he had: during 1958 the Squad carried out over 1,400 arrests and recovered stolen property to the value of £282,538 – both these figures were the highest on record and more than double those of 1954. Nineteen of their prisoners had been convicted of crimes involving the use of explosives and had received sentences totalling seventy years, and another thirty-nine had been arrested in connection with the theft of sixty-eight motor vehicles, valued at £37,450.

So the days passed, with Challenor being involved in run-of-the-mill Squad work and putting up work of his own. He was as noisy as ever, bellowing with laughter as he chased a lorry thief across back gardens off Thornton Heath High Street – although when the suspect surrendered, blood pouring from a cut on his hand, it is difficult to believe that Challenor brightly exclaimed, "Don't worry, me old darling, I'll see you get the best medical attention possible." Perhaps the prisoner was so exhausted and in such a state of shock that he did not object to being addressed as "Me old darling". Others, however, did.

On 2 November 1959 Tommy Butler returned to the Flying Squad as the detective superintendent. This was his third tour on the Squad; the first had been in 1941 as a detective constable, and he was a quintessential Flying Squad officer. Short, dark, with a receding hairline, Butler, who was unmarried, devoted practically every working hour to police work. When he was not actually arresting criminals, he was either meeting informants or typing reports. Fanatically secretive, he was also unemotional – years later, when Detective Inspector Jack Slipper brought him the evidence which smashed Ronnie Biggs' alibi for the Great Train Robbery, Butler, without a trace of enthusiasm, merely replied, "Right. Lovely. Now, here's your next assignment ..."

In a career with the Flying Squad which totalled seventeen years, he was commended on thirty-five occasions and appointed a Member of the British Empire. A non-smoking, virtual teetotaller, Butler was a workaholic who put in sixteen- or twenty-hour days and expected no less a commitment from his men. It worked. In 1959 the Squad hit new heights, carrying out over 1,500 arrests and recovered stolen property to the value of £312,716. Thirty-five arrests were made in connection with the thefts of sixty-nine stolen vehicles, valued at £46,205.

After Challenor had returned from attending St Thomas' Hospital in May 1960, having complained of experiencing loss of hearing of the higher tones, he found he was speaking louder than ever, and this cannot have endeared him to Butler, who one month later wrote on Challenor's annual appraisal:

> Continues to apply himself industriously to the job in hand. Is capable and willing but is inclined to noisy tactlessness. Room for improvement in this direction.

Some of this tactlessness may have been directed towards the Squad typists. John Simmonds (who with less than four years' service had been posted to the Flying Squad because of his skills with informants) recalls, "He did not mean to be aggressive but he put the fear of God into some of the young typists that used to come to the Squad office for dictation. He would chase them for fun (but not in a sexual way); it was not unusual for a girl to check if Harry was in the office and if he was, she would decline to attend and ask for an older woman to come down in her place. Some girls took his behaviour as fun and laughed at it. People laughed at Harry when he went after the girls, I do not think his motives were sinister and as most of the guys in the office were fathers, no one, to the best of my knowledge thought that Harry's capers were anything but simple fun. Today, I suspect there would be a different interpretation but I genuinely considered him to be harmless."

Simmonds was a member of 8 squad, while Challenor was attached to 4 squad. "Harry was always smartly dressed, with collar and tie, you had no doubt he was an ex-serviceman and he was as hard as a nut," Simmonds told me. "He had the appearance of being an ex-boxer and was reputed to walk to work, just to keep in trim. His wartime experiences as an escaped POW were known, and when you saw Harry, you could accept that maybe only he could have done it. Today, one might question his mental health but at the time he was still considered to be a hero and a character."

Challenor was working long hours, mainly on tip-offs from his informants regarding the whereabouts of stolen and hi-jacked vehicles. However, when Detective Inspector Reginald George Roberts, the officer in charge of 4 squad, was conducting an operation to arrest one of two men wanted for armed robbery, Challenor decided that he would approach matters his own way. This was a mistake. Roberts was enormously experienced, having spent half of his twenty-five years' service with the Flying Squad in all ranks: detective constable, detective sergeant second- and first-class and now, detective inspector. One of the robbers and his girlfriend were going to meet the girl's mother at Liverpool Street station. Roberts decided that the arrest would be effected when the three of them met – possibly to stop the girlfriend or her mother from warning the second armed robber; and if that was indeed the case, it made considerable sense. Despite having been told twice to stick to the original plan, Challenor thought otherwise. When the robber and his girlfriend went to meet the train upon which it was assumed the girl's mother was travelling, and before the meet could be kept, Challenor strolled up to the robber and hit him across the throat with a commando chop, cheerfully telling him – allegedly – as he sat astride him on the ground, "You are nicked, my old darling, and my boss will tell you that formally in a minute."

It was clear that Challenor loved the limelight; he paid the price on this occasion when he was soundly beaten across the back by an umbrella-wielding city gent who thought, with some justification, that he had witnessed a mugging. However, it all turned out well; the guns and ammunition were recovered, the second robber was arrested and both men were convicted. It led Butler to pen Challenor's annual report in July 1961 in which he wrote:

> Detective Constable Challenor has continued to work enthusiastically and well. Is capable and fearless in his dealings with criminals. Has improved in general bearing since working with present partner.

This new partner was Detective Sergeant (First-Class) David Clarence Dilley, who had joined the police after seeing wartime service with the Royal Navy. At six feet one, Dilley was thought to be tough enough to apply a brake to some of Challenor's behaviour.

Perhaps this was echoed by the new head of the Squad. Sparks had retired and his place was taken by Ernie Millen.

Millen had left the Squad as a detective chief inspector four months after Challenor's arrival, and now, as the detective chief superintendent in charge, he was back bearing a broom to sweep the Squad clean. This was Millen's third posting to the Squad, and although at heart he was really a Fraud Squad officer, there is no doubt that he knew the workings of the Flying Squad inside out. Aged forty-nine at the time of his appointment, Millen was known as 'Hooter', either because of the shape of his imperious nose or because, disdaining the use of telephone or intercom, of his preference for bellowing orders down the corridors of the Yard. Millen put a stop to the use of 'mugs' – where a stooge was arrested, driving a lorry-load of stolen goods – and 'participating informants', where a gang of armed robbers was arrested in the act of carrying out the crime, leaving the inside-man to escape, even though the numbers of police present were sufficient to subdue the most hostile of Notting Hill carnivals. This dictum must have initially caused considerable unease to the likes of Challenor and Alec Eist (as well as a few other Squad officers), although it would take another nine months before Eist was kicked off the Squad; however, like many bad pennies, he would return.

With Millen in charge and Butler as his second-in-command, there was an uneasy alliance between the two men. Because of the rise in Squad arrests, Millen wanted to keep it that way and encouraged the men to go for quantity rather than quality, something that would have roused Butler's ire. In fact, the arrest figures for 1961 dropped slightly, to just over 1,400, but the value of the stolen property recovered amounted to £484,931, or more than £170,000 over the previous year's total.

Challenor's three and a half years with the Squad had been good ones, but it was time to go. He and Dilley had achieved a number of successful cases, and Challenor was recommended for promotion. In February 1962 he appeared before the Chief Medical Officer to assess his fitness for the rank of detective sergeant (second-class); and since no mention was made of his odd behaviour he passed with flying colours, although in fairness, to pass the promotional medical examination in those days all one had to do was turn up at the surgery. Commander Hatherill decided that Challenor and the general public would profit from his being sent to a working-class environment, and therefore he was posted to Southwark, part of the Metropolitan Police's 'M' Division.

★ ★ ★

Situated just south of the River Thames, Southwark was, at the time of Challenor's arrival, an area of light industry and factories, office developments and council estates. It is an area of great historical interest; Shakespeare's original Globe Theatre had been built there and it is the home of St George's Cathedral and the Imperial War Museum. And on 5 March 1962 it became the home – albeit a short-lived one – of Detective Sergeant (Second Class) Harry Challenor MM. Southwark police station, built in September 1940, was situated at 323 Borough High Street.

"During the week, Harry generally wore a blue suit and a trilby-type hat," recalled Ron Cork, then an aid to CID. "At weekends, he sometimes wore a sports jacket and slacks." Challenor's reputation preceded him, especially tales of his exploits with the wartime SAS, but as Cork told me, "Harry never wore a regimental tie nor did he speak of his wartime experiences. I was aware that Harry kept in touch with his old Squad chums." Cork added, "He was quite a secretive individual and didn't suffer fools gladly." Cork recalled that Challenor was always industrious in the CID office, friendly, well liked and respected, with a sense of humour. "If you were going out on a job with him, he would say, 'You, you and you – come with me; we're going to nick someone' and he'd brief you on the way."

That was what happened after an associate of the Richardson gang had driven over a prostitute outside a club in Kennington because she had allegedly infected him with gonorrhoea; to re-emphasise his displeasure, he had then reversed over her as well. Given the case to investigate, Challenor had discovered via an informant that the man would be leaving a house in Walworth at a certain time. Taking two aids to CID – Ron Cork was one and his buck, the late Frank 'Chunky' Marsden, the other – in the CID Mini, Challenor sat up in the street and kept observation on the house. The gangster and his wife left the premises, got into a Ford Zephyr and drove off, towards Challenor. The story is taken up by Ron Cork. "Harry then drove the Mini towards the car as there was no way he could pass us as we had taken centre position and there were other parked cars in the street. Harry said, 'Get 'im', I was out of the car with 'stick' in hand and ran up to his car which he started to reverse and do a three-point turn. My only access was via the front passenger door, where his wife was sitting. I tried to open the door and found it locked, as was the rear door. As I started to try to break the side window with my truncheon, his wife was screaming at me, saying, 'He's got a gun, fuck off!' " To emphasise this assertion, she pointed to the area of the seat between her and her husband, and then the gangster swung the car around, knocked Cork against a parked car and drove off. It had happened in seconds; Cork's partner in the rear of the Mini had been unable to get out (since the Mini only possessed two doors), and Cork got back into the Mini and informed his colleagues of the possibility of the suspect being in possession of a firearm; although Challenor tried chasing the Ford, he lost it. Cork explained that he had been unable to get into the Ford because the doors had been locked, and Challenor affected astonishment. "What's the matter with going through the windscreen, me old darling?"

"I have no doubt," Cork told me, "that if Harry had been in my position, he would have attempted it." The last time Cork saw Challenor as a police officer was when they attended court in this case, for which the gangster was sentenced to a lengthy term of imprisonment, and he described Challenor as 'looking quite stressed'. By then, subsequent events had overtaken him, and when Cork asked him if he was all right, "He replied that he was fine but had reached a stage that his Number Ones[3] had overtaken his police commendations."

But certainly, during his days at Southwark, as Ron Cork told me, "I and many of the aids who worked with Harry held him in high regard and as the saying goes, 'would have followed him to hell and back'." Later, it appears that some of them did.

Des Prendergast had been an aid at Southwark, been posted off the Division and returned to uniform because of his long service, then was appointed detective constable and returned to Southwark, where he was thrown into the deep end of investigative work. He was resented by the majority of the rank and file, many of whom had been there previously. The only person to assist was the late Woman Detective Sergeant Henrietta Susannah (known as 'Anne') Dovey, the 543rd woman to join the Metropolitan Police. She died in 2011, just short of her hundredth birthday. "She was a stern, middle-aged lady who was not to be messed with," Ron Cork told me. "Harry used to tease and joke with her – she quite liked him."

The situation was less happy for Des Prendergast. "My life was a misery, I was drowning in a sea of paper and lumbered with cases I didn't know how to deal with," he told me. "Then out of the blue, Harry was posted in, on promotion from the Squad, he took me

---

3. These were official complaints against the police – so called because the number of the complaints docket issued from Scotland Yard commenced with '1', followed by the year of the complaint and then the consecutive number of the complaints that year.

under his wing and sorted out my tray for me and showed me what to do and how to do it! He was one of the kindest men I have ever known. He was a real go-getter and soon became unpopular with the old guard at Southwark." But Prendergast added firmly, "I will never forget the kindness of Harry."

While Challenor naturally kept his sources of information to himself, Ron Cork was on one occasion able to witness Challenor's informant cultivation at close quarters. "He went on a building site where they were losing a great deal of equipment. He walked around for a bit, looking the workers up and down, took down a few details for CRO (Criminal Record Office) checks, then selected a likely candidate and brought him back to the office. He sat him in a chair, brought another and turned it round so the back of it faced the individual, sat astride it facing the said individual and proceeded to tell him that he had a problem which he was hoping said individual could help him with. Suffice it to say that chummy was released and Harry received a number of phone calls." A number of Irish labourers were arrested for stealing a large amount of the site equipment, thanks to the precise information that Challenor had received, and as Cork remarked, "I witnessed the quickest confessions ever, on that one!"

Irishmen also featured in an arrest one Sunday morning when a Traffic Patrol car noticed a GPO van parked opposite Borough tube station which was causing an obstruction to the passing traffic. Challenor and Des Prendergast were called and they entered an old tube tunnel. "Hear that, me old darling?" asked Challenor. "Listen, hear that music? Sounds like someone playing the zither – Harry Lime must be down here, somewhere!"

It was not the intrepid black marketeer of Carol Reed's 1949 film, *The Third Man*, nor was it the sound of Anton Karas' music for the film that Challenor could hear. It was the noise made by the cutting equipment of two Irishmen employed by the GPO who were indulging in a little private enterprise, busily helping themselves to the tunnel's cabling. Both pleaded guilty at Tower Bridge Magistrates' Court and were committed to the County of London Sessions for sentence. The Chairman, Reggie Seaton, handed down punishments that were severe but nevertheless more merciful than the one tendered to the fictional Harry Lime.

Challenor was described as being 'a very capable and energetic officer and one who is completely loyal to the Service', by his senior officers at Southwark. Meanwhile, Harry's old boss from the Flying Squad, Detective Chief Inspector Ron Townsend, was about to be promoted to detective superintendent. Townsend had been a pre-war copper whose career was interrupted by the Second

World War, when he had served as a captain in the Military Police. Rejoining the Metropolitan Police after his demobilisation, he had ascended the promotional ladder, collecting commendations from the commissioner, various Magistrates' Courts, the Old Bailey and the Director of Public Prosecutions for his painstaking work in complicated cases of fraud.

Now, just approaching his forty-seventh birthday and having served two years with the Flying Squad, Townsend learned that on promotion he was going to be posted to 'C' Division, in the heart of London's insalubrious Soho. He needed somebody who was 'very capable and energetic' to rigorously enforce the law on those lawless streets.

A quick telephone call to a friendly face in Scotland Yard's C5 Department was made. A transfer was arranged, and after four months and four days on 'M' Division, and ten days before Townsend's arrival on 19 July 1962, Harry Challenor was waiting for him at the Divisional station, West End Central. Unknowingly, Ron Townsend had opened up the Metropolitan Police's very own Pandora's Box; and as the eponymous owner of that receptacle discovered, all that remained at the bottom of it was Hope.

CHAPTER 5

Soho and 'The Mad House'

Soho, in Central London, is not a large area; it covers approximately one square mile. Its boundaries are Oxford Street to the north, Regent Street to the west, Leicester Square to the south and Charing Cross Road to the east.

The area has for centuries been synonymous with the sex trade, which included strip-joints, clubs (licensed or otherwise), brothels, prostitutes and their attendant pimps – plus gangsterism and protection rackets. And just before the First World War two individuals arrived on these shores to supply London's glitterati with drugs. Chan Nan (otherwise known as 'Brilliant Chang') arrived from the East and ran a lucrative trade until 1924, when he was arrested for possession of cocaine, sentenced to fourteen months' imprisonment and deported the following year. From the other side of the globe came Jamaican Eddie Manning (dubbed 'The worst man in London'), who also ran a lucrative business in prostitution and drugs. His final prison sentence – one of three years' penal servitude for receiving stolen goods – was one from which he would never emerge. He died of syphilis in Parkhurst prison's infirmary in 1933.

A small French contingent frequented the Union Club in Frith Street; it was there in 1926 that Charles Baladda was shot dead by Emile Berthier, a pimp in the pay of a Spanish white-slaver named Juan Antonio Castanar. It was likely that Baladda had been mistaken for Casimir Micheletti, a violent French-Algerian pimp and a sworn enemy of Castanar. Berthier was found guilty but insane and was later deported, as were Micheletti and Castanar.

With the Sabini brothers – who had flourished from the 1920s as racketeers – interned during the war, the area was divided mainly between Jewish and Italian gangs. The Maltese Messina brothers, who had run a thriving prostitution industry before the war, had also taken out British citizenship to prevent them being deported in the event of their arrest; this rather backfired on them since they now became eligible for conscription into the armed services, so they kept a very low profile until the cessation of hostilities. An even lower profile was kept by the White family from North London; their leader, 'Big Alf' White, a hard man in his time, had been humiliatingly beaten up by a gang of tearaways outside

Harringay Greyhound Stadium in 1939, and he had formed an uneasy alliance with the Italian faction. When Italian Antonio 'Babe' Mancini was hanged (and rather unnerved the hangman when from underneath the hood which had been placed over his head he called out "Cheerio!") for the murder in 1941 of Jewish club owner and pimp, Harry 'Little Hubby' Distleman, peace reigned, for a time. Otherwise, law and order was administered in a fairly ad hoc fashion. Divisional Detective Inspector Arthur Thorp from West End Central was fairly unconventional; when punters complained that their wallets had been stolen by prostitutes and nobody would admit the identities of the owners of the rooms used by the women, Thorp would suggest that the aggrieved party "might like to work the room over a little"; he would then avert his eyes as the victim gleefully and systematically wrecked the premises. It was probably a cathartic experience for the punter, if a fairly irregular one for the forces of law and order.

In 1937 the deeply unpleasant Harry Raymond had been sentenced to ten years' penal servitude for running a blackmail ring out of a café in Lisle Street, where beautiful, moneyed, susceptible young men either paid up for their sexual peccadilloes or risked exposure. Barely had Raymond been released when he was at it again; he sought redemption by becoming a Ghost Squad snout whilst he was on the run for nine months, but nemesis, in the form of His Honour Judge McClure at the Old Bailey, caught up with him in 1947 and he received a sentence of five years' penal servitude.

In 1955 considerable friction erupted between the Jewish gangster Jack Spot and the Italian bookmakers, and there was a fight between Spot and 'Italian Albert' Dimes (who had been bound over in the sum of £5 to be of good behaviour for his part in the fight which preceded Distleman's murder) in Frith Street, Soho; although there was a great deal of blood spilt, neither man was convicted of any offence.

The Messina gang were wiped up, imprisoned, deported and died, as did the Sabinis; Jack Spot was savagely slashed with razors, at the behest of his former colleague Billy Hill, and gradually Spot and Hill drifted away from the scene.

But Albert Dimes stayed, and other gangsters with fingers in all sorts of different pies moved in. A club was opened in Old Compton Street by Jimmy Humphreys, a man with nine previous convictions who had just been released after a six-year sentence for safeblowing, and he was assisted in his enterprise by a ponce, later to be linked to the Maltese Syndicate, named Bernie Silver. The notorious landlord Perec 'Peter' Rachman ran La Discotheque in Wardour Street, and Ronnie Knight, at one time the actress Barbara Windsor's husband, ran the Artistes & Repertoire Club – it was known as the A&R – in Charing Cross Road. A club named 'The Stragglers' at Cambridge Circus had attracted the attention of two East End tearaways; their names were Reggie and Ronnie Kray.

Following the Street Offences Act, 1959, many of the hundreds of indigenous prostitutes were driven off the streets, and many of the clubs became fronts for prostitution. The gangsters behaved as they pleased, corrupt payments were being made to the police and crime was simply out of control. Conventional means were useless. Something – or somebody – extraordinary was needed to stop it. Someone very much like Harry Challenor.

★ ★ ★

The Soho area was in one of six police divisions under the control of No. 1 District Headquarters, the building next to Kensington police station in Earl's Court Road. 'C' Division comprised two police stations: West End Central (known in police circles as 'CD') in Savile Row, W1 and Tottenham Court Road, or 'CT'. That great detective Ian 'Jock' Forbes QPM named West End Central as one of eight police stations in the Metropolitan Police which consistently produced a crop of good detectives, and he based this premise on the fact that it was this type of station which provided the greatest variety of criminal investigation experience, due to the neighbourhood in which it was situated. However, over the years, West End Central had had its fair share of trouble.

In 1928 an investigation was launched by Scotland Yard into Kate 'Ma' Meyrick, the proprietress of the 43 Club in Gerrard Street, Soho, where the licensing laws were being systematically flouted, and into the very corrupt Station Sergeant George Goddard. The investigation team, led by Detective Sergeant Fred 'Nutty' Sharpe of the Flying Squad, revealed that Goddard had acquired a house valued at £2,000 on a weekly wage of £6 15s 0d, an expensive Chrysler motor car, two bank accounts containing £2,700, plus £12,000 in a Selfridges safe deposit box rented under the name of Joseph Eagles. When some of these notes were traced back to Mrs Meyrick it merited further investigation, and when one of Goddard's colleagues implicated him in taking bribes on a massive scale, in return for tipping off Mrs Meyrick when raids were planned on her establishment, Goddard, Meyrick and her manager, Luigi Rebuffi, found themselves in the dock at the Old Bailey. Goddard was sentenced to eighteen months' hard labour for corruption and ordered to pay £2,000 costs. The Superintendent of 'C' Division was reprimanded for negligence, fined and transferred; the resultant publicity ensured that the case became a cause célèbre, and it did the Metropolitan Police as a whole (and 'C' Division in particular) immense damage.

To replace Vine Street and Great Marlborough Street police stations, West End Central was opened in Savile Row, W1 on 14 July 1940. Hardly two months had passed before it was destroyed by a German parachute mine. Detective Sergeant Percy Burgess had been in the CID office chatting to a fellow detective sergeant named Frank Collins when the blast blew Collins through two internal walls; he was one of three killed, in addition to thirty other casualties. Astonishingly, three months later, the station had been rebuilt.

In 1954 a Maltese pimp named Joseph Grech had been arrested for housebreaking but claimed that the key which had been used to effect entry also fitted his own front door. He was disbelieved and was sentenced to three years' imprisonment. But from his cell at Maidstone Prison, Grech made a series of damaging allegations which were investigated by Detective Superintendent Herbert 'Suits' Hannam. Grech stated that he had paid a Detective Sergeant Robert Robertson £150 to ensure that a lock was manufactured for his front door to accommodate the key, with another £150 promised after Robertson had been recalled to the witness box to confirm that the key fitted. Grech also implicated his solicitor Ben Canter and his 'runner' Morris Page, and with Robertson all stood trial for conspiracy to pervert the course of justice; Robertson and Canter both received two years' and Page fifteen months' imprisonment. Someone else was implicated from the witness box by Grech: Inspector Charles Jacobs of West End Central of whom Grech said, "For months and years, I was a victim of blackmail."

With a fine sense of the theatrical, Hannam had handed Lord Goddard, the trial judge, a copy of his report, with the corollary, "I do not want to let this out of my hands", adding, ominously, "The report is highly confidential". He was right to express such reticence; the *Daily Mail* revealed details of Hannam's report which had been leaked to them, and if these allegations were to be believed – and by readers of that newspaper they undoubtedly were – they were far, far worse than anything disclosed in the Goddard/ Meyrick case, twenty-five years earlier. It was claimed that forty criminals, including pimps, who were serving prison sentences, had alleged that police officers from West End Central had received corrupt payments for tipping off the owners of brothels and clubs regarding impending raids and had watered down evidence about raids on brothels, and that prostitutes had a rota system for submitting to prosecution, with payments going to officers who could postpone court appearances. Some officers, said the article, were accepting up to £60 per week in bribes – this at a time when a police constable's weekly wage was £10 3s 0d – and one particular officer was said to be 'the richest policeman in the Force'.

Lord Goddard, upon being handed a copy of the offending article, dismissed it with the words, "It does not refer to this case." The Under Secretary of State at the Home Office, Sir Hugh Lucas-Tooth, damned the allegations as "deplorable" and James Callaghan MP, spokesman for the Police Federation, demanded that whatever the situation which existed, it should be "cleared up". The Commissioner, Sir John Nott-Bower, 'screwed his courage to the sticking place', jumped up on to a table at West End Central, informed all of 'C' Division's personnel that there had been no truth in the newspaper's allegations as to the content of Hannam's report and denied allegations that up to 450 officers were being considered for transfer.

Perhaps the commissioner was being a little premature; Hannam's report was not handed to him until two weeks later, and eight officers were identified as being involved in corrupt practices. Six of them were exonerated, which left just two: Robertson and Jacobs.

Jacobs was not prosecuted but he was dismissed from the Force on a police disciplinary board after being found guilty of assisting a prostitute to find premises for her trade or calling, failing to disclose in court the previous convictions of a ponce and failing to account for property taken from another ponce. Both Robertson and Jacobs continued to proclaim their innocence for many years thereafter; it did them not the slightest bit of good.

That there were a great many honest, hard-working police officers working from West End Central there is no doubt; it is a pity that the corrupt actions of a few had given the station a 'taint'.

★ ★ ★

To say that the CID workload at West End Central in 1962 was, as Commander George Horace Hatherill CBE put it, 'a bit too heavy', was rather like saying that the trenches in Flanders during the First World War were 'fairly uncomfortable'. At that time, the CID establishment was up to strength and was comprised of a superintendent and a chief inspector, three inspectors, four first-class sergeants, nineteen second-class sergeants and twenty-one constables. This number did not include aids to CID, who were uniform officers working in plain clothes. The establishment had remained the same since 1959; crime figures and caseloads had not. Correspondence since 1960 had increased by 65.8 per cent; in 1959, the caseload per officer was 264, in 1960, 261 and in 1961, 274. By the first six months of 1962 this caseload had increased to an astonishing 690 per officer, yet the arrest figures had only increased by 13.3 per cent from 1959. In addition, any correspondence generated by arrests made by the aids to CID had to be dealt with by a CID officer. Not for nothing was West End Central referred to as 'The Mad House'.

Shortly after his arrival, Detective Superintendent Townsend submitted a memorandum in which he suggested splitting the West End Central CID into two sub-divisions, 'CD1' and 'CD2', and by 1 October the CID had been reorganised, with each team under the control of a detective inspector. Harry Challenor would serve in CD2 – an area covering Oxford Street in the north, Old Compton Street, Brewer Street, Beak Street and Mount Street to the south, with Charing Cross Road to the East and Park Lane to the west; in other words, Soho. He had previously endeavoured to police the CD1 area of West End Central, which covered Mayfair; it was a disaster. The great and the good of Mayfair, already distressed after their homes had been broken into, further objected to being addressed by the investigating officer as 'your duchess'– just as Tommy Butler of the Flying Squad had when he was termed 'me old darling'. However, even before the sub-divisional split had been implemented, Challenor had already started his operations.

One criminal who frequented Soho was suspected of a number of serious offences, including an armed robbery which had been carried out just off Oxford Street; however, there was insufficient evidence to charge or even arrest him. Challenor went to work and received information that he was in possession of detonators and a quantity of gelignite. He acquired a search warrant and paid a visit to the man's flat in Hoxton. The premises were searched; no gelignite was found but detonators were discovered in the refrigerator. The criminal, knowing he was going away for a considerable time, asked Challenor if he could bid his wife farewell. "Make it quick," said Challenor. "You've got ten seconds." It was all the man needed to make a dramatic departure from the flat's second floor bedroom window.

He resurfaced three days later, together with a solicitor, and made no reply to any of the questions put to him during the interview which followed. Nevertheless, he was charged and at the

Old Bailey he produced a young, up and coming boxer to say it was he who had left the detonators in the fridge. Sadly, the boxer not only failed to produce an explosive punch in the ring, his explanation failed to deliver a significant impact upon the jury; and the man from Hoxton went down for three years.

CHAPTER 6

"It's Frighteners, that's all, Frighteners"

Wilfred Henry Gardiner was not, alas, a pleasant type of person; he had convictions for violence – assaulting a police officer and a traffic warden – and dishonesty, dating back to 1944. He was a strip club proprietor and since August 1960 had owned the Phoenix Club in Old Compton Street; two years later, he also acquired the Geisha Club around the corner in Moor Street, just off Cambridge Circus. Both clubs had flourished until 19 September 1962, when they were closed, due to threats of violence.

This, according to Gardiner, was because on 16 July that year he had been approached by John Charles Ford, leading a group of young men near the Geisha Club. Ford, looking at him in a threatening way, said, "Hello, Bill," and Gardiner replied, "I don't think I know you, do I?" – this was not entirely true. Ford then butted Gardiner in the face. Gardiner crossed the road, but the group followed him and Ford said, "Don't run away. I want to talk to you and do some business with you. Put a couple of my boys on the firm. I shall collect the wages or I might send somebody to collect them for me, and you might not even see me and you'll get no trouble." Gardiner suggested that they talk about it, and Ford replied, "Well, forget about it then. But watch where you walk and watch every way." There was another confrontation the same day, and again, claimed Gardiner, Ford butted him in the face and then a fight broke out. Police were called, but Gardiner refused to cooperate with the enquiry, not even providing his address, and the waters were further muddied when Victor Berrill, a doorman employed by Gardiner, later claimed that it had been Gardiner who started the fight.[4]

According to Ford, the first time he had met Gardiner was some six months previously when a girl who was a stripper in the show

---

4. Victor Berrill features on a number of occasions throughout this book, and none of what he had to say was to Gardiner's credit. Gardiner asserted that this was due to intimidation; from whom, it is not especially clear.

at the Phoenix Club had taken him and some friends there; there was some misbehaviour, and Gardiner stated that he would throw them out if they did not keep quiet. No confrontation materialised, and Ford and his companions left the club. It is possible that the trouble arose after Gardiner had stopped money from the stripper's commission, to pay for Ford's entrance fees to the club. Gardiner's account was that menacing groups of young men, including Ford, had been hanging about outside the club.

The following day, 17 July, Ford and another man, Lionel William 'Curly' King, approached Gardiner outside the Phoenix Club in an effort, said Ford, to 'patch things up'. This, in part, was later corroborated by Berrill the doorman, but Gardiner stated that another young man, Riccardo Mario Stefano Pedrini, was present and said, "If you try to nick Johnnie Ford, I'll cut you up. If I get nicked for it, I shall come out and cut you up, again." Pedrini – who worked as a waiter in one of the restaurants owned by his family – and Ford were childhood friends and spent much of their time together, drinking and dancing in West End clubs. However, King was unsure if that person was Pedrini; and both Ford and Pedrini denied that he (Pedrini) was even present. For the moment, 'Curly' King can be forgotten; he re-emerges later, in stunning style.

The next day, 18 July, the soft-top hood and tyres of Gardiner's car were slashed and its windscreen was smashed; Ford denied having anything to do with causing the damage. On 7 August there was a further incident, and here the waters became exceedingly muddied. Gardiner was in Old Compton Street in possession of a hammer, which he was using to knock out a dent in his car. However, according to Ford, he (Ford) was walking along the street with a Mr Turner when Gardiner drew up in his car in front of him, leapt out and threatened him with the hammer. Turner's memory appeared faulty; he could remember nothing of the incident. John Anthony Spiller would later say that it was he who was Ford's companion, and that Gardiner rose up from behind his car and threatened Ford with the hammer; Ford, however, denied any knowledge of Spiller. And if that were not enough, Gardiner's less than dedicated doorman, Berrill, said that Gardiner had run out of the club brandishing the hammer, and that in any event Gardiner's car was not in the street.

This was rebutted by Police Sergeant Alan Ratcliffe, who stated that Gardiner's car *was* in the street and that Gardiner was standing next to it. Having heard Ford's allegation of being threatened with the hammer, Ratcliffe asked him if he wished to prefer a charge against Gardiner. Ford replied that he did, and the parties present set off on foot to the police station. En route, Ratcliffe heard

Gardiner say to Ford, "I'm going to finger the lot of you when we get over there," and Ford replied, "You know what will happen if you do. That woman of yours won't want to be seen with you again," adding, "I'm going to fix the bastard, one way or another." Elizabeth Ewing Evans, who was living with Gardiner and was employed at the clubs, was probably 'that woman of yours' referred to; she was present and overheard that conversation. Ford and three of his companions ran off; the remainder were questioned by the police and were released without charge. Interestingly, Sergeant Ratcliffe stated that Gardiner had told him that Sergeant Challenor was dealing with an investigation into Ford's alleged protection racket; Gardiner later denied mentioning Challenor by name.

But a short while later, in the early hours of 8 August, Police Constable David Harris saw three men outside the Phoenix Club. Standing with his back to the wall was Wilfred Gardiner, looking, as PC Harris put it, 'rather white'. Facing him were John Ford and Riccardo Pedrini, who appeared to be threatening him. When the officer spoke to the men, Pedrini gave his correct name but Ford stated that his name was 'Williams'. Later, at the James Enquiry into this affair, both Ford and Pedrini denied any recollection of the incident.

Three weeks later, when Police Constable Patrick Goss was on patrol in Piccadilly Circus, an open-top car driven by Gardiner, with Elizabeth Evans as a passenger, drew up. Gardiner claimed that just previously, whilst he was stationary at traffic lights, a van had drawn up beside him, driven by Joseph Francis Oliva, with James Thomas Fraser as a passenger.

Here the connection between the two sets of men should be explained. Oliva had known both Pedrini and Ford since childhood and Fraser since 1962, when they had had a drink in Ford's company. Fraser said that he had first met Pedrini when Oliva had taken him to the restaurant where Pedrini was working; this was denied by Pedrini. However, with regard to Gardiner, Pedrini and Fraser said they did not know him; and Oliva said that he had heard of Gardiner, but did not know him.

On this occasion, Fraser shouted, "Are you still grassing?" and lashed out at Gardiner with a metal object which might or might not have been a bayonet. When PC Goss stopped the van shortly afterwards, both Oliva and Fraser denied any knowledge of the metal object, and when PC Goss searched the van, no such item was found.

Both Fraser and Oliva alleged dangerous driving by Gardiner, and interestingly, both men claimed to be the driver of the van. Another passenger in the van was Jean Murray, who told the officer that the driver of the van had been Oliva and that apparently there had been a vehicle trying to race them, which had been driven by Gardiner. She added that she had not seen a weapon of any description produced. And there, for the moment, we can leave Miss Murray, who reappears again at the arrest of Oliva.

Although Gardiner's passenger Miss Evans said she was unable to hear Fraser's actual shouted words at the traffic lights, she did say that after Fraser had been stopped at Piccadilly Circus, he said to her, "When we do your old man up, we will do you as well." And once again PC Goss recalled that Gardiner mentioned the name of Sergeant Challenor, who was investigating the activities of the occupants of the van – something that Gardiner denied.

The following night, 26 August, Gardiner claimed that he was approached by Ford and Oliva, the latter saying, "How's business? You won't be in business much longer if you don't look after us," adding, "If you try nicking us, I shall shoot you. You're a dead man, anyway. You won't live the rest of the year." As Ford ran his finger down Gardiner's back, Oliva stated, "You're going to get your back all cut up." However, Oliva later said that Gardiner started an argument with Ford and then that he, Oliva, offered to fight Gardiner, an offer that was refused. Ford, however, claimed that he personally was not even present.

In the early hours of the morning of 19 September, Gardiner stated, he had seen Oliva, in the presence of Ford, cutting the hood of his (Gardiner's) car outside his club, with Ford telling him, "That is what we will do to your face" – something later denied by both Ford and Oliva, who stated they were not even there. Gardiner had now had quite enough and he went to West End Central to formally complain – to Challenor, he said, although the statement was in fact taken by Detective Constable Desmond Harrison.

The reason for this was because on 28 August DC Harrison had received an anonymous letter stating that a gang of about seven men, under the direction of Joseph Oliva, had been meeting at the Coffee Pot in Brewer Street; and through DC Harrison's own informants, he believed that Oliva and his gang had been causing trouble and endeavouring to operate protection rackets in that area. DC Harrison's informants were being intimidated and believed that Wilfred Gardiner might be similarly subjected to blackmail.

But whilst the statement was being obtained, it appears there were shady goings-on at the Geisha Club. Elizabeth Evans – and there were no other witnesses – stated that she had been approached by Oliva, Pedrini and Ford. She told them that she did not know Gardiner's present whereabouts and would not tell them if she did; she said that Oliva and Ford threatened violence to Gardiner if he reported them to the police. This was entirely denied by the three men, who called witnesses of varying reliability to say they were elsewhere at the material time.

It appeared that a large number of the persons involved in this scenario were experiencing the utmost difficulty in giving an accurate version of events.

* * *

On the evening of 21 September two aids to CID, Police Constables 310 'C' John Bryan Legge and 309 'C' Allen David Wells, were keeping observation on the Phoenix Club from the opposite side of the road in Old Compton Street. Although both men were attached to West End Central, they had both been there for less than a week and neither had had any dealings with Harry Challenor. In the club's doorway they saw Wilfred Gardiner; he was being pushed by Ford, Pedrini and Alan John Cheeseman, to the accompaniment of shouting and swearing.

Cheeseman was an out-of-work salesman, who two years previously had met Ford through a friend of his father's, and through him, Pedrini. The men used to drink together in a pub in Theobalds Road, but the occasion of his arrest, said Cheeseman, was the first time he had visited the West End with them. He did not believe he had met Fraser or Oliva previously. This did not, however, accord with the recollection of Oliva, who said that he had known Cheeseman for years; they would drink in the pub in Theobalds Road with Pedrini and Ford, and sometimes the four would visit the West End together – at other times, he and Cheeseman would go to the West End alone. In addition, Cheeseman said that he did not know Gardiner.

As the two officers crossed the street, PC Legge heard Pedrini say to Gardiner, "You're going to give us £100, or what you going to do?" Prior to the arrival of the police, Gardiner stated, Cheeseman was in possession of a knife and had said, "Let's stripe the bastard. He's given us a lot of aggravation." He also said that Ford had nicked his ear with a knife, and the officers did confirm that Gardiner's ear was bleeding.

On telling the three men they were police officers and that they had heard threats uttered and a demand for money, Pedrini replied that Gardiner would not dare to charge them, whilst Ford took to his heels and escaped. Cheeseman stated, "I don't know anything about this. We were only kidding about doing him up."

The two arrested men, plus Gardiner, were taken to West End Central in a police van, and there PC Wells found a foot-long length of metal tubing in the inside pocket of Pedrini's overcoat – it was, claimed Pedrini, his 'cigar holder' – and, stated PC Wells, Pedrini offered him £100 if he (Wells) "would see him all right". PC Legge searched Cheeseman and in Cheeseman's pocket he found a flick-knife, which the prisoner claimed he carried "for his own protection".

A few hours later, at one o'clock in the morning, Police Constables David Leonard Harris and David Paul Stephenson (both aids to CID) were looking for Ford, who had run off earlier when Cheeseman and Pedrini had been arrested. They found him, together with John Anthony Spiller, in Shaftesbury Avenue, where Ford claimed his name was 'Assarati'; when he was told that he was being arrested for demanding money with menaces, he replied, "It's that bastard Gardiner; he's grassed on us," adding, "It's a nice club he's got; if he charges me, he won't have it for long." Taken to West End Central (accompanied by Spiller), Ford was searched and nothing of consequence was found.

But an hour later, Harry Challenor was taking down Ford's antecedents when Ford said, "Can I speak to you, guv?" Reminded that he was still under caution, Ford replied, "That's all right. I'm knackered anyway, but don't get the wrong idea, this is all a take-on. Joe Oliva and a few of the boys have been taking the mickey out of him, we wouldn't have had his money, it was just frighteners." Challenor made a note of these comments, at which Ford reiterated, "It's frighteners, that's all, frighteners."

★ ★ ★

Joseph Oliva was arrested the following day, 23 September. Harry Challenor had received information that Oliva intended to fire-bomb the Phoenix Club; he consequently instructed two aids to CID, Police Constables 373 'C' Peter Warwick Jay and 155 'C' George McIntosh Laing, to keep a watch for him, and if Oliva was seen, to keep him under observation. In fact, he was seen in the Coffee Pot in Berwick Street – the meeting place mentioned in DC Harrison's anonymous letter – and Challenor was informed and met the two aids in an unmarked police car. At 11.30 that evening they saw Oliva, together with two girls, Jean Marie Murray and Jane Anna Ryan, get into a white Renault and drive off. Oliva's car was followed but when it came to a halt, due to the amount of traffic in Brewer Street, Challenor decided to act. Getting out of the police car, he ran to the nearside of Oliva's car, while PCs Jay and Laing ran to the offside and Laing pulled Oliva from the vehicle; he was struggling and shouting to such an extent that Laing was obliged to draw his truncheon. PC Jay could detect a strong smell of turpentine coming from the car and found an oval bottle, two-thirds full of a colourless liquid, on the floor where Oliva's right foot would have been. Although the bottle was of the type to have been secured with a screw-cap, the neck was plugged with a piece of towelling material. Taking this bottle over to the police car, PC Jay could see Oliva being searched by PC Laing, who discovered a flick-knife in his pocket. Challenor had brought the two girls over to the car and remarked that the bottle was to be used to start a fire at the Phoenix Club, a suggestion which Oliva neither denied nor confirmed. Arrested for that offence, Oliva replied, "If I don't burn him, somebody else will", and when told he would be also be charged in respect of the flick-knife, he replied, "So what? I've got a repeating airgun at home, but I don't use it."

At West End Central the two girls were handed into the custody of the matron, and Oliva was placed in a detention room. PC Jay later entered the room and discovered Oliva cringing and whining, "Don't hit me". His disposition then suddenly changed, and picking up a chair, he shouted, "You're not going to hit me, because I've eaten bigger blokes than you."

A later search of Oliva's address by Challenor and PC Laing revealed that in his bedroom he did indeed have a repeating air pistol. It was wrapped in a piece of towelling, and when this was submitted to the Metropolitan Police Forensic Science Laboratory, together with the towelling used as a stopper for the bottle containing turpentine, a scientific examination revealed a 'mechanical fit' – that the stopper had been cut from the towelling found in Oliva's bedroom.

At midnight on 25 September Police Constables 491 'C' Donald Francis Gibson and 615 'C' Michael Margrave Trobridge Edwards, two aids to CID, were keeping observation on the Phoenix Club. PC Edwards was talking to Elizabeth Evans when she directed his attention to James Fraser, who was approaching Wilfred Gardiner at the junction of Greek Street and Old Compton Street. Gardiner stated that Fraser, who was holding something in his pocket, told him, "I've been looking for you, you bastard," and Gardiner, who was aware that PC Gibson was present, nodded to him. As PC Gibson crossed the road, Fraser saw him and walked away, but he was stopped. Telling Fraser he intended to search him, Gibson did just that and discovered a cut-throat razor in his pocket. Asked why he was in possession of the razor, Fraser – obviously referring to Gardiner – replied, "I suppose he put you on to me, did he? He doesn't know what's coming to him," adding, as he was arrested,

"He'll have to get more than you lot to look after him. His days are numbered."

All of this was compelling evidence to substantiate a charge of racketeering, although it would later be suggested by the National Council for Civil Liberties that because the charge of conspiracy was not added until twelve days after the prisoners' initial arrest and charging, the evidence was not as strong as might be thought. The answer is simple: at that time, a charge of conspiracy could not be preferred without the authorisation of the Director of Public Prosecutions; he had to study the evidence before authorising such a charge, hence the delay in assembling the evidence, passing it to the DPP's office for authorisation and then, the decision having been reached, adding the conspiracy charge at court. It was not until the Criminal Law Act 1977 was passed that it became possible to charge a prisoner with this offence without reference to the DPP.

Not, of course, that that was of the slightest interest to the prisoners; and what they had to say later differed considerably from the version given by the police.

* * *

Pedrini – a young man with a previous conviction for malicious damage – stated that at the time of his arrest he had said nothing to Gardiner and that he had been thoroughly searched by PCs Wells and Legge and they had found nothing; he insisted that Miss Evans had intervened to release Cheeseman – who later said that he had not even seen Gardiner – but that Cheeseman had been re-arrested at Gardiner's insistence; it was a matter denied by both officers and Miss Evans. Ford, on the other hand, would later say that he did not run off at all, but having wished Cheeseman and Pedrini a courteous "Good night" at the junction of Old Compton Street and Greek Street, he had strolled off along Moor Street, towards Cambridge Circus.

Pedrini said that at West End Central Challenor and another officer came to his cell and Challenor said, "Hello, my little darling. I don't want you. Where's your pals?" He then mentioned a number of names, including Oliva, and Pedrini said he knew none of them. Challenor then threw a metal bar on to the floor, saying, "That's yours, my old darling," and when he refused to pick it up, Challenor punched him half a dozen times in the face. His facial injuries – including a broken tooth – were quite visible, and when he was charged, he declined to sign for his property, which included the metal bar. However, Inspector Ernest Chidzoy, who charged the prisoners, did not see any signs of facial injury;

neither did any of the other police officers. The other prisoners said that they did. So, apparently, did Pedrini's sister, Mrs Antoinette Bellini, who said she saw her brother at court the following day and noticed his lips and eyes were swollen. He claimed he had been beaten up by the police, but she made no mention of this when she was interviewed by police on 4 February 1964; she did, a few months later, at the James Enquiry. Pedrini did allege at his trial that he had been assaulted but made no mention of the broken tooth "as it was not worth mentioning". Even more irrationally, as he later told the James Enquiry, either PC Wells or PC Legge, speaking of Challenor, told him, "That man is mad. He was a prisoner of war by the Italians and he hates Italians," an allegation which, given Challenor's wartime experience in Italy, was highly fanciful.

Cheeseman – who had no previous convictions – was in an adjoining cell at West End Central and was visited by Challenor, who, he said, hit him in the face, told him he was "in a right load of trouble" and later showed him a knife, saying, "That's for you" and pointed to an iron bar, saying, "That's for your mate, Pedrini".

Ford, who had been previously convicted for assault and possessing an offensive weapon – and who in 1964 would head-butt a police officer, something he mentioned (but later denied) that he was prone to do – was interviewed by Challenor at West End Central and denied knowing Oliva. Later, in the charge room, in company with Pedrini and Cheeseman, Ford said he saw an iron bar and two knives on the charge room table. Challenor pushed the bar towards Pedrini, who refused it, and then one of the knives towards Cheeseman's property, with the words, "That's for you". As a uniformed officer entered the charge room, Challenor closed the third knife and put it in his pocket, saying, "I want something bigger for you." If that was the case, whatever the 'something' was, it was not forthcoming. Ford claimed at the James Enquiry that he got the impression that the reason why Challenor failed to plant an offensive weapon on him was because Challenor hoped to extort money from his family. Precisely why Ford came to this conclusion is not exactly clear.

John Spiller, who had voluntarily accompanied Ford to the police station, duly noted Pedrini's injuries before he himself was slapped in the face by Challenor, for no apparent reason, and told that if he 'poked his nose in' he would get more bird than the others because he would have more iron bars than he had given the others. He did not mention the slap when interviewed by police, almost eighteen months later, but did at the James Enquiry when he was escorted to the tribunal from prison, to give evidence.

Fraser did not dispute any of the evidence at the trial, saying the razor was used in his employment at Covent Garden. He had previously been convicted for possessing a pistol and for not having a firearms certificate. He later alleged that the razor had not been in his possession when he was arrested, that he had not seen it until PC Gibson produced it when he was charged, but later still admitted that with the exception of his name and address the whole of the evidence which he had given at his trial had been concocted and was a lie.

Oliva was a different kettle of fish when it came to a background of serious criminality. This can best be described in an interview he gave to the *Daily Sketch*, published on 1 July 1959, which was accompanied by a grinning photograph of himself showing wounds to his chest which had been caused by shotgun pellets. This astonishing two-page document, each page signed by him, together with corrections which had been initialled by Oliva, reads as follows:

30th June 1959
JOSEPH FRANCIS OLIVA, aged 19, of 6 Radcliffe Buildings, Bourne Estate, Clerkenwell, N. says:

I was shot in the chest as I stood in the doorway of Carlo's Restaurant, Theobalds Road, Holborn, last night.

I am a Roman Catholic, educated at St Peter's Italian School in Clerkenwell Road, leaving at 15. Since then I have had four convictions – one at 15 for stealing a car; another at 16 for stealing a motor cycle; three years borstal reduced to six months on appeal for breaking and entering at 18, at 17 I was fined for causing grievous bodily harm.

I was used to be a fish porter but I have not worked for two years.

My father is a docker and I have two brothers, aged 22 and 29. The eldest one is married.

In the shooting last night I got about 16 lead shots in my chest. My mates picked them out with a knife.

This is what happened. Ten of us were drinking tea when a black Austin pulled up outside the cafe. A man stuck a single barrel shotgun through the window when I went out to see them. When I was two yards from the car, the man fired. The car raced off before I could get at the man. I am not disclosing his name to anyone, not even the police. I know who he is and I am out to get him myself. I will settle this my way.

I went to the Homeopathic Hospital. They gave me an injection but I insisted on leaving. My mates had washed the wounds and picked out the 16 shots. Perhaps there are one or two still in but this doesn't worry me.

The reason for the shooting is because I am the leader of a gang 400 strong. They call me King Oliva.

The shooting is in retaliation for a fight which took place in a dice speiler in a Camden Town club three weeks ago. It was a revenge attack because six of us cleaned up all the money, about £80. We just did it to show I was the "Guvernor". The money has gone on a car – a big Buick car, big enough to hold a lot of us.

I am going to be boss of the night clubs – and run the night clubs around the West End. I have got to shift one or two big gang leaders to do it. But I have got a man behind me financing me. I already work for him. We have got to have cars to get around in and "clobber" (clothes) to look the part.

We already get a nice little living from the East End clubs and some in the West End. And we look after about 12 clubs. We see no one takes liberties with the juke boxes and we make sure there is no trouble in the clubs. The club owners pay us for this and we give the money to the "Governor". He is a London business man who owns property and lives in a big house on the outskirts of town.

I command about 400 people. I can get them all at just 24 hours notice just by fifteen to twenty 'phone calls to individual top men in each gang. Then I am the Governor of them all. They are different gangs from all North and South London but mostly in the Theobalds Road Area.

All the 400 do not get paid. They do it for the kicks. They are all teenagers. They worship me – King Oliva.

We last called the 400 up six months ago for a big fight at the Memorial Hall, Camden Town. But the other side backed out.

I have two Lieutenants. I split equally with them. I am drawing about £30 a week at the moment.

We do not value our lives because without money we are nothing.

I am not worried about jail. If you do these things you have to expect "bird". It is one of those things. I am not afraid of prison or afraid of anything or anybody. When I am dead, that's it. I am not afraid of serving as much time as Billy Hill but I am not going to jail for nothing.

Look at Billy Hill. He was like us when he started. We admire him and look up to him. He's living easy. He is respected – feared if you like. I am going to be like Billy Hill one day.

We are going back at the fellows who shot me to give more than we got. In the death, they will fall in with me and I'll be stronger still.

It was Chicago come to London. A car pulled up … bang, bang. Men can get shooters easily in London if they know where to go. We are not afraid and not worried about the public. They don't worry about us.

We don't want to have a go at the public. Only gang governors like us in the underworld. I am going to be boss because there are some rich pickings. All a fellow needs is guts and backing – and I've got both. We are going to live good with cars, and fine clothes. A big showdown for power is coming and when it does come it will be a bloody battle.

I used to fight for fun but now I'm going to the top for money. Girls? I go out with a few but I don't go steady. I've not time for them in my business.

(Signed) JOSEPH OLIVA.

When he was later questioned at the James Enquiry regarding this document, he became extremely truculent, tearing up the transcript in the witness box and declaring that it was "lies and filth". It was not, he said, a series of juvenile boasts but a complete fabrication by the newspaper. Oliva had refused to give evidence about the shooting, but three of his assailants had been jailed for the attack. John Ford had been present at the shooting and two years later both men had been convicted of possessing housebreaking implements – these included a jemmy and face masks – for which Oliva had been sentenced to nine months' imprisonment. He had previously been fined for hitting a youth over the head with a milk bottle and in 1960 was sentenced to two months' imprisonment for assaulting two women whom he stopped in Holborn. The following year he was again sentenced to two months' imprisonment for assaulting an attendant at a Turkish Baths. In fact, by the time of his arrest for possessing the fire-bomb, his number of convictions had risen to ten.

His version of his arrest was that when his car stopped in Brewer Street, Challenor, sitting in the police car, said, "Well, if it ain't fucking Oliva" and told the aids, "Arrest the two girls in case he calls them as witnesses." One of the officers – presumably PC Jay – had a bottle on his lap, which Oliva had not seen before and which had a screw cap on it. Challenor told him, "It's for you. You were just going to blow Gardiner's Club up." When one of the girls protested about the arrest, Oliva said he told her to be quiet, as he "could get enough witnesses to square this little lot". At West End

Central, Challenor, together with PCs Jay and Laing, saw him in the cells, and Challenor, he said, was in possession of the bottle and a knife. He told one of the aids to tear off a corner of a towel, which he recognised as being from the boot of his car, and put the torn piece in the neck of the bottle, telling Oliva, "We are putting all this stuff on you. We have had your mates and now we will have you". Oliva later described Challenor advancing towards him with his jacket off, saying, "I'll give you something to scream about," whereupon Oliva picked up a chair and replied, "If you come any nearer, I'll hit you with this chair and then you can charge me with something"; he then said the officers ran from the room because they had guilty consciences at having framed him. This does not sound entirely credible.

But what of the two girls who were in the car, against whom charges were later dropped? Miss Murray had originally worked for Gardiner as a club hostess and was paid in accordance with the number of drinks purchased by the customers, but she was placed under supervision for being in need of care and protection, due to her tender years. She had been associating with Oliva for about a year prior to her – and his – arrest. She told the enquiry that she had seen Oliva put the towelling in the boot of the car on the day of their arrest. She saw the bottle in the car after they had been arrested, with a white rag in the top, and had not seen a knife in the car.

Miss Ryan had also worked for Gardiner when she was sixteen as a club hostess, as well as working at other similar clubs, until she was placed on probation, one of the conditions of her order being that she stayed away from London's West End. She had known Oliva since 1959 and through him had met Ford, Pedrini and Cheeseman. She also said she knew the towelling was in the boot of the car and when arrested she too saw the bottle with a white cloth stopper – but did not see a knife, the knife which PC Laing had found in Oliva's pocket.

And when Challenor searched Oliva's room, his father Francis Oliva would later tell the James Enquiry, on finding the repeater air pistol Challenor had exclaimed, "This'll get him ten years." Mr Oliva senior was adamant that the pistol was not wrapped in towelling, nor was towelling taken from the house.

However ... none of the prisoners alleged at the police station that the items had been planted. Nor did they allege it at the trial. What Oliva said at the trial was that the police *did* find the bottle in the car with the towelling in it, but it was not his; the bottle belonged to a Mr Darling, whom he had known for two years, as did the flick-knife found in his pocket. When PC Jay gave evidence, it was suggested under cross-examination that Oliva had said to him, "I've got witnesses to prove that I lent my car to a friend, and the bottle is not mine." PC Jay denied that Oliva had said those words, as well he might, because they were not spoken. Miss Murray told the court that she had seen the knife in the car but not the bottle. Miss Ryan attended the Old Bailey but was not called to give evidence. Mr Darling also gave evidence to the court that he had borrowed Oliva's car, that the bottle was his and that the flick-knife belonged to a friend.

That was not quite the truth. Oliva had not known Darling for two years; he had met him at Brixton Prison whilst on remand for his trial. Everything that Darling and Miss Murray and Oliva had told the court, on oath, was a pack of lies; this was later admitted by Oliva and Miss Murray. Not only that; Pedrini and Ford also later admitted that they had lied at their trial. When Oliva was charged, together with the charge of receiving a stolen car radio which had been found in the car, he replied, "No, thanks."

On 18 December 1962 at the Old Bailey, following a two-week trial and after the jury had deliberated for two and a half hours, the five men were found guilty. Passing sentence, His Honour Judge Maude said:

> It is necessary for the protection of the public that blackmail of any kind – particularly in the very heart of London – should be sternly dealt with at the earliest possible stage – that is, when persons have only gone as far as agreeing to commit such a detestable crime. In other words, when they conspire to commit blackmail.
>
> Moreover, the punishment must be of such severity as will show that the courts are of firm determination to strike fear into the hearts of persons who agree to acts as 'frighteners' and thieves. Doubtless you thought that with Mr Gardiner's disgraceful past, he would not dare to invoke the law and face the police and jury for the fear in his heart that the past would prevent the acceptance of the truth from his lips.

For conspiracy to demand money with menaces, demanding money with menaces and possessing offensive weapons, Pedrini was sentenced to seven years' imprisonment and Cheeseman to three. Ford, for demanding money with menaces and for conspiracy to do so, was sentenced to five years' imprisonment. Oliva, for conspiracy to demand money with menaces, possessing offensive weapons and receiving a stolen radio, was sentenced to six years' imprisonment. Fraser, who was acquitted of charges relating to demanding money with menaces, was sentenced to fifteen months' imprisonment for possessing an offensive weapon.

After the prisoners had been taken to the cells, Judge Maude addressed the court, saying:

> Woe betide anyone if anything happens to Mr Gardiner and woe betide anyone who tries to do this sort of thing again in the heart of London. The next time, the sentences will be doubled.

★ ★ ★

If the general public – and police and villains – had not heard of Harry Challenor before, they had now. 'Sergeant Harry topples "King" Oliva', reported the *Evening Standard*, which carried a photograph of a sunken-cheeked Joseph Oliva and a potted biography of Challenor, plus a photograph of him sipping a celebratory glass of Guinness. 'A Soho Gang Gets 21 Years', the *Evening News* informed its readers, with the sub-heading, 'Courts determined to strike fear into hearts of frighteners'. The newspaper also reported:

> Listening to the sentences being passed was forty-one-year-old Det.-Sgt. Harry Challenor, who had been assigned to break the protection gangs in the West End.
>
> Sgt. Challenor, holder of the Military Medal, heavyweight boxer and swimmer and an ex-Paratrooper, led a team of detectives. He was helped by his knowledge of Italian learned during the war, in interviewing Soho's cosmopolitan population.

Senior officers were delighted with his performance; Detective Superintendent Townsend had written on 4 December 1962, 'Detective Sergeant Challenor continues to work with industry and has developed a knowledge of the problems of the Division, well in advance of many long-serving officers.' And three months after the headlines, commissioner's commendations were awarded to Challenor and six of his aids: Police Constables Legge and Gibson (both of whom had by now been appointed detective constables, on 'B' & 'E' Divisions respectively) and Laing, Wells, Jay and Edwards for 'persistence and ability resulting in the conviction of a number of violent criminals for offences in connection with the paying of protection money'. John Simmonds attended a social gathering whose participants included Ron Townsend, who was singing Challenor's praises to the assembled company, telling them that Challenor was cleaning up the West End on his own and that with a few more like him, West End Central would be a better place. Referring to the plaudits being handed out by his senior officers, Peter Jay told me, "Harry soaked up their congratulations," adding, "He was certainly a man on a mission."

This was corroborated by Len Smith, then a uniformed officer working from West End Central's Clubs Office. "Harry was fearless," he told me. "I saw him walk into a club in Gerrard Street and he simply looked at the two minders in there; they just got up and walked out, without a word." Smith added, "Many of the 'faces' in there also beat a hasty retreat!"

"I was one of 'Harry's Boys'," Don Gibson – later a detective chief superintendent – told me. "I thought he was wonderful. He inspired confidence. Harry was just under six feet tall," he said, "heavily built, with fingers like bananas. I never heard him raise his voice but when he wanted to make a point, his face would change, it took on a different look, almost as though he was tackling a German sentry. His eyes would almost close, he would point his finger and he would say very quietly, 'I'm not going to tell you again'."

Challenor was not universally adored. One officer who wanted no details of his identity disclosed admitted, "I thought he was the sort of person whom it was better not to get mixed up with." Raymond 'Dick' Docking, who was an aid to CID, told me, "I don't think many people wanted to challenge him." And Frank Gutsell (then a uniform inspector and later Deputy Chief Constable of South Yorkshire) said, "He wanted to cleanse Soho of all evil; he was boisterous, a dangerous man to have around."

Just how dangerous, a number of Soho habitués were about to find out.

CHAPTER 7

"Don't Look Any Further, Sergeant"

On 21 January 1963 Challenor and Detective Sergeant Frank Evans were put in charge of the 'C' Division aids, who had an office on the fourth floor of the police station. Evans was responsible for the administrative side ("Frank was a bit like the Olympic torch," one of his colleagues humorously told me. "He never went out!"). However, on 22 April Detective Superintendent Townsend and Detective Chief Inspector Gerald McArthur (later to achieve great success with his investigation into both the Great Train Robbery and the Richardson Brothers torture enquiry) decided to introduce a special night-duty squad made up of thirty aids to CID, drawn from all over 1 Area, in order to combat crime in Soho. In fact, Challenor's old boss from the Flying Squad, Ernie Millen, now the Deputy Commander of the CID, had brought about an increase of a further 186 officers in the Metropolitan Police's CID, bringing the establishment to 1,774; this was a much needed boost to crime fighting.

Challenor was an obvious choice for one of the officers to lead the night-duty unit; on 5 March Superintendent Townsend had described his energy as being 'outstanding' and he had written in Challenor's annual report that he was, 'a very shrewd, deep-thinking officer who works with energy and purpose. Keen, competent and loyal.' Police Constable John Legge was one of the aids to CID who had been mentioned in Challenor's latest commissioner's commendation – his first – and was one who recalled the night-duty squad. "The first week saw over 120 arrests all for Vagrancy Act offences, burglaries, pickpockets etc." he told me. "Over a month, the crime figures were drastically reduced." Comparing the statistics of the first six months of 1963 to the same period in 1962, 580 fewer crimes were committed, 256 more were cleared up and there was an increase of 287 arrests.

This type of result was inevitable when Challenor was one of the officers in charge of the proactive role; the other was Detective Sergeant (First Class) Kenneth Howard Etheridge, who after seeing war service with the Royal Navy had initially joined the Cornwall Constabulary before transferring to the Met. Described to me as being 'One Hundred Per Cent', Etheridge would be commended on twenty-five occasions before retiring with the rank of detective chief superintendent in 1977. Etheridge was not a friend of Challenor's – in fact, not many people were. But Etheridge described his colleague as being "a police officer with a tremendous appetite for work, a good-natured man with a good sense of humour, noisy and a bit of a rough diamond".

Etheridge and Detective Constable Des Harrison often worked with Challenor and accompanied him on raids. Very little briefing was given. "'We're going to arrest some people for possessing guns or explosives,' Harry would say," recalled Don Gibson, "and off we went."

John Legge concurred with many of these sentiments. "His briefings were quick, 'follow me' type," he said. "A good leader. His hobby was working 24/7, if possible. Harry disliked supervision and loved freedom, to arrest as many as possible. He told me that everyone he arrested was a potential informant. His informants would have come from clubland, dives, Greeks in Soho. Harry maintained a good relationship by putting the fear into those who wished to operate in the Soho area."

For Challenor, paperwork was of secondary importance. "I can remember him at three o'clock in the morning, in the office, typing a prisoner's antecedents," Dave Parkinson told me. "They were to be presented at the Old Bailey later that morning – and in those days, there were no photocopiers!" This was true; copies were made by using carbon paper between the forms; a mistake meant that the error had to be erased on each copy, and the final copy was usually illegible.

Marlborough Street Magistrates' Court was where the prisoners from West End Central were initially taken. The building had originally been designed as the district's public wash-house, and in the years which followed a great deal of dirty washing was aired there. There were two main stipendiary magistrates in residence: Edward Robey, the son of George Robey, the comedian with the expressive eyebrows, and Leo Joseph Anthony Gradwell DSC, RNVR, who had served with distinction in the Second World War as the skipper of the trawler *Ayrshire* – a fact which became known to Harry Challenor. He purchased a dozen Merchant Navy ties and distributed them for the aids to wear in court; Gradwell later called Challenor into his office and asked him if he knew why so many former merchant seamen were joining the Metropolitan Police, with the majority of them being posted to 'C' Division. "He was always in command in the witness box," Don Gibson told me. "When called to give evidence, he would walk slowly to the witness box, carefully remove his specs from an inside pocket, put them on and adjust them, take the oath and get his notebook out. His reputation preceded him, and we all sat or stood (the courts were always packed when Harry gave evidence!) in anticipation of a lesson in how to conduct yourself in the face of hostile questioning! I recall an instance when he pulled out his notebook to recall a suspect's reply to a question and the defence told him to put his book away and give his evidence from memory. Harry's response was to tell the solicitor that he'd dealt with a dozen other cases since the arrest of the defendant, couldn't possibly remember every comment made by all the defendants, then totally ignored the solicitor and read from his notebook." The courts supported him, his senior officers sang his praises, his subordinates adored him and the villains trembled at his approach; Challenor was on top of his job.

★ ★ ★

On or about 8 October 1962 two betting shops, the property of a 'Major Collins', one in Greek Street, the other in Percy Street, were blown up. The following day, an employee, Lionel William 'Curly' King, a man with a criminal past, was told that the police wished to see him, and since Percy Street was situated within the boundaries of Tottenham Court Road police station, it was there that he went. At the station he saw Detective Sergeant Terry O'Connell (later Commander O'Connell QPM), whom King said he knew and trusted. O'Connell, a wartime lieutenant in the Royal Marines, would spend three tours – a total of almost ten years – with the Flying Squad. A very tough customer, who would be awarded twenty commissioner's commendations, O'Connell had known Challenor on the Flying Squad when he was serving as a detective constable and a second-class sergeant. Now, as a first-class sergeant, he was spending a very brief sojourn on 'C' Division before his return, once more, to the Squad. O'Connell knew nothing of a request to see him, but he made enquiries and established that it was Harry Challenor who wished to see King.

At West End Central, King was seen by Challenor and PC Jay. Before the matter of the betting shop bombings was mentioned, Challenor referred to the incident which had occurred on 17 July, when King had been in company with Ford, and Gardiner, the club owner, had been threatened. King's explanation was: "I'll tell you what happened. I came out of the betting shop with Ford and the other fellow. Ford pointed out Gardiner and said that Gardiner was going to nick him. The other fellow threatened to do Gardiner up and I stopped them. There was a lot of aggravation.

I told Gardiner not to aggravate Ford and make it up. I might have seemed nasty but I didn't join in the aggravation." Asked if he knew any of the others, including Oliva, King replied that he only knew them as customers in the betting shop. He was being less than frank. He had known Oliva since 1960 and had been released from prison, having served a sentence with Oliva, less than a year previously.

Told that the facts would be reported with a view to prosecution (as they were), King replied, "Don't you think I'm in enough trouble with all these bombs? I can't say anything – I'll get my throat cut. I'm getting it all ways."

Now, according to King, Challenor demanded information as to who was responsible for the bombings and said that in the event that no information was forthcoming, 'something' would be found in his (King's) possession. King subsequently recounted this episode to O'Connell, but O'Connell later said that whilst King had said that Challenor wanted information about the bombings, no mention was made of threats, and that King was the type of person whom Challenor might well have sought information from with regard to the bombings. PC Jay later agreed that no threats had been made, although he disagreed with O'Connell's view that King would have been a likely informant, believing that King would have been a most unlikely source from whom the police would solicit information.

A few weeks later, King alleged, he was taken to see Challenor again, with Challenor once more demanding that King should provide information; and following that exchange, in November, King was walking along Wardour Street when Challenor called him into a shop doorway, produced a photograph of a man and asked if he had seen him. King said he had not and that he was on his way to meet his wife, who was waiting for him. Challenor replied, "She'll have to wait a long time for you if you don't help me". King claimed then that, "He said he could find something on me and I'd have no chance, so I'd better be getting in touch."

But there is little doubt that Challenor would not have wished to solicit King to become an informant; he regarded King as a dangerous gangster, someone simply to be arrested. There, for the time being, the matter rested.

* * *

Harry Challenor was making himself just as busy as the aids; two days after the commencement of the night-duty squad, he and Etheridge were out on patrol when Challenor had occasion to speak to an informant. When he returned to the car, he told Etheridge that he had received information that Lionel King and other men were in the West End and that they were in possession of explosives. Returning immediately to West End Central, Challenor briefed the aids to search for King; he, Etheridge and Police Constables Jay and Owen Tweedy set off to search for King's car. During the early hours of 25 April Challenor and his team were on patrol when they saw and stopped a car in Charing Cross Road driven by King, who was accompanied by David Lewis Silver. Etheridge took Silver into a shop doorway, searched him and then placed him in the back of the police car. Challenor brought a cushion taken from King's car to the police car and asked Etheridge for a knife; he passed over a pocket knife to Challenor who slit open the cushion. Having returned the knife, Challenor reached inside the cushion and pulled out, one at a time, two detonators and some wire. When the detonators were found, King said, "Don't look any further, Sergeant. There's no 'jelly' here, now. You could score all this down to aggravation. We're unlucky; that's somebody else's gear." Silver said, "I must want my head examined. I shouldn't be mixed up in this."

When King's address was searched, a forged driving licence was discovered. King's explanation for this was: "It was for the nutter who was going to blast a certain spieler. He was going to use a nicked car with a dummy licence, in case he got a pull. All I had to do was to supply the necessary. The funny part about it though, I didn't get the dets [detonators]. I was just born lucky." (There was a little controversy at the trial as to whether that final word should have been 'unlucky').

At their trial, neither man alleged that the detonators had been planted by police. In his instructions to his solicitor, Norman Beach, Silver stated that 'someone' had planted the detonators but he could not say it was the police. However, when interviewed by the police in 1964, Silver stated that he had seen Challenor put his hand into his raincoat pocket, then into the slit-open cushion and produce the detonators, and this, he told the James Enquiry, was what he had told Beach all along. This was rebutted by Beach and also PC Jay, who witnessed the finding of the detonators and later told the enquiry that Challenor could not have planted the detonators and had no opportunity to do so.

King's evidence to the enquiry was that, having cut open the cushion, Challenor called him over, showed him the detonators and told him, "I've two detonators here. You're nicked. I've given you a chance; I could have found them in your pocket."

Charged with receiving stolen detonators, possessing detonators with intent to cause malicious damage to a building by explosion and conspiracy to cause malicious damage to a building, both men appeared before the Acting Deputy Chairman, Mr A.C. Munro-Kerr at the County of London Sessions, and on 20 June 1963 both were convicted. King was sentenced to two years' imprisonment, Silver to six months.

★ ★ ★

The night-duty squad had been a resounding success, but after three weeks, on 16 May, it had to be discontinued because the excessive hours on duty and the time spent at court would have had a detrimental effect on the personnel. Not that Challenor was letting up; his hours of work were astonishing. "As a CID officer, I thought he was great," Maurice Harding, who was a detective constable at West End Central, told me. "I had the greatest respect for him, he was nicking the right people at the right time."

One of those who slipped through the net was spotted by Challenor walking along Shaftesbury Avenue in the early hours of the morning. "There's Reggie Kray!" he roared, and Reggie, turned, took one look and sprinted away. Reg's sudden flight might well have been due to the presence of Challenor, who had previously visited a restaurant in Old Compton Street, escorted the brothers Kray to the borders of the East End and imparted certain cautionary words of wisdom to them as to what might be their fate should they return. Don Gibson recalled that he had accompanied Challenor to an address where the Krays had just set up a drinking club and put in 'front men' to run it. He informed the representatives of the Kray brothers that if they had not vacated the premises by four o'clock that afternoon, he would return with a search warrant. They took the hint. David Parkinson recalls Challenor receiving a call to say that the Kray twins were in a club in Gerrard Street. The caller, probably the owner of the club, innocently turned to the twins and said, "Harry Challenor just phoned up to see if you were here." "By the time Harry arrived," Parkinson told me, "they'd legged it."

Leonard 'Nipper' Read – who went to West End Central in 1966 as a detective chief inspector – told me, "Personally, I thought Challenor had an obsessive hatred of lower-class criminals and would do anything to get them off the streets."

Two years later, when Reggie and Ronnie Kray were brought to book for a miscellany of serious offences, including murder, they probably expelled a sigh of relief that it was Read who had arrested them rather than Challenor.

CHAPTER 8

"They Think I'm Mental"

Scarcely had the night-duty period finished when Challenor was in action again. Late in the evening of 24 May 1963, four men had gone to the Establishment Club in Greek Street. Ernest George Pink – known as 'Pinkie' – at six feet six, was a very large, intimidating, self-confessed strongarm man with convictions for violence; he was also a deaf mute. He was accompanied by Robert Joseph Brown (also deaf), William Francis and Frederick Steven James Bridgeman. None of the four was a member of the club. Admission was obtained after the door was answered by a doorman sporting a black eye; Pink threatened to black his other eye, although he later stated that this was a joke. In the bar, Pink accused the barman of fiddling the till, although how this accusation was actually made is unclear. "I don't have trouble, because most people are afraid of me," Pink explained later. "I am deaf and dumb and use exaggerated signs and they think I'm mental."

Quite possibly this was the impression which had been conveyed to the management, because the police were called, and at 12.20 a.m. Challenor, Ken Etheridge and a number of aids to CID arrived. One of the aids was Norman 'Nobby' Birch, who told me, "Personally, I found Harry was an enthusiastic leader, along with Ken Etheridge who was the first-class at the time, the two of them being implicated in several cases which became an obsession in Harry's endeavours to sort out Soho and the West End's untidy night life."

As Pink & Co were walking up the steps of the club to the street, and after a short struggle, Challenor arrested Pink for being in possession of a cut-throat razor. Brown also behaved violently as he was arrested by Police Constable Robb, assisted by PC Birch, for possessing a flick-knife. Francis was arrested for possessing a hatchet and Bridgeman for possessing a knife.

At West End Central, Francis stated later, Challenor told him that he could walk out of the police station providing he paid a bribe of £150; he also said that Challenor posed as a superintendent in front of the other officers and that he (Francis) had been assaulted by several of them. Francis claimed that Challenor had asked him if he had ever been in trouble before in the West End. When

Francis said that he had not, Challenor replied, "Well, you are now", and turning to another officer, had told him, "Charge them with carrying offensive weapons." However, at the James Enquiry, Francis, under cross-examination, 'showed himself to be a very unsatisfactory witness'. Bridgeman described Challenor as walking up and down, rubbing his hands together and saying, "Lovely, lovely, lovely. More and more."

There was a considerable delay in charging the men – it did not happen until half past five in the morning, but this was almost certainly because Challenor had followed Etheridge on to the Roaring Twenties nightclub in Carnaby Street to carry out a raid. Frank Rushworth, a Clubs Squad officer (and later a detective chief inspector), recalled raiding this predominantly black club. "Although there were hundreds of customers there, Harry jumped up on the stage and grabbed the microphone. One of the clientele tried to take it off him but was discouraged from doing so, as Harry warned him, 'You all know me, my old darling!'"

It appears they did. David Pritchard, then a detective sergeant with the Yard's Drugs Squad (and later a detective chief inspector), was brought in as an adviser when West End Central carried out the raid. A fluent German speaker, he was conversing with a German national to determine whether or not the pills she had in her possession were, as she claimed, to cure constipation, when a bearded West Indian decided to prove his innocence beyond question. Making himself the centre of attention, he dramatically tore his pockets inside out and, arms flung wide, screamed to the audience, "SEE? SEE? I AIN'T GOT NO DRUGS, MAN!"

One of the onlookers was Harry Challenor, who walked over to him and, nose-to-nose, said very quietly, "Are you sure, my old darling? Because I think I can see some weed hiding in your beard!" Pritchard, who, like many other officers had heard some of the unkind rumours circulating about Challenor, squeezed his eyes shut and offered up an urgent, silent prayer: 'Oh, don't do it, Harry!'

Harry didn't; and the chastened gentleman from far-off shores paled, and sat down very quickly without any further discourse. Besides, Challenor had more to concern himself with than pills which might or might not be used for alleviating pressure on the lower bowel.

At the trial of the four men charged with possessing offensive weapons, all of the prisoners would allege that they had been 'planted' with the weapons at West End Central, with Pink making a formal complaint to Superintendent Townsend on 4 June and Brown on 10 June.

But on 15 June Pink, on bail in respect of the offensive weapon charge, was arrested and charged with assaulting a Mr Bates, occasioning him actual bodily harm during a fight in the Limbo club, in Wardour Street. Clifford Ireland – also a deaf mute – met Pink the following day, and Pink asked Ireland to attend court on 18 June, to see if bail would be granted. It was not; and Pink was remanded in custody until 22 June, when he was due to appear in any event on the offensive weapons charges, together with his co-defendants, Brown, Francis and Bridgeman.

On 22 June at Marlborough Street Magistrates' Court, Ireland arrived in company with Frederick Steel – yet another deaf mute – together with Ronald William Braggins and Frank Matthews. This was the scenario: Ireland and Steel knew both Pink and Braggins. Steel knew Matthews as a person who worked for Braggins. Ireland and Steel knew Brown (Pink's co-defendant), and Braggins knew Pink but Matthews did not. Ireland and Steel knew Bates – the assault victim – by sight. All of this is rather confusing, but the upshot of it was that for a variety of reasons – which Mr James described in his report as 'a benevolent view of their evidence and the manner in which it was given [which] stretched credulity to its limit' – all four men arrived at court, and as they did so, the complainant, Bates, was talking to Challenor. PC Robb heard Braggins say, "Wait until they see the other mob, tonight," and Matthews had said, "He'll want a bigger bit of plaster than he's wearing now"; this was later hotly disputed by the men.

Challenor, approaching the men, said, "I heard there was going to be trouble up here; take their names and addresses." The reason for this request was because in the early hours of that morning there had been further trouble at the Limbo Club, where shots had been fired.

John Troon was at that time a uniformed police constable attached to Rochester Row police station; he was also a 'signer' – someone conversant with the use of sign language for deaf mutes, a skill he had learnt when a boy with this affliction was evacuated to his village in Cornwall during the Second World War. Troon's ability to successfully defuse disturbances involving deaf mutes had led him to become an interpreter for the police, after a rigorous examination by the RAAD – the Royal Association in Aid of the Deaf, as it was then.

The first time that Troon encountered Pink was when Challenor called him to Marlborough Street Court on that day, pushed him into Pink's cell and shut the door. "At this time," Troon told me, "Pink was very frustrated, jumping up and down, and as soon as I entered his cell, he punched me in the eye. But when I signed,

Harry Challenor enjoying a plate of escargots at an SAS reunion in France, 1980.

Harry and Doris Challenor just after their marriage, 1944.

Harry Challenor in wartime
France, 1944.

(L to R) Harry Challenor, Para. Dance (later killed in Germany), Louis Rousselet, Freddy Gosselin (SAS), Bernard Duaux and Jean Nicol, France, 1944.

Harry Challenor (right) in Bergen, Norway, June 1945.

(L to R) Lt. Col. Bill Stirling, Lt. Col.
David Stirling DSO, OBE, Major Randolph
Churchill MBE.

Lt. Col. Blair 'Paddy' Mayne DSO (left),
Major Roy Farran DSO, MC.

A Jeep of the type used by Challenor in France.

Aids to CID on 'M' Division, c. 1952

Thomas Proudfoot.

Arthur Porter BEM.

Ken Rexstrew.

David Woodland, aid to CID at Croydon.

Croydon police station.

The Flying Squad, c. 1962

(L to R) John Simmonds, Reg Roberts, Dave Dilley.

Det. Ch. Supt. Tommy Butler MBE.

New Scotland Yard.

Southwark police station.

Ron Cork, aid to CID.

Des Prendergast, aid to CID.

Claridge's Hotel, Brook Street, London W1.

West End Central police station.

Det. Sgt. Ken Etheridge.

Queen Frederika of Greece.

Three of the aids to CID commended, with Challenor, for the protection rackets case

Don Gibson.

Peter Jay.

John Legge.

Marlborough Street Magistrates' Court.

The Stipendiary
Magistrate,
Edward Robey.

The Old Bailey.

Villains of the Manor

Jimmy Humphries.

Reg (left) and Ron Kray.

Albert Dimes.

St. Lawrence's Hospital.

Netherne Hospital.

SAS reunion at Châtillon, 20 June 1982.

Roy Farran (left) and Harry Challenor, reunion at Châtillon, 20 June 1982.

Russ King (left) and Harry Challenor, two years before Challenor's death at his nursing home in Putney.

Harry Challenor's wartime medals.

Donald Rooum – the man who brought about Challenor's downfall.

'I'm here to help you', he immediately calmed down. We had a long chat and Pink was as good as gold." No action was taken about the punch to Troon's eye; Challenor just laughed and said, "I'll buy you a pint, me old darling."

Troon later interpreted for Pink during his trial at the Old Bailey and sat in the dock with him; the defence did not object, and Pink insisted on it. Much later, when the chief constable of Wolverhampton conducted an enquiry in respect of allegations of bribery regarding Challenor, Troon interpreted for Pink once again. The officers wanted Pink to incriminate Challenor, but he refused to do so. Troon (who later retired as a detective superintendent) told me, "I think Pink respected Harry; I certainly held him in high esteem."

The four men were arrested for an offence of 'insulting behaviour' and were taken to West End Central by PC Laing at 11.45 where they were detained. Challenor was still giving evidence in respect of his prisoners on the offensive weapon charges at Marlborough Street Magistrates' Court, and at the conclusion met an informer before arriving at West End Central at 1.30. Here he was confronted by the duty officer, Inspector Robert Thomas, who was annoyed that the men had not been charged and that he had not been informed by Challenor as to why they were being detained; this disagreement became heated, until Detective Superintendent Townsend was called in as an arbitrator. The four men were remanded at Marlborough Street Magistrates' Court, a report was sent to the Director of Public Prosecutions and they were later committed to the Old Bailey on charges of conspiracy to pervert the course of public justice.

But by now, concerns were being voiced about Challenor's behaviour by his senior officers. It was not that he was simply loud or ebullient or spoke out of turn; it was beginning to appear to be rather more serious than that.

★ ★ ★

It was during April that Challenor had seen his GP, Dr Stern, regarding a ringing sound in his ears; once again, he was referred to St Thomas' Hospital. It is possible that this was tinnitus, caused by gunfire and/or explosions during Challenor's war service; it was also thought that the very heavy dosage of quinine, administered by Signora Eliseio to combat Challenor's malaria whilst he was on the run in wartime Italy, might have been responsible. But whatever the reason, it was suggested that he might use a hearing aid. This was brought to the attention of Superintendent Townsend, who was already aware of Challenor's increasing deafness because he had been informed that during a court hearing Challenor had misheard or perhaps misunderstood questions put to him. The deafness was also causing him to speak louder. Townsend suggested that Challenor might wish to be transferred to another station; but this Challenor was quite unwilling to countenance.

In the twelve months he had spent at West End Central, Challenor had brought terror into the hearts of the gangsters and racketeers who infested Soho. They had never encountered anyone like him; he could not be frightened and he could not be bought, so it was decided to frame him. Terry O'Connell told me that he had been approached by the gang leader Albert Dimes, who stated that Challenor had attempted to extort a bribe of £1,000 from him. O'Connell told Dimes to keep him apprised of events, but since Challenor had never approached Dimes in the first place, no further information was forthcoming. There were other unsubstantiated murmurings that Challenor had accepted bribes. But what was known was that there would be a suitable reward for someone with no previous convictions who could lure Challenor into a compromising position, under the guise of giving him information, and then hand over money (the notes would naturally be marked and the handover photographed by the tabloids) in order to thoroughly compromise him. This was a 'win-win' situation; such an allegation would almost certainly result in Challenor's suspension from duty, and if charges – criminal or disciplinary – could be brought, so much the better. But even if they were and those charges were dismissed, it would certainly result in Challenor being posted elsewhere; and the problem would thus be solved.

This was the gist of the conversation that Detective Superintendent Townsend had with Deputy Commander Reg Spooner at the Yard on 26 June 1963. He later recounted it to the James Enquiry:

> The discussion was that Challenor had been working very, very long hours, he had done some good work in the West End, he was going deaf, getting boisterous ... he might have to wear a deaf aid, but the criminal fraternity were, as I have heard, preparing or trying to stop his activities, and I felt it was time for his own good to move him to a quieter station where he could take a rest, perhaps work much shorter hours and have a quieter way of life and also for the good of the job, the good of the police force, because it was obvious to me at that time that the criminal fraternity were endeavouring to take some action to stop his activities.

Townsend added that 'desperate men were prepared to take desperate remedies'; he described Challenor as being 'a thorn in the side of the criminal fraternity' and told the James Enquiry:

> There is a limit to everything, and if a man is doing a job of work and is being continually complained about, then as a senior police officer, one must take notice of the position and try to take him away from the scene until the thing is clarified. Quite obviously, it is a position which cannot be tolerated.

And therefore it was felt that when a suitable vacancy arose, Challenor should – like it or not – be moved to a quieter station. He was looking 'drawn', he was extremely tired through working such long hours – during one thirteen-day period he had worked 187½ hours[5] – and on 29 June a complaint had been lodged by Irvine Shine, a legal representative, to whom Challenor had raised his voice and called 'an imposter'. This was because Shine had given the impression that he was a qualified solicitor when he was not, and because when he arrived at the police station at 6.30 in the morning, he was unshaven and of a rather dishevelled appearance. He demanded to see a Mr Jarvis, whom Challenor had arrested for causing grievous bodily harm and demanding money with menaces; Challenor refused Shine access to Jarvis until his identity could be confirmed, which Shine was reluctant to do. Unfortunately, this took some considerable time. Shine's home telephone number had been found in a diary owned by Jarvis, which included the names of criminals; and since other people were being sought in respect of the offences for which Jarvis had been arrested, it was thought – quite properly – that it would be unwise to permit Shine access to a man arrested for serious offences until his identity could be established beyond doubt. An explanation, covering Challenor's long hours (he had at that time been on duty for twenty-one hours) and his increasing deafness, plus an apology, was tendered by Detective Superintendent Townsend, and it was accepted.

But on top of his long hours, he had for some time been walking the fifteen miles home after finishing duty. He was spotted on one occasion by his old contemporary from Mitcham, Thomas Proudfoot, at one o'clock in the morning in London Road, Mitcham. It was, Challenor told his wife, "to keep fit", but when he

---

5. Although, incredibly, Etheridge had worked even longer hours than Challenor.

arrived home on the day that the Shine complaint had been made, he was soaked through from the rain and his feet were bleeding.

Doris Challenor was very concerned about her husband's long hours, but when she mentioned this to him, he replied, "If someone tells you I'm having a breakdown, you mustn't worry about it. It's all part of a plan." He also mentioned to her that he was 'toughening up' for a special job, but what this was she did not know. Knowing of her husband's wartime activities, she assumed that he was indeed engaged on some specialist work which required complete fitness; but since in those days detectives generally did not discuss their work in detail (if at all) with their wives, she did not enquire about it, nor did she mention it to anybody else. On or about 3 July Challenor mentioned to his wife their forthcoming holiday to Yugoslavia, due to commence on 19 July. He told her that one aspect of the holiday must be cancelled: they were not to travel through Italy and instead they must go to Switzerland. When she asked why, he told her that there might be someone waiting to kill him, because of his current work. That was worrying enough – but before the holiday could commence Harry Challenor's life would spiral completely out of control.

CHAPTER 9

'Bongo, Bongo, Bongo'

The Boulevard Club was situated at 16 Frith Street, Soho. It was regarded as a 'near beer' establishment (where the beer was watered down to less than two per cent to avoid the need for a liquor licence), and a 'clip joint', where customers were lured in to purchase drinks for the hostesses at an exorbitant price on the promise of sexual intercourse, which would not be forthcoming; thus the customer was 'clipped'. The owner was Broulio Dario Oliva (no relation to Joseph Francis Oliva, mentioned previously), who described himself as a gambler and had several criminal convictions. Oliva had sublet the premises to a Mario Requena. All of Oliva's convictions were to do with his activities at 'clip joints'; moreover, three of these convictions related to violence towards customers at the Boulevard.

One person who appeared to have been 'clipped' was a Swiss national named Beck. On 4 July 1963 he engaged one of the hostesses, Jean Browne, in a conversation at the door of the club and then spent a total of £8 18s 0d on drinks for her (for which she received a commission), on the understanding that sex would follow. This was agreed, and Miss Browne told Beck to meet her in a coffee bar in Wardour Street; when she failed to materialise, Beck went to West End Central to complain that he had been defrauded.

A few hours later, early the following day, the club was visited by Challenor, Etheridge (who had considerable experience of clip joint offences) and Beck, who identified Miss Browne. She told the officers, "I have to earn a few pounds somehow. We kid the punters that they can have a bit of the other and then send them down to Wardour Street where friend Padmore speaks to them about his girl. They don't come back. Have a word with Mr Oliva, he's the real boss here." Whoever 'friend Padmore' was, he was not someone who was known to the officers, nor had he been present when Beck had visited Wardour Street earlier.

The officers then spoke to Mrs Patricia Violet Hawkins, aged thirty-eight and described as a waitress. Etheridge asked if she had assisted Miss Browne to defraud Beck on the false promise of sexual intercourse, to which she replied, "Yes, but don't take the girl, she takes her instruction from me. I told her to send him down to Wardour Street, and if a man had been there, as he should have been, this wouldn't have happened. Why don't you speak to Mr Oliva?" Told that a warrant would be obtained for her arrest, she became hysterical, pleaded, threatened, then grabbed hold of Beck and tried to stuff money in his pocket. Challenor took the money to hand back to her, and Mrs Hawkins fell to the floor.

Her version of events was in complete contrast to Etheridge's, who, she said, brusquely demanded to know if she was 'Big Pat' or 'Fat Pat' and if Dario Oliva was the owner of the premises. She added that Challenor, who was drunk, had foully abused her and knocked her to the ground. She begged the officers to take her to the station but to leave Miss Browne and had tried to reimburse Beck with £9, which Challenor ordered him to return to her. Mrs Hawkins, shocked at such immoderate behaviour, said to Challenor, "May God forgive you," which elicited the reply, "He probably won't."

The following day, warrants were obtained for the arrest of Miss Browne and Mrs Hawkins on charges of obtaining money by false pretences with intent to defraud; Challenor, Etheridge, PC Robb and other officers went to the club at 11.15 to execute the warrants. Miss Browne was not there but Mrs Hawkins was, and Robb described how she advanced along the passageway of the club, screaming hysterically, the fingers of her outstretched hand shaped in a claw. With the assistance of a woman police officer she was placed in a police van and conveyed to West End Central. The van driver, Police Constable David Powell, stated that Mrs Hawkins was crying and hysterical, saying, "I'm rather a sick woman;" and these were the words heard by Woman Police Constable Maureen Holland, who accompanied her.

Mrs Hawkins' version of subsequent events once more varied considerably from that of the officers. She described how Challenor had vulgarly told her that she was 'nicked' and that she was then subjected to a series of punches and digs from both him and Robb, including a blow from the latter which knocked her from her seat on to the floor of the van. Challenor, she said, had sworn at and abused her, telling her that 'he would get her two years' imprisonment'. But imparting all this information to the James Enquiry, Mrs Hawkins also said that she felt sorry for Challenor, because his colleagues were aware of his unacceptable behaviour but did nothing to help him. Mr James came to the conclusion that he did not think these sentiments were 'the product of her own mind'.

At midnight there was an imposing caller at West End Central. His name was Sydney Harold Dacosta Padmore, a Barbadian, six feet three and a half inches tall and weighing in the region of sixteen stone. Padmore had originally arrived in England as a member of the Provost Corps of the Canadian Army; after the war he had returned to Canada, where he worked as a bodyguard and a chauffeur. Since 1955 he had lived in England and was employed as a railway shunter. He and Mrs Hawkins lived at 11 Islington Park Street, N1, and he had stated – this was not accepted as being the truth at the James Enquiry – that he had returned to that address earlier to discover that Mrs Hawkins had been arrested. At West End Central he was taken upstairs by Police Sergeant Walter Trump to see Challenor, in the hope that he could obtain bail for Mrs Hawkins. This was the 'friend Padmore' to whom Miss Browne had referred, although any connection with the club or its activities was later vehemently denied, both by Padmore – a man with no previous convictions – and Mrs Hawkins; but not according to Detective Sergeant James Cruse, who at that time was manning the telephone switchboard in the CID office. He was present when Padmore told Challenor, "I'd like to speak to you about Pat, the woman you took from Frith Street, she is my friend," to which Challenor replied, "What do you mean, 'your friend'?"

Padmore said, "Well, Sergeant, I think you know my friend Dario Oliva who has a clip at Frith Street. Now, this is rubbish and only a few pounds owing. If I could have been at Wardour Street when the Swiss boy turned up, you would not have this trouble." When Challenor mentioned that this had caused him extra work, Padmore replied, "Look, I know that, Sergeant. That is why Dario asked me to come and see you. Leave it to us, man. Dario will pay the Swiss boy, and when the punters come to Wardour Street, I will make sure that if they're still unhappy, I will take them to Dario and he will pay them and you will get no more trouble." Told that a warrant for conspiracy to obtain money by false pretences would be applied for, Padmore replied, "Very clever, Sergeant, but you forget we have the girl. You won't get her and where is your case, then?"

Told he would be detained, Padmore turned out the contents of his pockets. He was still in the CID office when Dario Oliva entered. Oliva was interviewed by Challenor in the presence of Sergeant Cruse, and in the course of the interview Oliva said, "What can I say? I know you know the routine and there's no answer to it if the Swiss boy goes the whole way. We have got the girl and if the big spade had been doing his job at Wardour Street, the boy would not have bothered you. I will be generous to the Swiss boy and I will tell you, Sergeant, that there will be no more complaints." He, too, was told that a warrant for his arrest would be applied for and that he would also be detained.

Challenor made enquiries of the owner of the Venus Rooms in an effort to trace Miss Browne, but without success; there was also an argument between him and Inspector Ernest Willars regarding the amount of time the two men had been detained. But at about seven o'clock in the morning Padmore and Oliva were released by Inspector Willars, to re-attend the station on 11 July. The inspector subsequently noticed the two men conversing with two or three others in the street outside the police station. One of these was named Ralph James Rodriguez. In the light of what happened next, he would later provide an interesting input into the proceedings.

* * *

Padmore gave an entirely different version of proceedings at West End Central on the night of 6 July. He stated that upon entering the CID office, Challenor had demanded to know who he was and what he wanted; when Padmore explained his reason for being there, Challenor replied, "What does a black ponce like you want in a white police station?" Padmore again stated that he had come to stand bail for Mrs Hawkins but thought he had better leave. Challenor ordered that the office door be closed, saying, "We'll have some fun with this coon; he looks big enough." However, this could not be true; evidence was later given by Detective Inspector Taylor that the top hinge of the door had been defective for weeks; it could not be closed and therefore had to be propped open. Padmore then said that he was seized by three or four officers and repeatedly struck by Challenor, causing both a tooth and his tie-pin to be broken and his shirt to be torn. Challenor then said to PC Robb, "Take that black bastard out of my sight. I wish I was in South Africa; I'd have a nigger for breakfast every morning," and then started to sing Hilliard and Sigman's song 'Civilisation', made popular by Danny Kaye and the Andrews Sisters sixteen years previously, which contained the words:

So, bongo, bongo, bongo, I don't wanna leave the Congo,
Oh, no, no, no, no, no,
Bingo, bangle, bungle, I'm so happy in the jungle,
I refuse to go ...

This, said Padmore, caused considerable amusement to the assembled officers, and Challenor told him that he would get him seven years' imprisonment, he would think of something with which to charge him and whatever he told the magistrate would be believed, "because he was a white man". Challenor stated that he wanted to find Jean Browne but had been unable to do so, and he told Padmore, "If you don't find her, I'll have your guts for garters."

When Dario Oliva entered the CID office, Padmore said he saw Challenor hit him in the face and abuse him. Oliva would later say that when he entered the office Challenor said to him, "Ah, you've saved me a lot of trouble," told him he was going to 'book' him and get him five years' imprisonment, and punched him in the stomach and face. Challenor had blood on his hand, said Oliva, which Challenor referred to as 'black blood' or 'poncey blood'.

So the two men were released, both having been told to reappear at the station on 11 July, with no police officer having seen any sign of injury on either of them. What is interesting is that prior to their being released Inspector Willars got into conversation with Padmore, who, he told the James Enquiry, he had seen around the West End on several occasions previously, although this was the first time he had actually met him. It was a convivial discourse; they spoke about sport in general and wrestling in particular, and Inspector Willars told the enquiry that he thought that Padmore was 'a fine figure of a man', dressed in a well cut navy suit and a white shirt.

It cannot be said that Inspector Willars was one of Harry Challenor's greatest fans. He was not happy with the fact that the two men had been detained for so long, especially since he believed that they would be charged with some offence, and two days later he told Challenor so; there was then an argument, because Challenor told him that the full facts of the case had been reported. In fact, Challenor was surprised that Willars should even mention the incident, not believing that he had done anything to be reproached about – although it is fair to say that Challenor had this effect on several of the uniform inspectors at West End Central.

The animosity between Inspector Willars and Challenor makes it all the more strange that following Willars' amiable conversation with Padmore, in which he scrutinised him quite carefully, he could see nothing in his appearance to suggest he had been assaulted. This was in complete contradiction to Oliva, who told the James Enquiry that outside the police station Padmore complained of his ill treatment, and said that Padmore had, "A hanging tooth, a few loose teeth. He had a mouth bleeding and swollen". Just to make the point quite clear, he was asked, "A hanging tooth?" and Oliva replied, "Literally hanging."

Having left the station, Inspector Willars saw Patmore and Oliva meet up with some other men. One was Mario Requena – the man who was the sub-lessee of the Boulevard Club, another was a man named Ralph Lopez and the third was Ralph James Rodriguez. The latter would later give evidence to the James Enquiry, and if Padmore and Oliva's accounts differed markedly from Challenor's, the evidence of Rodriguez would be even more divergent.

★ ★ ★

Rodriguez – known to Padmore as 'Spanish Jim' – knew Harry Challenor. He had previously given him information regarding a protection racket and he was a petty criminal who had served sentences of up to four years' imprisonment for assault, forgery, theft and receiving stolen goods. Rodriguez, in his times of liberty, worked as a source of information for Fleet Street reporters. On the evening of 6 July Rodriguez had met the four men in Frith Street; they were talking about the arrest of Mrs Hawkins, and Padmore volunteered to go to West End Central to see if she could be bailed. When he did not return, Oliva went to the police station; and when he, too, failed to return, the remaining three men went to West End Central. Rodriguez alone entered the station and spoke to Challenor, who told him that Padmore and Oliva were being detained and that he wished to know the whereabouts of Miss Browne. Rodriguez discussed this with Requena and Lopez, who formed the opinion that without the girl the police would have no case. Later, both Padmore and Oliva were released and formed the group that Inspector Willars saw talking in Savile Row.

The time at which Rodriguez claimed that he spoke to Challenor and of the release of the two men did vary from other accounts, but then he was giving evidence to the enquiry a year after the event. What he did have to say was this: both men were angry, Padmore because Mrs Hawkins had been detained and Oliva because he had been refused permission to smoke. However, neither Padmore nor Oliva complained of being assaulted whilst they were in the police station, nor did they exhibit any signs of any ill treatment; Requena said the police had made a 'big mistake' in not charging the pair there and then.[6] Requena suggested that Padmore – because he had no previous convictions – should report back to

---

6. In fact, Challenor had wanted to charge the men but Inspector Taylor declined to do so, saying that a warrant was necessary. He was wrong; since an indictable offence had been committed during the hours of darkness, under the provisions of Section 11, Prevention of Crimes Act 1851, the men could have been charged, and this was later confirmed by Detective Chief Inspector McArthur.

the police station on 11 July, in the presence of a solicitor, and he should remain in custody overnight and harm himself by biting his lip and pinching his cheekbone, then in the morning complain immediately to his solicitor that the police had beaten him up. Padmore suggested that Lopez and Rodriguez should support this by stating that he had been abused prior to his leaving the police station on this occasion; Lopez and Rodriguez declined, on the grounds that they had previous convictions, but Requena agreed to provide the necessary evidence; however, he did not.

On the evening of 7 July Rodriguez met up with Oliva and Requena again; Oliva left the group to gather some information about Challenor. But when he returned, Oliva told the men that Challenor could not be paid off and that whoever had provided that information also told him to clear off out of the country. And that was what Oliva did; he did not return to West End Central on 11 July and only when he heard that the case against his co-defendants had collapsed (Miss Browne was eventually arrested in September) did he decide to return from Spain, on 27 January 1964.

On 8 July Padmore took a statement typed the previous day by an Indian friend known simply as 'Raj', who by chance had visited him and coincidentally had brought his typewriter, to Bernard Solley & Co, solicitors. The typed version was, said Padmore, taken from a handwritten statement which he had made; later, he wrote a further statement from the typescript. He was dealt with by Abraham Joseph Stoller, a solicitor, part of whose evidence at the enquiry was described as being 'entirely incredible'.

On the same day Superintendent Townsend spoke to his and Challenor's old boss from the Flying Squad, Detective Chief Superintendent Tommy Butler, now the officer in charge of No. 1 District's CID. Townsend was clearly concerned at Challenor's behaviour, which he put down to overwork, his long hours of duty and his increasing deafness. He had addressed Challenor on this subject, instructing him to limit his hours of duty and not to undertake any fresh investigations, and reminding him that he was due to commence his annual leave on 19 July; until then it was his intention to 'nurse' Challenor so that he could recoup his full fitness during his period of leave. Butler agreed that deafness could be the root cause of Challenor's illness; he said as much in his minute to Commander Hatherill.

A rather different interpretation was offered by one of the rank and file. Ron Cork told me, "I was aware that the pressure on Harry to produce results by 'those above' was intense. This was without doubt affecting his mental state as I noticed a dramatic change in him when I last saw him at court."

Challenor discovered that at the fourth attempt he had passed the educational examination to permit him to sit for promotion to detective sergeant (first class). This would have been the last examination he was required to pass; after that, further promotion would have been determined on selection boards, based solely on his abilities as a police officer.

He received this welcome information on 10 July 1963. It was the last piece of good news he was to receive for some considerable time.

* * *

Just about everybody to whom I spoke agreed that Harry Challenor was incapable of foreseeing the consequences of his actions. To Challenor, making arrests was the be-all and end-all of his work. He would dash out, make an arrest, insert the culprit in a cell, often telling no one, and rush out again to make more arrests, not necessarily in connection with the same case, leaving the station inspectors raving because there were prisoners in their cells for whom nobody could satisfactorily account. This would be demonstrated on the evening of 11 July at about six o'clock, when Padmore arrived at West End Central together with his solicitor, Abraham Stoller. They were met by Challenor, who told them that Padmore would be charged and would be staying in custody. He then read the men what purported to be a warrant, but would not let either of them inspect or read it; it is possible that what he referred to was not the warrant, which may have been mislaid. Stoller asked to speak to his client; this was refused, and Padmore was searched and placed in a cell. According to Padmore, when a uniformed inspector asked about charging the prisoner, Challenor replied that, "He was too damned busy." If the warrant had indeed been mislaid, charging would have presented considerable difficulties. In any case, in Challenor's eyes Padmore's charging could come later; he was going nowhere. Besides, there were fresh arrests to be made.

Nobby Birch – who at this time was on holiday in Scotland – told me, "Ken Etheridge was, as I'm sure you know, a tremendous stabilising influence in holding Harry in check, on certain occasions." But at that time of night on 11 July 1963 Etheridge was nowhere to be found, because he was conducting other enquiries, quite separate from Challenor's. In the light of what was to happen, his stabilising influence could not be exerted. This was a pity. More than that, it would become a tragedy.

CHAPTER 10

The Brick Incidents

At the time of the 'Brick Incidents', the Prime Minister was Maurice Harold MacMillan OM, PC, FRS, later 1st Earl of Stockton. He was in his sixth year of office and was a statesman noted for his wit and imperturbability. He had successfully weathered the impending storm of the Cuban Missile Crisis in October 1962, but on 21 June 1963 he had instructed the Master of the Rolls, Lord Denning OM, PC, DL, to launch an enquiry into what had become known as the 'Profumo Affair'. At this time, with the emergence of the 1960s, the number of political demonstrations in Central London grew. Quite often, the reason behind a demonstration was spurious; in fact, many of those who took part had little or no idea what it was they were protesting about. It mattered not – anarchist groups simply had a wonderful opportunity to attack property and the police. Not unnaturally, the Government wanted them suppressed, but in so doing police manpower and the public purse were stretched to breaking-point – as were the tempers of some police officers. Grossly outnumbered and fed up with being sworn and spat at and pelted with bricks and bottles, seeing fireworks thrown at police horses and marbles tossed under their hooves, some reacted impetuously and were treated to whining accusations of 'police brutality', made to just those authorities whom the demonstrators claimed to despise.

With the 'Brick Incidents' about to become headline news, the Prime Minister would need all the humour and unflappability he could muster.

★ ★ ★

Claridge's Hotel is situated on the south side of Brook Street, Mayfair, and since the 1860s its five-star opulence has attracted the great, the good and the crowned heads of Europe. The hotel has been a great favourite of Her Majesty the Queen, and after guests were received at Buckingham Palace, they often returned the hospitality by hosting a banquet at Claridge's. Therefore, when King Paul and Queen Frederika of Greece arrived on a state visit in July 1963, it was natural that they would stay at the hotel.

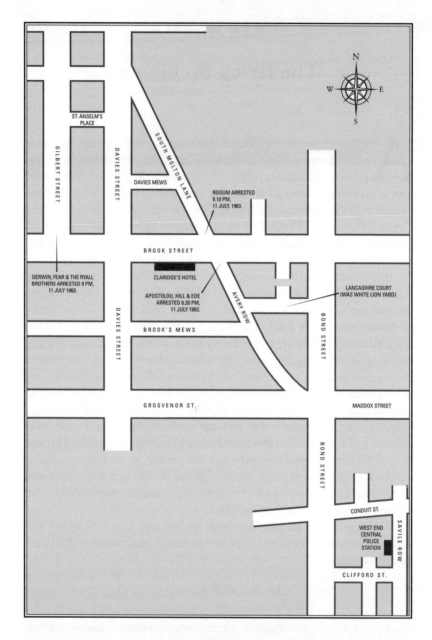

Queen Frederika, the great-granddaughter of Queen Victoria, was also the great-granddaughter of Kaiser Wilhelm II; having lived in Germany as a girl, she had out of necessity in the political climate of the time joined the Nazi youth organization, the *Bund Deutscher Mädel* (League of German Girls). Following her marriage to Prince Paul of Greece in 1938, she and her husband settled in Athens, but after war was declared much of the Greek royal family's exile was spent in London. In 1946 the Greek people restored the monarchy, and following the death of King George II, Frederika's husband ascended the throne. This coincided with communist-inspired political instability in the country which led to a two-year civil war, and the new King and Queen toured Greece to appeal for loyalty. Although Field Marshal Alexander Papagos was largely responsible for the defeat of the communists in the civil war, when he successfully ran for the office of Prime Minister in 1952 he was bitterly and vociferously opposed by Queen Frederika. It is possible that she thought him too popular with the people; but whatever the reason, she interfered – many thought unconstitutionally – in Greek politics for many years. A large number of communists had been imprisoned following the end of the civil war, including one Tony Ambatielos, who in 1945 had married Betty Bartlett, a member of the British Communist Party. Betty Ambatielos had produced a pamphlet which read, 'Give me back my husband: release Tony Ambatielos and all the political prisoners of Greece.'

Although Queen Frederika was a third cousin to Her Majesty the Queen, protests against the state visit were whipped up to the level of hysteria by anarchist groups, and by the 'Committee of One Hundred', famed for their sit-down protests. The flames of discontent were fanned both by Queen Frederika's pre-war connection to the Nazis and the ridiculous, communist-inspired assertion that children who had been orphaned during the civil war and whom Queen Frederika had lodged in 'Queen's Camps' had been illegally adopted by Americans. Following the assassination of Grigoris Lambrakis, a left-wing Greek MP and activist, it was clear that the protests aimed against the Greek royal family were not going to be of a passive sit-down nature – despite the later assertion of the National Council for Civil Liberties (formed in 1934 to promote fundamental rights and freedom in the United Kingdom), that, 'There was no suggestion the demonstrators were likely to be violent, in fact quite the reverse. At the worst, Queen Frederika would have been confronted with hostile stares, slogans on placards and some booing.' This was utter nonsense.

For three days, the West End of London became a battleground, and what was known as 'Commissioner's Regulations' was invoked; this meant that under Section 52, Metropolitan Police Act 1839, certain named streets could be closed and vehicles and pedestrians prohibited from entering them. Thousands of police officers were on duty, hundreds of arrests were made, Queen Elizabeth II was booed by the mob and Betty Ambatielos chased Queen Frederika out of Claridge's, shrieking, "Release my husband!" Former

Police Constable John Grey, who was present, remarked, "Had they reached Queen Frederika on that occasion, she would have been killed." Frank Pillinger, then a uniformed police constable, drafted in as aid from the East End's 'H' Division, was kicked as he went to assist a Special Branch officer making an arrest near India House. Jim Smith BEM, also aid from 'H' Division, recalled running battles in the same location; later, having heard that an attempt was going to be made to storm Buckingham Palace, his serial were lined up and were pelted with lumps of earth. And these were demonstrators who were 'not likely to be violent'? The whole suggestion that the protest was going to be peaceful was risible.

During the evening of 10 July Police Inspector George Brooks, who had been on duty outside Claridge's, was hit in the face by a thrown brick; the wound required nine stitches, and as Harry Challenor looked at the inspector's white face, with blood pouring down it, he decided that decisive action should be taken.

* * *

At about 8.20 on the evening of 11 July, 1,480 officers were on duty to police the demonstration. Of these, 1,355 were uniformed officers, the remainder being CID, Special Branch officers and approximately twenty-eight aids to CID. During that evening, a total of ninety-five arrests would be made (of which nine were dealt with by means of summons), and thirty-four of the arrests were dealt with at West End Central. Nine of the arrests were for possession of offensive weapons; eight of them were carried out by Challenor and his officers.

Challenor was in Brook Street in the thick of the protest. He was in company with one of his aids, Police Constable 376 'C' David John Oakey, a single man who lived with his parents in Coulsdon, Surrey and whose family owned the Oakey Sandpaper Company. Aged twenty-two, six feet one tall and previously a police cadet, Oakey had joined the police four years previously. He had been an aid to CID since April 1962 at West End Central.

They were met in Brook Street, on the south footway at the junction with Avery Row, by Police Constable 176 'C' Frank Edward Battes, who was six feet tall, twenty years of age and had married four months previously. He was not then an aid to CID, but had submitted his application to become one the previous month. He had been engaged on uniform duties between 10.30 a.m. and 6.30 p.m. that day, had taken a meal in the canteen at West End Central and then had passed the time talking to his colleagues until eight o' clock. He put a blue mackintosh over his uniform and strolled off towards Claridge's, because he knew that the royal families of Greece and England would be visiting there.

Battes stopped to talk to the two officers and then saw the royal cars approaching from the east, along Brook Street towards them. At the same time he saw a group of young men in front of him carrying banners and wearing badges of the Committee of One Hundred; as the royal cars approached, he heard one of them call out, "Get your stones ready; they're coming." At this, the group became very excited and started jumping up and down, trying to see over the top of the spectators and police officers in front of them. Challenor told Battes and Oakey, "Quick, search those men," and Battes seized hold of one of the group, who gave his details as George Constantine Stylianou, a shop assistant of 10 Medina Road, N4. This was a lie; he later admitted, after he had been charged in the name of Stylianou, that his real name was John Constantine Apostolou, of 71 St Thomas' Road, N4. Searching him in a doorway, Battes said that he found a piece of brick in seventeen-year-old Apostolou's right-hand jacket pocket; asked why he had it, Apostolou shrugged and made no reply. He was then arrested for possessing an offensive weapon.

Challenor had seen fair-haired Gregory John Hill put his hand in his pocket just before he grabbed hold of him; he told Hill he was a police officer, searched him and found a segment of housebrick in his right-hand jacket pocket. "You must realize," said Challenor, "that this brick is an offensive weapon, you will be arrested for possessing it." When he was cautioned, Hill replied, "I was only obeying instructions."

Oakey, dressed casually in a black blazer, had stopped Ronald George Ede, who was smaller than Hill, with jet-black hair and spectacles, and upon searching him, found a piece of brick in his right-hand pocket. Asked why he had the brick, Ede replied, "We were just going to have a bit of fun." When Ede was asked where he had got the brick from, he replied, "We found them near a building site." He, too, was arrested for possessing an offensive weapon. The pieces of brick were put into the officers' own pockets and later produced and labelled.

All the men were taken to West End Central and were shown into the female charge room, since it was there that prisoners arrested in connection with the demonstration were to be processed. They were later charged, and although Apostolou and Ede signed for the property in their possession as being correct, Ede replied when charged, "That's nothing to do with me." Hill and Apostolou made no reply.

Having lodged the prisoners, Challenor felt there were others from the same group whom he could identify. He called out to Detective Constable Maurice Harding, "Quick – I need some help!" but Harding was dealing with a prisoner in the CID office and was unable to go; so instead, Challoner called upon Battes and Oakey, and one other officer was conscripted to join them.

That third officer was Police Constable 607 'C' Keith Stanley Goldsmith, attached to Tottenham Court Road police station, a single man living in Trenchard Section House and a native of Norfolk; "A good copper", as Dick Docking told me. Goldsmith was twenty-five years of age and, like Battes, had been both a grammar school boy and a police cadet; he had over four years service on 'C' Division. He had been an aid to CID since January 1961 and his courage was beyond doubt; in January 1962 he and another officer had been highly commended by the commissioner for their outstanding courage and determination in arresting a violent criminal armed with a sawn-off rifle, as well as being commended at the Old Bailey. And six weeks later, both officers were awarded £20 from the Bow Street Metropolitan Magistrates' Court Reward Fund.

On the day of the demonstrations, Goldsmith had been the junior member of the early turn (i.e. 9 a.m.–5 p.m.) 'C' Division 'Q' Car, and he had been engaged with the processing of a prisoner named Walder up until the time that he, Battes and Oakey left West End Central at about 8.45.

The officers told Goldsmith that they were looking for demonstrators who were part of the same group whom they had arrested earlier. They went to Davies Street, where they saw four young men: Colin George David Derwin, aged eighteen, Richard Ian Fear, aged sixteen and brothers John Ryall and Ronald Alfred Ryall, aged nineteen and eighteen respectively, who entered Davies Street from Davies Mews, crossed the street and passed a line of uniformed officers. Then Derwin was heard to say, "Let's go round Brook Street; we can get them over there." They then ran into St Anselm's Place, and the officers noticed that each of the men had pieces of brick in his right hand. The three officers ran into Brook Street and at the junction with Gilbert Street they stopped the youths, with PC Goldsmith producing his warrant card and saying, "We're police officers; what have you got in your right hands?" The youths' open hands revealed that all of them were in possession of broken pieces of brick; when Goldsmith asked, "What have you got these for?" John Ryall replied, "In case we get in a bundle" and Derwin said, "We picked them up round the corner," whilst the other two made no reply. Told they would be arrested for possessing offensive weapons, Ryall replied, "They're only bricks, not weapons." Once again, the pieces of brick were pocketed by the officers, those from Derwin and Fear being placed in the right-hand pocket of Goldsmith's brown, lightweight raincoat and later produced and labelled, showing the prisoner's names. They were conveyed by police tender to West End Central, taken to the female charge room and later charged, Fear in the presence of his father, who advised him not to sign for his property; Ronald Ryall and Derwin similarly declined to sign. In response to the charge, John Ryall replied, "I had no weapon on me", and his brother replied, "I am not guilty to that charge", whilst Derwin simply replied, "Not guilty."

Meanwhile, Harry Challoner had gone his separate way, first to the Burlington Public House where he purchased a pie and then to Brook Street to search fruitlessly for the remainder of the group he had previously seen. However, at about 9.10 p.m., opposite Claridge's in South Molton Lane he saw a bearded man in company with two girls who were carrying CND banners. The man's name was Donald Rooum.

* * *

Rooum was born in Bradford in 1928 and became an anarchist prior to registering as a conscientious objector; he later gave way to family pressure and completed two years' National Service in 1949. After studying commercial design, he worked as a layout artist, typographer, cartoonist and lecturer, and had fathered four children. By 1963, as well as being an anarchist, Rooum was also a member of the National Council for Civil Liberties, and on the evening of 11 July he was with two friends and was carrying a banner marked 'Lambrakis, R.I.P'. Although he would later say that his intentions were peaceful, he agreed that it was also his intention to make the task of the police more difficult, and further, that he was 'consciously playing the brinkmanship game with the police'.

Challenor heard Rooum say, "I don't care, they shouldn't push us around like that. I will throw my stone, not in revenge but as a demonstration of my ideals." Challenor went over to Rooum, the girls moved away, and he told Rooum that he was a police officer, said what he had heard and asked if he had a stone in his pocket. Rooum then tried to run past him but was grabbed by Challenor, who felt a hard object in his right-hand jacket pocket. Rooum shouted, "Take it, but you must take all the stones in London to stop me." Satisfied that Rooum was in possession of an offensive weapon, Challenor arrested him for that offence and cautioned him, to which Rooum replied, "Down with the monarchy". Taking Rooum to a police coach nearby, Challenor searched him and discovered a piece of brick in his pocket. Having transferred him to a police tender, both men were conveyed to West End Central, where Rooum was later charged with possession of an offensive weapon.

So in a short space of time eight arrests had been carried out by Challenor and his aids of people in possession of offensive weapons and intent on civil disobedience involving the monarchy and visiting royalty. It looked as though some very ugly incidents had been nipped, very smartly, in the bud.

Or so it appeared; unfortunately, the police evidence was deeply flawed.

★ ★ ★

The persons arrested had a very different version of events to tell. At the time of his arrest, Gregory John Hill was just fourteen years of age and a supporter of the Committee of One Hundred. He stated that he had met up with Ronald Ede, then aged sixteen and a member of the Campaign for Nuclear Disarmament and a supporter of the Committee of One Hundred, who had attended the demonstration which he believed to be against the Fascist element in Greece, and John Apostolou, neither of whom, Hill said, he had met before. Making their way to Brook Street, they saw the approach of the royal family and Hill said, "Is anyone going to boo her?" This, it appeared, was quite enough for Challenor, who grabbed him from behind, saying, "Right, me young son, you're nicked." Ede was grabbed from behind by Oakey, and together with Apostolou the youths were taken to West End Central. Both Ede and Hill stated that Ede was told to remove his glasses by Challenor, before both of them were struck around the head. Ede was kicked, and pieces of brick were placed on a table with Challenor saying, "This is for you, and this is for you; a present from Uncle Harold." In the charge room the three youths had their personal property placed on a table, and pieces of brick were placed alongside their property; in respect of Apostolou, Challenor said, "The biggest brick for the biggest boy." According to the prisoners, Apostolou made the extremely cocky (and rather unwise) reply, "Thank you very much but Christmas is over and I don't particularly want the gift." But if this was the case, none of the police officers appeared to hear it.

Superintendent Frederick Harry Burdett DFC was attached to Tottenham Court Road police station and he did not know

Challenor; on this particular evening he had been sent to West End Central to supervise the charging of demonstrators. Hearing raised voices in the male charge room, he entered and saw Hill and Ede in the presence of Challenor and another officer in plain clothes. Upon his arrival, all noise stopped except for Challenor, who continued shouting, his words coming out in a rush and tumble. Burdett demanded to know what was going on and who was in charge; Challenor replied that he was, but continued shouting until finally his eye came to rest on Burdett's badges of rank and medal ribbons, whereupon he came rigidly to attention. Burdett took him outside and delivered a severe dressing-down, telling him that he was not prepared to tolerate such behaviour. It was clear that Challenor was under tremendous strain and, clenching and unclenching his fists, appeared to be controlling himself only with the greatest difficulty (which Burdett would later say was "like a spring gradually uncoiling"). Eventually he walked away, downcast, whilst Burdett had other urgent business to attend to. The shouting had also been overheard by Detective Superintendent Townsend, Detective Chief Inspector McArthur and Detective Inspector Bruce, who were in an adjoining room interviewing a prisoner in connection with a shooting. Bruce emerged from the room, only to find that Burdett was dealing with the matter, and when Burdett later saw Challenor in the charge room, his behaviour was normal.

Shortly afterwards, Challenor and the three constables separately left the station to try to arrest more demonstrators.

The four youths whom the police constables had arrested in Davies St. were not demonstrators at all; following a game of tennis they had left their racquets at the Ryall's home in Davies Mews and crossing into Gilbert Street they were on their way to Derwin's home in Brooks Mews. They were looking for a gap in the crowd to cross the road when they were stopped by three police officers in plain clothes; they stated that they were browbeaten, that PC Battes threatened them with his truncheon and that when they reached the police van one of the officers said, "Shall we give them a boot up?" When they arrived at West End Central, pieces of brick were put with their personal belongings.

According to Rooum, his banner was snatched from him by Challenor, and when he asked, "Can I have my banner back?" he received the reply, "Can you have your *what* back?" "My banner," replied Rooum meekly, only to be told, "You're fucking nicked, my old beauty," be grabbed by the collar and propelled towards a police van. "Please, officer, I'm coming quietly," piteously whimpered Rooum, but was told, "Don't say please to me, my old darling. I've got a stone heart."

Pushing Rooum into the tender, Challenor commented, "We've got a desperate one, here," and during the journey to the police station he called out to a group of officers, "Haven't you got yourself a prisoner, yet?" According to Rooum, Challenor propelled him up the stairs with a series of blows and kicks, knocking him to the floor and saying, "Boo the Queen, would you?" "No," replied Rooum, "not at all," and received another blow round the ear. "There you are, my old darling, have that with me," said Challenor, adding, "and just to make sure we haven't forgotten it – there you are, my old beauty. Carrying an offensive weapon. You can get two years for that." From his own pocket Challenor produced a segment of brick, wrapped in a newspaper.

Inspector Arthur Munns was concerned about the delay in charging Apostolou, Ede and Hill; two of them were juveniles whom he wished to be charged without further delay, and he and his colleagues wanted to complete their tour, since they had been on duty at the demonstration for some considerable time. Challenor stated that he was not yet ready to charge them, since there were other people concerned. Munns was told by Challenor that he intended to leave the station to effect other arrests, but when he returned, Challenor told him he wanted a meal; Munns then spoke to Superintendent Burdett, having been informed that Challenor had another person – this was Rooum – in custody. Burdett told him to find Challenor, who was having a meal in the canteen. When Challenor did appear at 9.30, he was with Rooum, and Burdett intercepted his entrance to the charge room because Challenor was now behaving worse than before, shouting incoherently, shaking and waving his arms. Challenor was again rebuked and calmed down, but at the same time appeared sullen and resentful at being admonished. Burdett brought this breach of discipline to the attention of Detective Superintendent Townsend; when Challenor offered an explanation for his behaviour, Townsend had to rebuke him for shouting. However, after Townsend and Burdett had discussed the matter, it was decided not to institute disciplinary proceedings.

Eventually, between 10 and 10.15 p.m., Apostolou, Hill and Ede were charged; but not before another argument ensued between Inspector Munns and Challenor, because the latter wished the three to be jointly charged, enabling them to be dealt with at the same court. DCI McArthur was the arbitrator and he agreed with Munns' point of view. Ede and Hill were bailed to appear at Chelsea Juvenile Court on 17 July (when they were further remanded until 4 September); Apostolou was kept in custody.

Rooum was charged at 10.25 p.m. and refused to sign for his property.[7] He had the sum of 5s 2d in his possession and also, he stated, a diary, from which pages had been torn out whilst he was in the police station. On one of the pages Rooum had helpfully written down the divisional number of a police constable which had been shouted out by another demonstrator on 9 July. However, Challenor denied pulling out the pages or, indeed, seeing a diary, which was not shown on the charge sheet. Rooum had heard the officers giving the inspector formal evidence of arrest, inasmuch that pieces of brick had been found in his pocket. Challenor said the same about his arrest. But Rooum knew that this was not the case; the brick never had been in his pocket. A book entitled *Science and the Detection of Crime* by C. R. M. Cuthbert had been published the previous year by Arrow Books, and Rooum realized that if he stayed in custody overnight and if the portion of brick was not placed in his pocket, then the following morning, his jacket could be submitted for scientific forensic examination to prove that there was no brick-dust in the pocket. Challenor would later tell Marlborough Street Magistrates' Court that the reason why Rooum had not been admitted to bail had been through an oversight; it was an omission which suited Rooum down to the ground.

---

7. Rooum would later tell the James Enquiry that three different bricks were attributed to him: one which Challenor had shown him in the charge room, another which was shown to the inspector and a third produced at court.

CHAPTER 11

"What Do You Expect Me To Do Next, a Handstand?"

At midnight Etheridge was carrying out an enquiry when he happened to meet Challenor, whom he later described as being "obviously dejected and in low spirits". They walked and talked, and it became clear to Etheridge that Challenor's dejection was twofold; it stemmed firstly from being rebuked by Superintendent Burdett, and secondly from being obliged to arrest and charge some youngsters who, said Challenor, "ought not to have been mixed up in the crowd they were with." By the time they returned to West End Central at 3 a.m., Challenor's depression had lifted, but because he was very tired, Etheridge took him home by car. However, that must have been some considerable time later.

Padmore stated that he was taken from his cell by Challenor at 5 a.m. to have his fingerprints taken, a course of action to which he objected; but, he said, Challenor called him, "A black bastard" and punched him in the mouth, upon which he believed that a further portion of tooth had been broken. He then agreed to have his fingerprints be taken, to save himself further punishment. This was at variance with the testimony of the gaoler, Police Constable Donald MacLean, who stated that at 4 a.m. Challenor and two aids to CID told him that they were ready to charge Padmore and it was he, PC MacLean, who brought Padmore from the cells, not Challenor; he then, at Challenor's request, left to look for Inspector Willars, so that he might charge Padmore. However, Police Sergeant Walter George Trump told the enquiry that at 4.15 a.m. he had heard and seen Challenor shouting at Padmore in the charge room, telling him that he was going to have his fingerprints taken, and Padmore had refused. Sergeant Trump rushed off to find Inspector Taylor, since he believed that Challenor might "exceed his duty", but Inspector Taylor's recollection of the incident – and that of Police Sergeant Mervyn Hanlon – was in marked contrast to that of Sergeant Trump; both were unable to remember anything out of the ordinary occurring in the charge room, with no complaint being made – except, of course, by Sergeant Trump. Nevertheless, Trump told the enquiry, in some detail, of Challenor's personality and reputation and also of his often unconventional way of dealing with paperwork, which tended to cause the uniform branch "a headache".

Inspector Willars – who, it will be recalled, was certainly no great fan of Challenor – charged Padmore at 4.30 a.m., received no complaint from him and noticed nothing out of the ordinary regarding his appearance. Neither did 'Nobby' Birch, who took Padmore's fingerprints. Dave Parkinson, who typed out a Form CRO 74, in which the full, detailed description of a person charged was noted, similarly did not notice any injuries. And lastly, neither did the gaoler, PC MacLean, who had been present during the fingerprint-taking and who conveyed Padmore back to his cell.

Police Constable Frank James Harris was the early-turn gaoler who took over from MacLean on the morning of 12 July, and he saw no injuries either. Later that morning at Marlborough Street Magistrates' Court, Rooum saw Padmore, who, he said, alleged that Challenor had assaulted him; he noticed that Padmore had a swollen lip and spots of blood on his cuff. Rooum made reference to meeting Padmore at court when he provided a detailed statement to Du Rose on 20 November 1963; however, he mentioned no details of assault, injuries or bloodstained clothing – rather an oversight for the person described in the James Report as having 'apparent enjoyment' in the giving of evidence.

Padmore's counsel was Claud Geoffrey Allen, instructed by the solicitor Abraham Stoller, who was also present. Padmore alleged to both men that Challenor had punched him in the face, knocking out a tooth, and Mr Allen did notice that his client had a swollen lip and some blood on his shirtsleeve; reference was also made to an injury to his arm. However, Stoller's recollection was far more vivid: he recalled both of Padmore's lips being swollen, a gap in his mouth where a tooth had once been, a black eye and an arm dangling in a bloodstained bandage, as though it were broken. Padmore was examined by Dr Hassan Mahoud Bayoumi, who found no injury to his eye or arm. He did find a small wound to the inside of his lower lip which was consistent with someone biting the inside of his lip. A tooth which had been substantially filled in the past had been broken, but such a tooth could break under slight pressure as well as with a blow to the jaw. This was on the left side of the jaw, but Padmore had stated that the blow which he received from Challenor on 6 July had been on the right side. The piece of 'broken tooth' which Padmore had preserved was subjected to forensic dentistry; it turned out to be a piece of dental filling.

Nevertheless, on his client's instructions, Mr Allen applied to the Bench for a summons, alleging assault by Challenor. This application was observed by Police Constable Alfred Chaney, the court's assistant gaoler, who had taken Padmore from the cells, stood beside him in the dock and returned him to the cells afterwards. He therefore looked at Padmore and later recalled thinking, 'Well, I cannot see anything wrong with him." And that, it seemed, was the view of the magistrate, who refused the application. Padmore was released on bail the following day. But during the court appearance Mr Allen noticed that Challenor looked strained, and it appeared to be an effort for him to stand up straight in the witness box. (Since Challenor had not left the police station until 4.45 a.m. that morning, had been driven home and then left again to be in the office by 8.45 a.m., he had probably had a maximum of two hours sleep; so his tiredness in the witness box was perhaps understandable.) And following the application, the barrister saw Challenor sitting on a bench, his head in his hands, saying, "I must have my Guinness" or "I must have my beer".

Rooum and Apostolou were represented by the solicitor Stanley Clinton Davis. He had been instructed by the National Council for Civil Liberties after Ede had telephoned them that morning; Clinton Davis would become Ede's legal representative, too. Rooum was remanded on bail until 18 July (as was Apostolou, who spent three nights in Ashford remand centre until a suitable surety could be found), and Rooum's jacket was submitted for independent forensic analysis.

On the same day as this court appearance, Ronald Ede made a formal complaint to his Member of Parliament in respect of Challenor's conduct; also on the same day, Superintendent Townsend sent for Challoner and gave him a direct, unequivocal order that he was to limit his hours of duty and to restrict his work to pending matters.

The same did not apply to Betty Ambatielos, who was still working flat out for her cause; on the day that Challenor was being censured she was granted a forty-five-minute audience with Panayotis Pipinelis, the new Greek premier. It met with limited success. Shortly afterwards, nineteen political prisoners in Greece were released, but her husband was not among them.

Following the court appearance, Clinton Davis, together with Martin Ennals, the General Secretary of the National Council for Civil Liberties, arrived at West End Central, saw Challenor and demanded to inspect the bricks which had formed the basis of the charges against Rooum, Ede, Hill and Apostolou. Challenor refused. There was an angry exchange, and finally Detective Inspector Leslie Bruce intervened but was accused by Clinton Davis of being similarly obstructive. Bruce recalled that Clinton Davis excitedly waved his papers in front of Challenor's face, claiming, "You are used to cautioning people, Sergeant and I now caution you that you are being extremely obstructive." It appeared that Inspector Bruce either thought – or had been given the impression – that Mr Ennals was Clinton Davis' clerk, and he told the solicitor that since the papers had been forwarded to the Metropolitan Police's Solicitors' Department, he ought to seek their permission to view the bricks. After consultation with Superintendent Townsend, an inspection of the brick segments was eventually carried out.

On Saturday 13 July Detective Inspector Ronald Taylor, in an effort to reinforce Superintendent Townsend's dictum regarding Challenor taking things easy, interviewed him; but Challenor 'appeared to go to sleep on his feet', and Taylor and Detective Inspector Bruce persuaded him to go home and rest. It appears he did; the following Monday, Bruce made a point of seeking him out in the office and decided that Challenor appeared fully recovered, bright and well.

The next day, 16 July, at a remand hearing at Marlborough Street Magistrates' Court in the case of Steel, Braggins, Matthews and Ireland, who had been arrested for insulting behaviour at that court, Challenor, according to Ireland and Steel, produced to them a length of metal attached to which was a piece of paper bearing the word 'Limbo'. Nothing was said to them by Challenor, nor, due to their disabilities, would they have understood him if it had been, so if this did occur it is difficult to understand why. In addition, the trial commenced at the Old Bailey of Pink, Brown, Francis and Bridgeman, all of whom were accused of possessing offensive weapons; all pleaded not guilty on the grounds that the weapons had been planted on them. Two days later, the charges against Rooum and Apostolou were due to be heard at Marlborough Street Magistrates' Court (as was the case of a man named Jarvis, who had been arrested for inflicting grievous bodily harm), and Challenor, who was at the Old Bailey, received an urgent summons from Mr McCrory of the Metropolitan Police's Solicitors' Department to go straight to Marlborough Street.

Quite obviously, Challenor could not be in two places at once, and in any event the Old Bailey took precedence over a Magistrates' Court. It was quite clear that Michael Sherrard, counsel appearing for Rooum and Apostolou, was aware of the reason for Challenor's absence, because either Kenneth Richardson, the counsel briefed for the prosecution, or Ken Etheridge, would have told him. However, Sherrard took this golden opportunity to utilise the type of rhetoric he had employed during his unsuccessful defence of the murderer James Hanratty two years previously, and shouted to the court, "After all this, we arrive with our army of witnesses, the prosecution does not even appear!"

However, due to the length of the court list to be heard that day, plus Challenor's absence, it seemed highly unlikely that the case would be heard; it was therefore adjourned until 8 August. As the legal representatives, together with Etheridge, were about to leave court, so Challenor arrived hot-foot from the Old Bailey, perspiring freely; seeing him, Clinton Davis suggested that application be made for the case against Rooum to be reinstated. "What do you want me to do next, a handstand?" roared Challenor (although he later said that this was a jocular remark to Etheridge rather than addressed to the lawyers), and then, "What is this ruddy case? I'll bloody well go back to court." Etheridge recalled Clinton Davis saying to Sherrard, "What an offensive officer. Something will have to be done about him" – and he was as good as his word. The same day, Clinton Davis sent a letter of complaint regarding Challenor to Scotland Yard, recommending disciplinary action; however, when he was questioned about the incident on 12 August by Detective Chief Inspector Harry Pike, Challenor's recollection of the matter was that he had merely said to Etheridge, "Well, if you don't need me, I will get back to the Old Bailey."

On 19 July Braggins and Co were committed to the Old Bailey to stand their trial for conspiracy to pervert the course of justice by the intimidation of witnesses; and three days later, the trial judge at the Old Bailey, Sir Gerald Dodson, summed up the case against Pink and Co, saying:

> In this case, you are not troubled with any question of whether there was any lawful authority or reasonable excuse for the possession of offensive weapons. The defence is that there was never any possession at all. That being so, the question of lawful authority or reasonable excuse does not arise. I only mention it because it simplifies your task if indeed your duty can be regarded as a task at all, in a case in which it has been rightly said the issue is so very clear cut and simple.

The jury's task seemed to be simplified, indeed; all four men were found guilty, with Pink being sentenced to two years' imprisonment (the maximum sentence possible) and Brown, Francis and Bridgeman each receiving twelve months' imprisonment.

Not that Challenor was there to hear the verdict; earlier in the week, having given his evidence, he and his wife had left to go on holiday.

CHAPTER 12

The Gathering Storm

While Harry and Doris Challenor were experiencing the clean air of Switzerland, Challenor's colleagues were hard at work endeavouring, albeit with limited success, to clear up the mess he had left behind him, including allegations about his behaviour which were coming in thick and fast.

On 25 July Superintendent Townsend received the letter of complaint (via Scotland Yard) from Clinton Davis regarding Challenor's conduct at Marlborough Street Magistrates' Court; this he handed for investigation to Detective Inspector Davis, who reported back to Townsend on 1 August; nothing in the report suggested mental illness in Challenor.

On 26 July Townsend stated that he had received a report from Detective Chief Inspector Harry Pike in respect of the complaint made by Ede; the report could not be completed, since Challenor was on leave and Ede still had yet to appear in court. It would have been quite improper to have interviewed Ede or any witnesses he might call, until the evidence had been tested. Therefore, apart from keeping senior officers briefed, there the matter temporarily rested.

However, Townsend was possibly mistaken regarding the author of the report, or perhaps the date when he received it, because although on 26 July Pike's promotion to detective chief inspector was shown in *Police Orders*, as was his transfer to West End Central on 1 August to replace DCI McArthur, Harry Pike was then still a detective inspector on 'D' Division. Knowing of his impending arrival (and of DCI McArthur's departure), it is possible that Pike was asked to undertake the initial investigation; however, this matters little.

It is clear that Harry Raymond Pike was a thoroughly decent man, a meticulous investigator and a plodder, not a kicker-in of doors or a firecracker of a crime-buster. Joining the Metropolitan Police in 1937 (his standard of education was so high that he did not need to take either of the Civil Service examinations, necessary before one could take the police promotional examinations), he had seen war service with the Special Investigation Branch of the Military Police, and during his twenty-six years' service he had slowly and industriously climbed the promotional ladder to reach his present rank. In addition, from 19 August to 6 September, he would assume the role of acting detective superintendent at West End Central. That temporary promotion would not have added one penny to his forthcoming pension, which was a pity, because given what was to occur he would have earned every bit of it. He was now aged forty-seven, and the remaining four months of Harry Pike's service would be the longest of his career.

On 27 July Townsend and Acting Chief Superintendent Lyscom saw Victor Mishcon, who was Irvine Shine's principal, and apologised for Challenor's behaviour on 29 June when he had dubbed Shine "an imposter". The explanations of deafness and overwork given by the two senior officers were accepted, and Mr Mishcon regarded the incident as closed.

On 2 August Messrs Bernard Solley & Co, solicitors acting on behalf of Padmore, wrote to the commissioner of the Metropolitan Police alleging that on both 6 and 11 July, 'Grave assaults and even graver indignities' had been inflicted upon their client. They demanded an investigation, and two weeks later a detailed statement, with the permission of his solicitors, was obtained from Padmore by DCI Pike.

Meanwhile, Detective Chief Superintendent Tommy Butler had sent a report through to Commander Hatherill suggesting that Challenor should be moved from West End Central; and due to Challenor's increasing deafness he had issued instructions that Challenor should be medically examined by Sir John Richardson Bt, MVO, MA, MD, MB, B.Ch, FRCP, MRCS, LRCP, the consultant physician of the Metropolitan Police. (That was Butler's last contribution to Challenor's welfare; a few days later, the Great Train Robbery occurred, and Butler was back to his beloved Flying Squad, never to return.) In a covering note for Sir John, Harold Victor Ettenfield, the Medical Branch Secretary, using information he had gleaned from Hatherill, wrote that the case was one of 'a very good detective sergeant whose increasing deafness is leading to embarrassing and possibly dangerous situations'.

But a transfer from 'C' Division was the last thing Challenor wanted. "If I don't go out and break the villains," he said, "I will not hold up my head in the West End again." In fact, and quite apart from his deafness, Challenor had been behaving oddly for years, but much of his behaviour was put down to pardonable eccentricity. He once walked into West End Central at one o'clock in the morning, unrecognisable in a Homburg hat, a cape, and glasses. Using a mid-European accent, he then told the bemused desk sergeant, "I vant to claim political asylum!" This sort of behaviour was considered the norm for Harry Challenor.

Challenor returned to work on 6 August looking refreshed, and DCI Pike had the opportunity of witnessing him in action, cross-examining an expert witness in court; Pike described his performance as 'superb'. During the hearing, Mr Hillman, a solicitor of Messrs Clintons, asked Challenor if a solicitor had recently complained about his conduct; this type of question was regarded as nothing more than a cheap trick, known in the trade as 'frightening powder', and Challenor, feeling (quite correctly) that this referred to the incident at court involving Clinton Davis on 18 July, simply stated that a letter had been received.

DCI Pike had also informed Challenor of the other complaints which had been lodged in respect of his behaviour, and told him he would be required to attend the Medical Branch on 16 August. Since Challenor had told his wife, whilst they were on holiday, that he was being tested, hypnotised and brainwashed regarding a special job for which he had been selected, the appointment at the Medical Branch could not come quickly enough as far as she was concerned. Doris Challenor was now frantic with worry at the state of her husband's mental health. Was he, in fact, on 'some special duty'? She considered approaching one of his senior officers, but her husband had told her that she must trust him and that she must not worry. If she were to communicate with a senior officer, would this not be disloyal to Harry and perhaps put him in the wrong? His behaviour was becoming more and more erratic, he was short-tempered, agitated, excited and speaking louder than ever. So, rightly or wrongly, Doris did not communicate her fears to anybody; but she was at her wits' end.

On the morning of 8 August Harry Challenor arrived at Marlborough Street Magistrates' Court in a buoyant, cheerful mood, asking Rooum if he was "ready for the fight"; but his joviality would not last for long. Before the stipendiary magistrate, Mr Robey, Challenor gave his evidence that Rooum had been in possession of a piece of brick, and Rooum gave his, that he had not been; so far, stalemate. But then evidence was given for the defence by a scientific expert, Mr J. F. Kayser, who had examined Rooum's pocket which had allegedly contained the brick. There was not a trace of brick dust in there. In fact, Mr Kayser went further than that; he stated that if a brick segment of the size suggested had been present in Rooum's pocket, it would have both stretched and scratched the pocket's lining – and no such indentations and striations had been found. The magistrate was passed the segment of brick, together with the pieces of brick which had allegedly been found in the possession of Ede and Hill; placed together, the now (almost whole) housebrick spelled out practically all of the word 'MARSTON', the name of the manufacturers, the Marston Valley Brickworks. Challenor agreed with the magistrate that it was quite possible that the segments were from the same brick, which suggested that the defendants were all acting in concert. However, due to the length of time between the two sets of arrests – almost an hour – and given the large numbers of demonstrators on the streets, Mr Robey obviously decided otherwise; saying that there was an 'element of doubt' in the case, he dismissed the charge against Rooum. He also refused Rooum's application for costs for his defence.

Challenor appeared rather disconcerted at the court's decision; after all, he was not used to his cases being dismissed. Rooum later said, "I am sorry to say I was not sorry to see him shaken."

It was, however, a different matter in respect of the other defendants, at the same court, on the same day, in front of the same magistrate: having been convicted of possessing pieces of brick as offensive weapons, John and Ronald Ryall were each fined £5, Colin Derwin was conditionally discharged for twelve months, and Apostolou was fined £10.

Later the same day, DCI Pike interviewed Challenor regarding the assault on Padmore, and two days later Superintendent Burdett submitted a report in which he said he thought that Challenor 'might be bordering on mental illness'.

On 12 August Challenor was interviewed by DCI Pike in respect of the complaints made by Ede and Clinton Davis. It was an interview beset with difficulties; on several occasions Challenor appeared to be falling asleep, he was unable to grasp the seriousness of the complaints, and although the statement was nine pages long, it took a very long time – four and a half hours – to record it. The same day, the father of John and Ronald Ryall wrote to his Member of Parliament (and the Speaker of the House of Commons), Sir Harry Hylton-Foster, to complain about his sons' treatment by the police and the courts.

On 16 August Challenor was examined by Sir John Richardson, and the following day Sir John informed Superintendent Townsend that Challenor was fit for duty. He felt that there was nothing wrong with Challenor's hearing and there was no indication that he was mentally disturbed; he requested, and was sent, a report from the Ear, Nose and Throat Department of St Thomas' Hospital, which stated that Challenor was suffering from a minimal loss of hearing in the higher tones. Challenor did not consider a hearing aid necessary.

On 19 August Deputy Commander Spooner contacted DCI Pike to ask how his investigations of Challenor were progressing. When

Spooner was told that Pike thought Challenor was 'a sick man' – he had formed this view after the interview of 12 August and was therefore surprised when Sir John Richardson had pronounced him fit for duty – he was directed to pass this information on to Commander Hatherill. This led to the Medical Branch Secretary, Mr Ettenfield, being informed that when Challenor was next examined by Sir John Richardson on 23 August, Sir John should apply his mind to Challenor's mental state.

Harry Challenor was experiencing grave difficulties in obeying the official order restricting his hours of work, and on 20 August DCI Pike felt impelled to underscore this dictum by recording the directive in Challenor's official diary. Two days later, DCI Pike again interviewed Challenor regarding the Padmore allegations; Pike felt that his mental state had deteriorated even more, since he was staring into space and appeared unable to comprehend the questions. Once more, Pike reinforced his orders about restricted duties.

But when Challenor arrived for his medical examination the following day, Mr Ettenfield noticed nothing about his behaviour which would suggest mental illness; and neither did Sir John, who did indeed apply his mind to the question of mental instability but could find no evidence of it. 'This man again declares he has no trouble with his hearing. He says he sleeps well, feels well and has no tensions,' he wrote and communicated his feelings to Commander Hatherill the same day, adding that the hearing defect was minimal, and that Challenor denied any existence of hearing problems and had told him that he was 'without any tensions, troubles or anxieties'. In addition, Sir John felt that there was nothing to suggest that Challenor needed the services of a psychiatrist. Mr Ettenfield described Challenor's demeanour as being 'calm and dignified' and recalled hearing him say to Sir John, "I am a mature man. If I'm in difficulties, I can manage them myself."

Mr Ettenfield might have changed his opinion if he had been in the CID office at the same time as Detective Constable Maurice Harding, when Challenor suddenly stood up in the middle of the office on night-duty and started shouting, "They're here! The aliens are here!" Mr Ettenfield might have thought his judgement seriously flawed had he been present in the CID office at Sutton police station, together with Detective Constable David Eager, when the door suddenly burst open and Harry Challenor started crawling between the desks of the CID officers with a knife between his teeth, saying – probably indistinctly – "You know, they think I'm mad!" But the fact was, many of the officers who knew Challenor and who witnessed this extraordinary behaviour, thought this to be the norm.

So when, on 24 August, Challenor arrived at West End Central to inform DCI Pike that he was 'fit for duty', his senior officer was not only flabbergasted but sceptical, so much so that he telephoned the Medical Branch and was astonished to discover that what Challenor had told him was indeed the decision of Sir John Richardson. Pike decided to keep a very close grip on Challenor's activities, although he had apparently kept to the limits of his duties as had been laid down by Pike and Superintendent Townsend.

But on the afternoon of 3 September Pike informed Challenor that Clinton Davis would be arriving at the station for the service of a writ on behalf of Rooum, and sensibly advised him to say nothing when this was done. He was unprepared for what followed; Challenor became very emotional, clenching and unclenching his fists, saying that to keep silent would be difficult because there was so much he wanted to say; this was followed by an incoherent outburst. From what Pike could understand, Challenor was saying, "I'm a simple man but I know what I'm paid for and I'm just not being allowed to do my job. I can't go on remaining in the office because I feel I'm getting money by false pretences." He then went on to say that there was a criminal conspiracy in the West End to destroy his character and get him transferred so that the protection racketeers could take over.

It was whilst this outburst was going on that DCI Pike was informed that the solicitor had arrived, so he told Challenor that they would continue to discuss his problems later and to wait in the CID office. Instead, Challenor tried to leave the police station and had to be physically restrained from doing so by Pike, who took him to Chief Superintendent James Starritt's office and informed the chief superintendent of what had occurred. Starritt (six feet four tall, known as 'Big Jim', a captain in the wartime Royal Marines and later to receive a knighthood as deputy commissioner) was a firm disciplinarian. Challenor reiterated his comments about being confined to the office, said that his hands were being tied behind his back and told Starritt, "These villains are doing their best to crucify me."

"Do you consider yourself fit for duty?" asked Starritt, and Challenor, who had been standing rigidly to attention throughout the interview, replied, "Fit as a fiddle, sir. All I want to do is go out and get some thieves."

Satisfied that Challenor now had some control over his emotions, Starritt permitted the service of the writ to go ahead, and in the presence of DCI Pike this was carried out without incident; but immediately afterwards, Challenor broke down in tears.

It was possibly about this time that Nobby Birch recalled hearing that, having been admonished by a senior officer, Challenor stormed out of his office shouting 'that he wasn't appreciated and that after all his efforts, he was being made a scapegoat'. He stamped along the corridor shouting uncontrollably, before sitting down on the stairs and bursting into tears, saying 'it was all a waste of time and effort'. "He was," Birch told me, "I believe, in the first stages of a nervous breakdown."

Pike left the room to ask Ken Etheridge to look after his colleague, but when he returned, Challenor had gone. When Challenor returned shortly afterwards, Pike informed Starritt, and Challenor apologised for his behaviour. For the next hour Starritt calmly discussed the situation and told Challenor that he should consult a doctor, because he clearly needed help and advice. Starritt was not prepared to rely on Challenor's assurance that he would seek medical help – by now he, too, had formed the opinion that Challenor was 'mentally ill' – and he sent a full report, the same day, containing the background leading up to these events to the Commander of No. 1 District Headquarters. (At the James Enquiry, it was unwisely suggested by one of the barristers that the report had not been sent on the date given, if indeed it had been sent at all; this prompted Starritt to forcefully reply, "Sir, may I tell you that in the whole of my thirty-odd years of police service, I have never had my integrity doubted!" The barrister hastily withdrew his allegation.) It was this report which was on Sir John Richardson's desk when he examined Challenor on 6 September.

But before that could happen, on 4 September Challenor turned up at Chelsea Juvenile Court to give evidence in respect of Hill and Ede. Understandably, DCI Pike accompanied him to court. Rooum was also there; he intended to act as a witness for the defence, although due to lack of time the case was adjourned until 9 October. But Pike was astonished when Challenor approached Rooum – who had been responsible for the serving of the writ on him the previous day – and said jocularly, "Wotcher, me old darling – what about playing football for us on Sunday?"

In respect of the direct orders – both verbal and written – which he had received regarding his hours of duty, it is highly likely that Harry Challenor was simply showing eight hours duty in his diary but then going out to conduct his own enquiries. He was certainly not going home at the completion of his restricted duty, because at one o'clock the following morning, 5 September, whilst walking home to Sutton, he arrested three youths who were lurking in the shop doorway of a vacant premises in Clapham High Street, during which time he sustained a slight injury. The station officer at Clapham police station refused to accept the charge, the youths were released, Dr Dymond the Divisional Surgeon was called, examined Challenor and certified that he was unfit for duty for twenty-four hours. An urgent telephone call was made to West End Central, and DCI Pike (who by now, must have felt that he would be inextricably tied to Harry Challenor for the rest of his life) attended Clapham police station, where he spoke to Challenor, who was puzzled and unable to understand why there was a delay about taking the three youths he had arrested to court. His bewilderment turned to rage when he discovered that, far from going to court, they had been released.

This story is taken up by Fred Faragher, then a detective constable at Clapham police station, whose first meeting with Challenor was that morning when he entered the station. Faragher found himself confronted by an extremely irate man who demanded to know, "What sort of a fucking nick is this?" After Faragher was apprised of the youths' identities, he realized that they were a gang of tearaways who had long been suspected of carrying out street robberies on lone pedestrians in the early hours of the morning. This was confirmed after Challenor told him, "Those three bastards tried to blag me when I was walking home. I nicked them and they've let them go."[8]

Challenor was the National Health patient of two general practitioners, Doctors Arthur Henry Stern and Otto Meerapfel. He had last seen Dr Stern in April 1963, when he complained of 'feeling lousy', a ringing in the ears and loss of energy. Nothing abnormal was detected and no treatment was prescribed, except for the suggestion of a hearing aid, although it was thought this would be of limited assistance.

Now DCI Pike arranged, via Doris Challenor, to have Harry examined that afternoon by Dr Meerapfel. The doctor was simply told by Doris that her husband was 'not well, sometimes elated, sometimes depressed and was not normal'. She made no mention of his delusional behaviour before and during the holiday in

---

8. He wasn't the only one to express surprise; about a year later, the ringleader was arrested again for theft by Faragher, who mentioned the previous incident – the youth agreed with Challenor's account and was still taken aback that one man "had kicked the shit out of the three of us". He was also at a loss to explain why he and his associates had been released.

Switzerland. No physical examination was carried out, but after a 15–20 minute interview the doctor concluded that Challenor was a worried but not a sick man; and at the conclusion of their discourse, Dr Meerapfel was politely but very firmly told by his patient that he could leave.

So it was just as well that DCI Pike reported the situation to Chief Superintendent Starritt, who was now so concerned that he informed the Deputy Commissioner, Douglas Webb CVO, OBE, *Légion d'honneur*, who in turn telephoned the Medical Branch Secretary, Mr Ettenfield. When he discovered from Dr Meerapfel that Challenor had refused a physical examination or to discuss his health, Mr Ettenfield recorded the tentative diagnosis 'Hypomania?' and immediately made an appointment for Challenor to see Sir John Richardson the following day.

By now, Harry Challenor could not be trusted in any investigations into his health, so when he attended the Medical Branch on 6 September he was accompanied there by Detective Superintendent Leonard Woolner from No. 1 District Headquarters. In fact, the superintendent did more than accompany Challenor; he addressed Sir John directly, informing him of the full facts of his companion's behaviour prior to the service of the writ on 3 September and the arrest the previous day of the three youths (which at that time was thought to have been unlawful). These facts, together with the report from Chief Superintendent Starritt, assisted Sir John in reaching a decision; what might have helped him even more would have been the information held by Doris Challenor, but he was unaware of this. Nobody knew of it.

However, the information which Sir John possessed was sufficient for him to conclude that Challenor needed psychiatric advice and treatment, and his report read: 'This man is unfit for duty. I have advised him to see a psychiatrist and this he refuses to do. He also refuses to go sick or see his own doctor. Paranoia.' Due to Challenor's refusal to see his own doctor, Sir John took the unusual step of placing him off duty on the grounds of sickness.

During Harry Challenor's career, both in the army and the police, he had not hesitated to bend the rules when he wanted to achieve his own ends, and now was no exception. The following day, he called on Dr Meerapfel, who was quite ignorant of the fact that twenty-four hours previously his patient had been examined by Sir John Richardson who had reached certain conclusions regarding his health, and Challenor did not inform him of this fact. But he allowed Dr Meerapfel to examine him and take samples for laboratory analysis, and he did admit to working very long hours. The doctor certified that Challenor was unfit for work due to 'general exhaustion' but later admitted that nothing in his patient's demeanour suggested paranoia, being unaware, of course, that the previous day Sir John had recommended that he see a psychiatrist. In fact, he thought that a holiday might restore his patient, who wore a tired and haunted look, to health.

So Harry and Doris Challenor went off on holiday to the seaside town of Swanage in Dorset. While they were relaxing there, on 11 September, Richard Ian Fear appeared at Chelsea Juvenile Court in respect of the brick offensive weapon charge, in which PC Battes gave evidence; the case was dismissed.

One week later, on 18 September, Ronald William Braggins, Frank Matthews, Clifford Ireland and Frederick Steele appeared at the Old Bailey in respect of charges of conspiracy to pervert the course of justice by the intimidation of witnesses. No evidence was offered, due to Sir John Richardson's assessment that Challenor had to be regarded as an entirely unreliable witness, and they were acquitted. None of the men had complained of police action prior to their acquittal; later, it was a different matter, and they claimed compensation for being unlawfully arrested. Braggins received £750, Matthews, £574 and Ireland and Steel, £250 each.

The Challenors returned from holiday, and on 21 September Harry Challenor saw Dr Meerapfel again. He appeared fit and healthy from the holiday, but the doctor persuaded him to agree to see a psychiatrist; he was reluctant to issue another certificate stating that Challenor was still unfit for duty and wanted a psychiatrist's opinion. Therefore he contacted Mr Ettenfield at the Medical Centre in order to expedite matters. Until then there had not been a full flow of information between the Medical Branch and Challenor's GPs; now, that changed.

But this was not the case as far as the psychiatrist was concerned. Mr Ettenfield immediately wrote to Dr J. J. Bradley of the Psychiatric Department of St Thomas' Hospital and briefly set out the background and circumstances of what had occurred at Sir John Richardson's examination. Because he was treating the matter – quite properly – with great urgency, Mr Ettenfield did not delay by forwarding the police files which Sir John had had the benefit of seeing. He anticipated that the psychiatric personnel at the hospital would form their own conclusions. He had not, however, foreseen Harry Challenor's cunning.

On 24 September – in the absence of Dr Bradley – Challenor saw Dr Erasmus Darwin Barlow MB, B.Ch, MRCS, LRCP, DPM, the consultant psychiatrist and senior lecturer in the Department of Psychological Medicine at St Thomas' Hospital. Challenor blandly stated that he felt fit and wanted to get back to work. He told Dr

Barlow that his present troubles had arisen as a result of people he had arrested in June [sic] and that a conspiracy hatched by the CND, which had resulted in some adverse publicity, had caused him to become angry. He candidly admitted walking the fifteen miles home to Sutton every night, but said that because he was engaged in sedentary office duties, it provided him with exercise and the opportunity to think matters over, and helped him to sleep. Contrary to what he had agreed with Dr Meerapfel, he now stated unequivocally that he was not prepared to undergo psychiatric treatment. Dr Barlow made a provisional diagnosis: 'Paranoia with a monosymptomatic delusional system' and made an appointment for two weeks' time.

With Challenor still off sick, matters were still progressing behind the scenes. On 7 October Pedrini, serving his seven-year sentence, appealed to the Court of Criminal Appeal for leave to appeal out of time; his original appeal against sentence had been refused on 15 May 1963. This fresh application was duly considered.

Two days later, Gregory John Hill and Ronald George Ede appeared at Chelsea Juvenile Court, and no evidence was offered by the prosecution, a letter from the Director of Public Prosecutions having been read to the court, giving Challenor's illness as the reason for dropping the 'brick' charges. Clinton Davis was triumphant. "I wonder with what accuracy the situation of Sergeant Challenor is described?" he brayed, adding, "This is a palpable fraud on the court"; a remark which the Chairman, Thomas Edie, told him was "improper".

The fact that Rooum had issued a writ against Challenor was reported in the press, as was the dismissal of the charges in respect of Hill and Ede. Challenor gave an interview to a reporter from the *Guardian* – many might have thought this to have been a clear indication of the extent of his illness – in which he said:

> There are certain people who have got it in for me. I can say that I have no regrets for anything I have done. There is not the slightest reason for me to reproach myself. It should have been mentioned that a number of other people had been convicted of this offence.

And on 12 October John Ford's father, Charles Ford, now jumped on the National Council for Civil Liberties bandwagon, writing to them and alleging that Challenor had been paid bribes.

The *People* newspaper was fed a story by the National Council for Civil Liberties which was published on 13 October, and this dealt with the dismissal of the charges in respect of Hill and Ede (who, being juveniles, were not named) and Apostolou's existing conviction; the newspaper stated: 'If indeed the boys are victims of a miscarriage of justice, it is also in the public interest that the boys be proclaimed innocent.'

Seeking a quote from Challenor, the newspaper published his reply: "At the moment, I am not working. I am being treated by a psychiatrist for overwork"; but the following Sunday, the *People* followed up their previous week's lead story with the second 'brick case' involving the Ryall brothers, Derwin and Fear.

On 15 October Challenor again saw Dr Barlow, who much later would say, "I have never seen a single case like this before." But he did not say so on that day in October 1963. His examination revealed no evidence of persistence of delusions, and to all intents and purposes Challenor was leading a perfectly normal existence. The following day Barlow wrote to Sir John Richardson:

> I do not see how I can keep him off sick any longer and I am therefore referring him back to you. I suppose it is possible that future court cases may indicate how disturbed he has been, and he may need treatment in the future.

Three days later, Sir John saw Challenor again, but he was convinced that Challenor was suffering from a paranoid illness and therefore he wrote to Dr William Walter Sargent MA, MB, B.Ch, FRCP, MRCS, LRCP, DPM, the eminent physician in charge of the Psychological Medical Department at St Thomas' Hospital.

Dr Sargent's investigation was three-pronged; first he spent some considerable time with Superintendent Townsend obtaining the background to the case – he also learnt that Challenor was in the habit of drinking seven to nine Guinnesses a day – and then he spoke to Doris Challenor. It was from her that the missing pieces of the jigsaw fell into place. And thirdly, he spoke to Harry Challenor himself.

On 25 October, the same day that he had interviewed Challenor, Dr Sargent wrote to Sir John Richardson:

> I am certain that Harold Challenor is very mad, indeed. His affect is very discrepant. I am sure he is covering a mass of delusional ideas which were given to me by his wife. I consider him certifiably insane.

On the same day, Dr Sargent wrote to the deputy commissioner, telling him that Challenor was unfit to return to work, that it was debatable that he would ever be able to return to work and that he was quite mentally unfit to defend a civil action brought against him.

By now, Apostolou had appealed against his conviction; no evidence was offered by the prosecution, and Apostolou, his conviction expunged, walked free from court.

There was then an incident at a dinner held at the Café Royal when an unwise remark was made, and due to a combination of alcohol and the pressure he was experiencing, Challenor lost control. Detective Inspector Dave Dilley was told to take him home, and on 26 October Dr Stern was called. He had not seen his patient in almost exactly six months, but he had no hesitation in ordering his admission to Netherne Hospital under the provisions of Section 29 of the Mental Health Act. By now Harry Challenor was excited, aggressive, difficult to restrain and in need of urgent, expert and prolonged treatment. His demons had finally consumed him.

CHAPTER 13

The Investigation

Even in its formative years, Netherne was regarded as a progressive hospital for the treatment of mental illness. Founded in 1905 at a cost of £10,000, what was then Netherne Asylum (and later, Netherne Mental Hospital) was situated in Hooley, Surrey. It was originally designed to cater for 960 patients, but by the 1950s numbers had swollen to 2,000. Patients were encouraged to work on the hospital's large estate or in the workshops and laundry. There were sporting activities, monthly dances, and pantomimes at Christmas. By the time of Challenor's arrival, the perimeter fence had been taken down and drugs and tranquillizers were in use. A plumber who had been contracted to work at Netherne at that time used to fetch the tea for the builders in a billy can. After six months there, feeling very 'down', he went to his GP. Discovering where he had been working, the doctor advised him to tell the staff in the canteen that the tea was for his personal use; the patients had bromide added to theirs.

More than bromide would be needed to calm down Harry Challenor; locked in a secure ward, he received strong tranquillisers and electric shock treatment. Many people thought that Challenor's illness was simulated; it was not. The diagnosis of Dr Niall Farnan, the consultant psychiatrist at the hospital, was that Challenor was a paranoid schizophrenic, and his opinion concurred with that of psychiatrists who had examined him prior to his admission to Netherne and subsequently. It was difficult for the experts to assess when the schizophrenia had actually commenced. The symptoms were possibly apparent by April or May 1963, but due to Challenor's eccentricities, his boisterousness and his loudness, it was difficult for those who knew him to distinguish them from his normal behaviour. However, it was generally agreed by the consultants that Challenor had been mentally ill for some considerable time, but that from September 1963 there was very clear evidence that he was suffering from the full-blown symptoms of paranoid schizophrenia – or, as Dr Sargent had so succinctly put it, "He was very mad, indeed."

Challenor's condition would undoubtedly have worsened if he had received a book posted to him. By Ralph Partridge and entitled *Broadmoor. A History of Criminal Lunacy and its Problems*, it was inscribed, 'From the chaps and slags. With love, you nut case'; and on a photograph showing the old cemetery was written, 'Poor ol' Harry', and a grave was marked, 'Reserved for you'. Fortunately, it was intercepted by the medical staff.

With allegations of malpractice gathering momentum, it was announced that an enquiry would be set up. The Home Secretary had received a written report on 9 October, and on 24 October he announced to the House that he had requested an investigation from the commissioner into all that was known about the 'half-bricks' case. The enquiry was headed by Detective Chief Superintendent John Valentine Ralph Du Rose, who had joined the Metropolitan Police in 1931. As a career detective he had taken part in the Haigh murders investigation and had played a decisive part in the smashing of the Messina gang in Soho. Nicknamed 'Four-day Johnny' because of the speed with which he cleared up murder investigations, he had been commended by the commissioner on fourteen occasions. He would go on to play a decisive part in the Kray brothers' enquiry, achieve the rank of Deputy Assistant Commissioner and be appointed OBE; but now, since August 1963 he had been one of the senior officers at C1 Department (dubbed the 'Murder Squad') at Scotland Yard. He was eminently suited to such a task, although it was an assignment beset with difficulties. Several people serving prison sentences refused to say anything to the police without a solicitor being present; in a letter to the Home Office dated 18 March 1964 the National Council for Civil Liberties pointed out, 'We were able to assist in this matter.'

Next, on 2 November, Pink complained to the Commissioner of the Metropolitan Police that he had been 'fitted up' by Challenor, and on 14 November it was widely reported in the press that Rooum, Apostolou, Ede and Hill were to receive *ex gratia* payments to settle their cases for malicious prosecution out of court; and they did. Rooum received £500, Apostolou, £400, Ede, £250 and Hill, £200. On 20 November the television programme *Fair Play* gave the Pedrini case wide coverage, and two days later the Home Secretary, Henry Brooke, faced questions in the House. The Sunday newspapers for 24 November had a field day, with the *Sunday Express* featuring the Pedrini case and the *People* stating, 'Police pay £250 to deaf mutes.' Three days after that, 'Curly' King complained to his MP, Mrs Joyce Butler, that he, too, had been 'fitted up'.

* * *

Complaints were now flooding in to the National Council for Civil Liberties from those who had been convicted on Challenor's evidence, or from their relatives on their behalf, and others alleged impropriety by Challenor. In addition, what was now being referred to as the 'Challenor Affair' was becoming regarded as the straw that broke the camel's back. The 'Rhino Whip' case in Sheffield, other cases of alleged police brutality in Coventry and the Woolf case in London had engendered a sense of public disquiet regarding the police; and now, with these latest allegations, the Home Secretary's Police Bill was debated in Parliament and passed. By 1 August, the Police Act 1964 would be on the statute books, and Section 32 of the Act would enable a statutory enquiry to be set up, with authority to compel the attendance of witnesses and to take evidence under oath.

Joyce Butler, 'Curly' King's MP, was now working closely with the National Council for Civil Liberties and was compiling a dossier of the complaints; the Home Secretary informed the House of Commons that enquiries were still being made. One week later, on 20 December, Pink, Brown, Francis and Bridgeman all had their sentences quashed by the Court of Criminal Appeal on the grounds of misdirection of the jury by the trial judge. And on 26 December the television programme *What the Papers Say*, hosted by Bernard Levin, mentioned the case of Rooum. The following morning, Challenor absented himself from his hospital ward and arrived at West End Central, shouting and raving that he had not received any support from the police.

The TV programme, together with the press reports he had seen, brought Challenor to breaking point. He made his way to the busy Caterham bypass and walked out in front of a lorry, which smashed into him. Rumours about his condition spread like wildfire. Many police officers thought he had been killed. Other more anarchic members of society smugly dismissed that assertion, claiming that 'he wasn't hurt at all'. Both were wrong. Challenor was rushed to Redhill Hospital, where it was established that his pelvis was broken and he had sustained head injuries which led to concussion. Later, when he saw his erstwhile aid Peter Jay, he told him, "I thought I was indestructible." But as Challenor was later to admit, it was also a suicide attempt.

On 8 January 1964 Padmore, Hawkins and Browne stood trial at the Old Bailey on charges of conspiracy to defraud in the clip joint case. Challenor, of course, did not give evidence, and the jury failed to agree upon a verdict. There was a retrial on 20 January, but Mr Beck, who had already travelled to England from Switzerland to give evidence on several occasions, refused to attend. Since he was such a crucial witness, the prosecution was obliged to offer no evidence, and the three were acquitted. Padmore claimed damages for assault and false imprisonment via his solicitor, and the claim was settled when he received £750.

By 15 January 1964 Du Rose had submitted his detailed report to the Director of Public Prosecutions, who felt there was sufficient evidence to issue summonses on Challenor, Goldsmith, Battes and Oakey for conspiracy to pervert the course of justice. At 1.20 p.m. on 13 February 1964 service of three of these summonses was carried out by Detective Chief Inspector John O'Connell of New Scotland Yard at West End Central police station. After being cautioned, Goldsmith replied, "Nothing to say sir, except that I completely deny the charge." Battes replied, "Nothing, except that I am innocent of that" and Oakey made no reply.

Although former PC Ken Walker worked in another part of the Metropolitan Police and had no personal knowledge of Challenor, he recalled that this was the only time an unofficial, unauthorised collection was made on any matter. Arrangements were made to collect funds to help pay for the officers' legal defence.

The committal proceedings commenced at Marlborough Street Magistrates' Court on 17 March before the stipendiary magistrate, Edward Robey, and the case for the prosecution – the eight arrests involving bricks – was outlined by John Mathew QC. The eight persons who claimed bricks had been planted on them by the police, plus the witnesses whom Chief Superintendent Du Rose had traced and interviewed, provided their depositions – including Rooum, who with almost unbelievable arrogance told Mr Robey, "I have a conscientious objection to being a prosecution witness. I only came here under penalty of paying £100. I am not going to turn up at the Old Bailey unless I get a similar penalty." Rooum was being disingenuous; he would no more have missed turning up at the Old Bailey than he would have walked to the moon. He was the centre of attention, giving evidence against the despised police, and there is little doubt that he was loving it.

So Rooum and the seven others who had been arrested by Challenor and the aids on the evening of 11 July 1963 were important witnesses. But Detective Chief Superintendent Du Rose had been meticulous in his investigations. There was a wild card in the pack: he, too, was an aid to CID and his name was Police Constable 512 'C' Richard Raymond Jones.

* * *

Jones had become an aid to CID in April 1963 at West End Central, under Challenor's control, and in common with many other police officers he had made a brief statement to Du Rose on 20 September in which he stated he had neither seen nor knew anything of the arrests on 11 July. But it was not true. He made a further statement to Du Rose on 15 November, which contradicted the first, and an even more detailed one on 20 December.

What Jones had to say was this: on 11 July he had been detailed by DCI McArthur to undertake patrol duties in respect of the demonstration, but he had seen Challenor in the CID office beforehand, who had pointed to part of a brick on his desk and told him, "We've got to stop them throwing stones at Royalty." He said in his statement of 20 December that on the evening of 11 July:

> He [Challenor] was in a nervous state. He was a fanatic as regards work, long hours, then walking home, and remembering seeing the brick in his locker and his remarks about it, I thought it possible he may or might go too far as regards prisoners. I have heard lots of allegations made about him and it worried me. This is why I did not want to get mixed up with him that night.

Jones was at the junction with Bond Street and Grosvenor Street when Challenor approached and told him to accompany him to Brook Street. He did so unwillingly, walking about ten yards behind him, and then saw Challenor, together with PCs Battes and Oakey, approach three youths – these were obviously Apostolou, Hill and Ede. Jones then left the scene on his own. He would later say that he did not wish to accompany Challenor because it was in contravention of the directions given to him by DCI McArthur and because he had heard gossip that Challenor had planted a detonator on a criminal.

His evidence at the committal proceedings was said to be 'pitiful', and he contradicted himself to such an extent – the position of the brick in the CID office varied, from a desk to a locker to a drawer, and wherever it was, Challenor had made no reference to it – that John Mathew requested he might be treated as a hostile witness and be cross-examined about his statements. This was permitted by the magistrate, but Jones later said that when he saw his colleagues in the dock, he "went to pieces" because of his strong sense of loyalty to them and because he could not believe that the charges against them were true.

"I don't know why he did it," one officer commented. "I think he might have found religion." Nowadays, Jones would be lauded as a hero for daring to speak out against malpractice. However, this is now and that was then. Jones later resigned.

Challenor was faring badly at the Magistrates' Court. He had to be helped out of the dock by a doctor and a male nurse from Netherne. "The strain of this week has caused a deterioration in his condition," Robin Simpson, counsel for Challenor, told the court. "It was causing concern to the doctors looking after him and they thought he might not be able to come to court today. He has just about had it." And so it appeared. "I took meals to him when he was awaiting committal to the Bailey from Marlborough Street," Maurice Harding told me. "He appeared to be out of it, as if drugged."

The four were committed to stand their trial at the Old Bailey. This was inescapable; there had been immense discussion in the media (and Parliament) for weeks, and there was another reason as well. After Edward Robey had dismissed the case against Rooum seven months previously, he had convicted Apostolou. The reason for his decision was because Battes had given such compelling evidence, and Robey was convinced that he had told the truth. However, having heard the case for the prosecution, he realized that he had been completely deceived by Battes and he was furious. In fairness, there was no chance that the four officers would *not* have been committed. It is likely that if the station cat had wandered into the courtroom, Robey would have committed the unfortunate feline for trial as well.

Du Rose concluded his investigations, which also covered 'other matters', and the file, containing 1,200 pages, was received by the Director of Public Prosecutions on 19 May.

But by the end of May Challenor was still too unwell to attend court, and the trial judge agreed to postpone the trial until 4 June. Prior to this, Challenor had been examined at Brixton Prison by Dr William Calder, the Principal Medical Officer, on 29 May; and on the date of the trial Dr Calder informed the judge that in his opinion, Challenor was not fit either to stand trial or defend himself and that he was suffering from paranoid schizophrenia. The judge asked, "Are you satisfied that he has been mentally abnormal for a considerable time?" and Dr Calder replied, "A very considerable time, yes sir." And when the judge asked, "Are you satisfied that his mental condition deteriorated rapidly from September of last year?" Dr Calder replied, "Yes, sir." This conclusion was confirmed by Dr Sargent from St Thomas' and Dr Farnan from Netherne Hospital.

As he sat in the dock at No. 1 Court at the Old Bailey –
coincidentally, the same dock occupied by Thompson and
Bywaters, who at the time of Challenor's birth were plotting to
murder Edith Thompson's husband – it took only one minute for
the jury to find that he was unfit to plead. Challenor was ordered to
be detained until Her Majesty's pleasure was known and was taken
back to Brixton prison, there to be held in custody until a decision
was made as to his ultimate destination: Broadmoor or Netherne.

CHAPTER 14

The Trial

On 16 June 1964 the trial of the three aids commenced at the Old Bailey before the Honourable Mr Justice Lawton. The prosecution was conducted by John Mathew QC and Henry Pownall; the three defendants were represented by Victor Durand QC and Robin Simpson. The case for the prosecution was of course quite simply that the aids had planted segments of brick on innocent young men; the three officers denied it.

Ede stated he had been assaulted and had signed for the brick, but only 'out of fear'. Hill was unable to say who had searched him. Rooum gleefully imparted his testimony to a packed courtroom, and his evidence was corroborated in part by witnesses who had been in South Molton Lane. A less enthusiastic witness was Police Constable Ray Jones, who limped unwillingly through his evidence.

John Apostolou told the court that during the course of the demonstration, when he had been arrested with Ede and Hill, he had been initially seized by an officer other than Battes, an officer, he said, whom the other officers had "chosen to ignore ... he was supposed to be non-existent". It was an early example of the cockiness which would soon bring him into conflict with the judge. Bricks, he said, were added to his and the other prisoners' property by Challenor, who said, "One for you, one for you and [referring to Apostolou] the biggest brick for the biggest boy."

Being asked if he realized the significance of this act was the perfect feed line for Apostolou, who replied, "It was pretty obvious to any intelligent person to see a piece of brick suddenly taken out of the blue and put amongst your things that it was not put there for decoration, was it?"

When asked why he had given a false name, he replied, "Well, there was a sort of combination of reasons. First of all, I did not want to worry my mother, I did not want to really get into trouble, and the other reason is that I was so disgusted with what had happened I just could not really give my name."

Apostolou engaged in some verbal fencing during cross-examination by Mr Durand; after he told the court he had seen Hill in Trafalgar Square a couple of days before their arrest, Mr Durand asked him, "How close to Mr Hill were you on that occasion?" and

Apostolou replied, "Do you mean as regards position or as regards relationship?"

Apostolou told the court that he intended to wave his banner and shout 'Boo!', and when he was asked if he felt very strongly indeed about the demonstration, he replied, "Not strong enough to hold a banner up like that and throw a brick at the same time." It was one smart remark too many. "Mr Apostolou, I have been watching you and so have the jury and they may have formed an impression of your behaviour, as I have," observed the judge frostily. "From now on, answer the questions you are asked and no others and do not answer back."

The cross-examination came to an end when Apostolou was asked if the officer was a little annoyed with him when he admitted giving a false name and address. "He did say he would have to stay up late that night," replied Apostolou, adding, "and he said ..." The sentence trailed off.

"Have you finished?" asked Mr Durand.

"No," replied Apostolou, before adding, "It does not matter if you do not want me to."

Mr Mathew for the prosecution got to his feet. "Could you just finish what you were going to say?" Mr Durand, quite obviously annoyed, added, "You tell us."

"Mr Durand invites you to finish", said Mr Mathew, which elicited the reply from Apostolou: "He obviously did not want to hear me."

And that was quite enough for the judge, who snapped, "He never said anything of the kind. You answer the question", to which Apostolou told the court that Battes had told him, amongst other matters, that he was lucky that he (Battes) was not Challenor.

If the rest of the evidence had been of a similar nature, it is quite possible that the three defendants would have been acquitted. In the early 1960s juries at courts of assize were middle class, usually middle aged home-owners. They did not take kindly to those they perceived to be left-wing layabouts who spent their time going to demonstrations in Central London in order to boo the Queen. They most certainly would not have approved of someone like Apostolou making a series of point-scoring wisecracks to eminent Queen's Counsel. And whilst police officers were to be respected, the sight of PC Ray Jones stumbling through his evidence would represent someone more to be pitied than scorned. This was, to a degree, backed up by the judge, who would later tell the jury, "You may think that demonstrating for many of us, at any rate – if not all – is a polite way of saying making nuisances of themselves. If you want to demonstrate, the police very often do not let you."

So it was unfortunate for the three aids to CID in the dock that the rest of the evidence was of a different nature: mainly from the police officers who had formed cordons for the demonstration and from the four young men who had been framed.

★ ★ ★

John Stanley Ryall described how on the evening of 11 July he, his brother Ronald and their friends, Richard Fear and Colin Derwin, having finished a game of tennis in Bayswater, had returned to their family home at 1a Davies Mews, but were initially prevented from entering the mews by a cordon of police officers. This barrier stretched from one side of Davies Street in an arc finishing on the north side of Davies Mews, thereby effectively blocking off entry into both the Mews and Brook Street. Police Constable 160 'Y' Lawrence Brown, one of a number of officers drafted in from other divisions to help police the demonstration, recalled four youths carrying tennis racquets who were eventually permitted to enter Davies Mews, where they stayed for approximately for ten minutes. It was their intention thereafter to go to Derwin's home in Brooks Mews, and the most direct route would be to leave Davies Mews, turn left into Davies Street, cross the junction with Brook Street and continue along Davies Street before turning left into Brooks Mews. This evidence was confirmed by John's brother Ronald, Richard Fear and Colin Derwin.

Charles Edward Brown, who at that time was living at 1b Davies Mews, had not seen the youths arrive at the Ryall home, but looking out of his bedroom window he did see them leave and walk towards the police line. They had nothing in their hands, he told the court.

Police Constable 524 'Y' George Stobbs was one of the officers on the police line who saw the youths emerge from Davies Mews, intending to walk off along Davies Street and thence into Brook Street. But PC Stobbs turned them away and made a circular movement with his hand suggesting the route that they should take, and they walked off towards St Anselm's Place. Like Charles Brown, PC Stobbs did not see anything in their hands. Neither did PC Brown, who having seen the youths arrive, saw them leave as well, and described them as 'slouching' as they set off towards St Anselm's Place and turned left.

The four youths walked through St Anselm's Place, turned left and walked south along Gilbert Street towards the junction with Brook Street; there, they could have crossed Brook Street, turned right into Davies Street and continued their journey to Derwin's home, but another police cordon awaited them. This barrier stretched right across Gilbert Street, effectively blocking anyone wishing to enter Brook Street from the north or Gilbert Street from the south. One of the officers here was Police Constable 341 'Y' Stanley Thoroughgood, who said that he had seen the youths walking down Gilbert Street towards him when he was approached by PC Goldsmith, who told him the youths had been causing trouble outside Claridge's; they had been booing the Queen and he (Goldsmith) intended to arrest them. He asked for Thoroughgood's help. Whilst PC Thoroughgood stated that he did not see anything in any of the four youths' hands, he did mention seeing a grey flat object, two or three inches in diameter, initially in PC Goldsmith's hand but also in the hand of one of the youths; this was an odd matter that was not satisfactorily cleared up either in examination in chief or cross-examination. However, it did not resemble any of the brick portions found in the youths' possession, said PC Thoroughgood, because they were too large – and since he had been a bricklayer prior to his police service, his word could be accepted on the matter.

Police Constable 206 'Y' Ralph Maslin was another officer on the cordon who told the court that he was approached by PC Battes, who asked him to help stop the youths, and he did so. Asked if he noticed anything about their demeanour, PC Maslin replied, "Possibly slightly surprised." He, too, did not notice anything in their hands, and had there been, he said, "I would imagine I would have seen it, yes."

No bricks were seen in the youths' hands by Police Constable 549 'Y' David Henderson either, although he was aware of their supposed existence because he heard one of the three defendants saying that they were "carrying bricks or stones". Police Constable 325 'Y' Desmond Tilly was part of the cordon and was told by one of the defendants, "Hold that man and put him in the tender," and he did so. Oddly, he was never asked if he saw anything in the youths' hands; it must be assumed he did not, because he told the court that he had no idea why the young men had been arrested.

John Ryall denied that he and the others had run into St Anselm's Place or that they had anything in their hands, and this was confirmed by the other youths as well as by the police officers on the cordons. He told the court that they intended to go to Derwin's house for an hour, then go on to the Barley Mow public house in Duke Street.

Ryall described how he was grabbed by Battes, who put his arm up his back and said, "You're nicked!" His brother Ronald asked, "What's this all about?" As they reached a police tender to transport them to the police station, one of the defendants said, "Shall we give them a kick-up?" and another said, "The first one who opens his mouth will get my fist in it." Battes drew a truncheon and said, "You won't use your fist, you'll use your truncheon; it's much harder." Ryall told the court that he mentioned to sixteen-year-old Richard Fear that "he had better be quiet".

At West End Central Ryall said that Battes put his personal property into a brown envelope and that he saw a piece of brick sticking out of it. When he was charged with possessing the brick as an offensive weapon, he interjected, "It's not mine," but was told to be quiet. Asked by the prosecuting counsel why he refused to sign for the property, Ryall replied, "Because of this brick. Well, the brick did not belong to me."

Cross-examined by Mr Durand, Ryall agreed that the company which he worked for had a dump at White Lion Yard, and that rubble was discarded there; the inference was that the youths had indeed been in possession of brick pieces, and they had been acquired at the dump. William Henry Beagarie, the general manager of George Smith, Avery Row Ltd, where John Ryall was employed as an apprentice carpenter, stated that bricks and general rubble were in the yard on 11 July. But White Lion Yard was at the opposite end of Brook Street, and the youths had not walked from that direction; moreover, White Lion Yard (it is now referred to as Lancashire Court) could only be accessed from Bond Street. And although Mr Beagarie had been shown the bricks used as exhibits in the case and admitted they could have come from his yard, he was also obliged to admit that the bricks could have come from just about anywhere.

Ronald Ryall corroborated his brother's evidence but identified Goldsmith as the officer who had made the 'fist' threat and informed the court that the first time he had seen a portion of brick was when it was placed with his belongings at West End Central. Asked why he refused to sign for his property, he replied, "Well, the brick was not mine and I never had it before."

Some brisk cross-examination from Mr Durand revealed a few inconsistencies between what had been said in evidence and what had been recorded in the deposition at the Magistrates' Court, and this resulted in Ronald Ryall becoming slightly confused – as possibly were the jury, too.

Richard Fear – a student at a grammar school who the previous June had obtained four 'O' levels and was preparing to take 'A' levels in 1965 – agreed with what the two previous witnesses had said: he identified Goldsmith as making the 'fist' remark and Battes as producing the truncheon. He gave evidence that whilst he was sitting on a bench in a corridor at West End Central he saw an envelope on the floor with pieces of brick in it. "It was open at the top," he said, and when he was asked how he knew they were pieces of brick, he replied, "You could see them quite clearly." Like the other youths, he had not been told why he had been arrested, and when he was taken into the charge room his personal possessions were on the charge room desk, as was a piece of brick. He also noticed an envelope with pieces of brick in it on a bench close to the charge room desk; his father, who had attended the station, had to move the envelope before he could sit down. Asked if he had signed for the property, he replied, "No, sir. I refused because of the piece of brick." He reported that his father had said – referring to the brick – "That's not yours, is it?" to which Fear replied, "No, Dad." When the charging had been completed, Fear senior demanded to know, "What bloody trumped-up charge is this?"

Sydney Fear told the court that he arrived at West End Central at ten o'clock on the evening of 11 July in consequence of being told his son had been detained there. He went to sit down on a bench near Inspector Chidzoy's desk and saw there was a brown envelope on it. Asked if there was anything inside it, he replied, "Yes, sir, some bricks inside. I had to move it to sit down. I pushed it further along the form." Referring to a portion of brick on the table, Mr Mathew asked, "I do not think there was any dispute that brick was in your son's possession and he was charged with being in possession of it?"

The question was phrased rather clumsily, because Mr Fear firmly replied, "No sir, it was not in my son's possession. It was on the table." Quickly correcting himself, Mr Mathew said, "I suggested the allegation was that it had been in your son's possession?" and Mr Fear agreed with this. "Did you say anything to your son when you realized that that was the suggestion?" asked Mr Mathew, and Mr Fear replied, "Yes, sir, I said to him, 'Is that right, you've been carrying this brick?' He said, 'No Dad, I haven't seen the brick before'." "What did you say to the officer?" asked Mr Mathew, and Mr Fear corroborated his son's testimony when he replied, "I turned around and said to him, 'What bloody trumped-up charge is this?' and I was told to be quiet."

Richard Fear later described sitting on a bench with Mrs Ryall, when her sons and Colin Derwin were appearing at Marlborough Street Magistrates' Court, and seeing Oakey and one of the other defendants being approached by Challenor, who told them, "There's nothing to worry about." This was in part corroborated by Mrs Kathleen Ryall, who stated that she saw all three defendants approached by Challenor and heard him say, 'Now, this is what I want you to say' – she did not hear the words which Fear had heard.

By far the most compelling witness was Colin Derwin. He was now a trooper in the Queen's Royal Irish Hussars and had flown in from Malaya to give evidence; he would rejoin his regiment in Germany after the conclusion of the court proceedings. He corroborated the other three witnesses' statements that they had not run into St Anselm's Place, they had not been in possession of any pieces of brick, they had been abused, roughly handled, pushed into the back of a police tender and not informed why they had been arrested. Trooper Derwin stated that he had seen the envelope containing segments of brick in the corridor at West End Central, that a piece of brick had been added to his belongings and that when he was charged with possessing the brick as an offensive weapon, he replied, "Not guilty, sir" and refused to sign for his property. He added that when he was convicted at court, the magistrate had been told that if he were to be fined this would debar him from joining the army. However, the magistrate had conditionally discharged him, which permitted him to join up after all.

So that evidence was very compelling, but there was more to come. Trooper Derwin stated (as had the other witnesses who had been arrested with him) that he had no interest in Greek politics, and it had already been confirmed that none of them were in possession of political literature of any kind, Greek or otherwise. But also on the evening of 11 July he had been with his parents at 18 Brooks Mews, behind Claridge's Hotel. He and his father had helped erect a ladder so that Special Branch officers could keep observation from the roof of the mews on Claridge's ballroom; this was hardly the action of a political activist or someone with a grudge against the royal families of England or Greece. This assistance was confirmed by Police Constable Michael Ferguson of Special Branch. It was also corroborated by Trooper Derwin's father William, who in response to a question from the judge stated that, like his son, he had been a cavalryman and agreed with the judge that it had been in "Sir Winston Churchill's old regiment" – an unimportant point but one which must have played well with the middle class and probably Conservative-voting jury. The day following their son's arrest, Mr and Mrs Derwin retraced the route which he had taken the previous evening. They found no trace of bricks or rubble en route. Mr Derwin also stated that he had seen PC Goldsmith at Marlborough Street Magistrates' Court and had said to him, "This is a nice state of affairs. My son is due to join the army on Monday", and that Goldsmith replied, "Oh, you bloody parents are all the same. You think your children are angels. They are not when they're outside and not at home."

One aspect of the four young men's testimony conflicted with the evidence of witnesses who were part of the police cordon: these officers were quite clear that during the arrests there had been no impropriety by any of the arresting officers, no objectionable language and no rough handling in getting the four prisoners into the police tender. However, unlike the defendants, those officers in the cordon did not see any lumps of brick in the four youths' possession – and there was one other important matter.

When Harry Challenor had arrested Donald Rooum, he said in his statement that he had searched his prisoner in the police tender and had discovered the brick in his pocket. But when former Police Constable Samuel Salter gave evidence during this trial, he revealed that he had been in the back of the tender at the time, and whilst he recalled Challenor and his prisoner Rooum being there, he did not recall Challenor searching Rooum, nor did he see a portion of brick in either's possession. He did remember (as Rooum did) Challenor shouting something like, "Have you made any arrests?" or "Make some arrests!" to three plain clothes officers, who might have been aids to CID, but he was unable to identify who it was that Challenor had shouted to. But whether he imparted his remarks to the three defendants or not, it is clear that within minutes, if not seconds, of Challenor's roared instructions, the four young men were under arrest.

Shortly after policing the demonstration, PC Salter resigned from the police and became a car salesman.

* * *

So much for the arrests; now the action moved on to West End Central. It would be fair to say that in common with several other supervisory officers at West End Central, Inspector Arthur Munns of that police station – with over twenty-eight years service – was not Harry Challenor's biggest devotee, and certainly not on the night of 11 July, when he was manning the special charge room for arrested demonstrators. Having brought in Ede, Hill and Apostolou, Inspector Munns told Mr Pownall for the prosecution that, "Detective Sergeant Challenor told me that he was anxious to go out again in order to obtain witnesses and further possible prisoners." By the time Challenor arrived back at the station with his latest prisoner, Rooum, Munns was anxious to get on with the charging, but when Challenor told him he wanted some refreshment, "there was some discussion." Asked if he thought it proper that the three first prisoners were still in custody without being charged, Munns replied, "I did not. I told him so and I brought it to the attention of the superintendent who was in overall charge."

He went on to say that the pieces of brick had been placed on the charge room desk by Challenor following the time the first three prisoners were brought into the police station. Initially, only their personal possessions were on the desk; the bricks were added later. When they were charged, Challenor and Detective Chief Inspector McArthur were present, and although the three prisoners denied knowledge of the bricks, he (Inspector Munns) did not at the time make a note of their replies. He told the court, quite correctly, that it was the arresting officer's job to do that.

Mr Justice Lawton asked, "When these young men were brought into the station at half-past eight and charged [sic] and searched and you were told by Sergeant Challenor what they had been arrested and what they had been brought in for, why did you not put your foot down and insist upon them being dealt with at once?" To this Munns replied, "Well, he suggested that there would be more serious charges to follow and also two of them were juveniles and it seemed desirable to have their parents there. The parents were sent for, although they did not arrive at the time. I did not agree to the delay readily but he was so insistent that there would be further charges or further prisoners, that I accepted that for the time being."

Inspector Munns could not recall the first time he saw the brick alleged to have been in Rooum's possession, but thought that it would have been after Ede, Hill and Apostolou had been charged, when Rooum (he described him as being "A very quiet, inoffensive man") was about to be charged and the brick was placed on the desk by Challenor.

Mr Justice Lawton said, "You had this situation: four prisoners, all very different types – one, really a mere boy, Hill, who was fourteen and a half. Then there was the Greek-Cypriot, and the jury saw him and formed their own impression of him, and then there was the other youth, a rather unlikely type the jury might have thought, and then Rooum – all denying that these bricks had got anything to do with them. Did that not strike you as being an odd situation?"

"It did strike me but it is common for a prisoner to deny any knowledge of property found on him," replied Munns. "It is not unusual. There was no direct complaint against the officers. They just said, 'It is not my brick'."

"Four with one arresting officer and one of them arrested at a different time and place," said the judge. "Did that strike you as being odd, or did you think that is what prisoners tend to do?"

"If you are asking for my personal opinion," replied Munns, "of course I did think it odd," which prompted the question, "What investigations did you make there and then?" Inspector Munns replied, "None, my Lord."

In fact, Munns was quite right; no complaint had been made and he had been provided with credible evidence upon which to formally charge the prisoners; had he not been, he would have refused the charge, and he told the court, "I have done so on many occasions."

Cross-examined by Mr Durand, Munns explained that there was a canteen open twenty-four hours a day at West End Central and that was why he was annoyed at Challenor's telling him he wanted to obtain refreshments. "I criticized it because I told him that he could have got his refreshment before he went out. He had the opportunity," said Munns, and he went on to say that if any of the prisoners had requested a solicitor he would have provided every facility for them to receive one.

Inspector Ernest Chidzoy was next; he, too, was in the specially convened charge room and he dealt with the next four prisoners, the Ryall brothers, Derwin and Fear. He described to the court how an arresting officer would give brief details to him regarding the circumstances of the arrest and produce evidence supporting the charge – in this case, the portions of brick – and said that this had happened on this occasion. Chidzoy had no recollection of Mr Fear Senior having to push an envelope containing brick segments away to permit him to sit down on a bench, neither could he remember him saying 'What bloody trumped-up charge is this?' "I think I would have remembered that statement," said Chidzoy. He did recall Mr Fear saying something to the effect, as he and his son left the station, that 'he was going to tan his boy if he thought this was true.'

Some police officers had been critical of Challenor's conduct, but Superintendent Frederick Burdett was the first police witness to give utterly damning evidence. He was the senior uniform officer in charge on the evening of 11 July and had previously circulated copies of the Commissioner's Regulations to all of the appropriate police stations. As he was walking along the ground floor corridor at West End Central police station at 8.30, he heard the sound of shouting – "an angry voice; the words were quite indistinguishable" – coming from the male charge room. "There were two prisoners sitting on the bench immediately beside the door," he told the court. "Detective Sergeant Challenor was to the left as I walked in and another officer who I did not recognise was standing in front of the prisoners but rather to the right of them." Burdett had not met Challenor before but quickly determined that he was responsible for the arrest of the two youths ("Their faces were flushed red and they appeared to be excited; they were fidgety," he said) and he called Challenor into the corridor, where he reprimanded him for his behaviour. Upon discovering that they were demonstrators, he ordered Challenor to take the prisoners upstairs to the charge room set aside for those arrested in connection with the demonstration.

It was later – when he discovered that the prisoners had not been charged – that Superintendent Burdett sent for Challenor. "How did you find Detective Sergeant Challenor when he returned to you?" asked Mr Pownall.

"He was completely unable to control himself," replied the superintendent. "He was shouting." In response to questions from the judge, he said, "In appearance, he was red-eyed, looked particularly tired."

"Were you able to discern what he was shouting?" asked Mr Pownall and received the reply: "Not at all. He was like a person who was mental. Very, very difficult to speak and to make him understand anything."

"That must have made you wonder what in the world was happening?" asked Mr Justice Lawton, and the superintendent admitted, "It did, yes."

"A man who brought youths to the station, who appeared to be mental and difficult to get him to understand or to get from him what was happening," mused the judge, then he asked, "That man preferred charges against people that night?"

Seeing the way the wind was blowing, towards possible words of condemnation for himself, Superintendent Burdett swiftly replied, "Under the supervision of the detective chief inspector."

"You were in charge of the charging?" persisted Mr Justice Lawton, but Burdett was ready for that one. "I was in charge of the overall arrangement but these were criminal charges, CID charges and in that case my responsibility was handed over to the detective superintendent, who in turn directed his chief inspector to hold a watching brief," replied the superintendent, adding, "which he did."

The judge expressed 'grave concern' regarding the whole scenario regarding Challenor, although he said, "I am not going to criticize. I am here to get at the facts" and then asked if Superintendent Burdett had written to a senior officer on his side of the Metropolitan Police about the events of that night. The superintendent was also ready for that one: he had been responsible for the charging of prisoners from the demonstration – but in charge of Harry Challenor or anything to do with the CID, he was <u>not</u>.

To explain why he had not submitted a report, he told the court: "I was assured by Detective Superintendent Townsend that the man had been working very long hours. He had had a number of testing cases at court, was living in a state of suppressed excitement. The youths were charged and I understand that the evidence that had been offered was credible to support the charges and that I was also assured that Sergeant Challenor was shortly, very shortly going on annual leave, and I was told that no doubt he would recover from his suppressed excitement by his return."

★ ★ ★

Now much of the rest of the prosecution's case dealt with the medical condition of Rooum, plus the submissions of various items of clothing and the forensic examination of the bricks.

Doctor Jeremiah Mortimer Slattery had for several years been Donald Rooum's medical practitioner. On the evening of Friday, 12 July 1963 he visited his patient at his home address and examined him. "I found he had bruising and abrasions on both ears, the left ear more than the right," he told the court, and asked what could have caused it, he replied, "An accident or a blow."

Stanley Clinton Davis, the solicitor who featured largely in this case, told the court that he had the conduct of the case of Rooum, whom he saw on the morning of 12 July at Marlborough Street Magistrates' Court. He described how he left court to return to his office and how, some fifteen minutes later, Rooum followed, wearing the same suit that he had worn in court. Rooum's wife brought in another suit, and the suit which Rooum had been wearing was handed to his solicitor. This in turn was handed to James Stafford, a commissionaire employed by the firm of Clintons solicitors.

In fact, continuity in respect of Rooum's jacket – and those belonging to Apostolou, Hill and Ede – appeared to have gone out of the window. Clinton Davis stated that he had not marked Rooum's jacket, that the other garments were handed in "within a matter of days after that … it would only be a matter of a few days … not more, I would say than nine or ten days at the most".

Mr Stafford described receiving the clothing from his employer, locking it in a cupboard, then removing it a few days later and taking it as a parcel to the Department of Forensic Medicine at London Hospital for examination. He also took two other parcels; it is not clear what they contained.

One of the parcels was opened by a senior technician at the hospital, Sidney Arthur Day, revealing a suit and a plastic mackintosh, and this was kept in a locked cupboard until it could be examined the following day. The lack of continuity of the exhibits (and consequent opportunities for cross-contamination) would not be countenanced nowadays; and yet there was very little cross-examination on the point by the defence.

The next witness was John Ferdinand Kayser. It was he who had been called by the defence at the Magistrates' Court to prove the brick could not have been in Rooum's pocket. Described as a Fellow of the Institute of Metallurgists and an Associate in Metallurgy at Sheffield University – therefore an expert witness – he also told the court that he was "a member of a number of societies, such as the British Academy of Forensic Science, the Iron and Steel Institute and the Institution of Metallurgists, which is a professional qualification, and the International Society for Serology." He was also, he admitted, a Member of the Institute of the British Foundrymen. It would be fair to describe him as an eccentric, and many of his responses appeared to be as impertinent as Apostolou's had been. In all probability, they were not; it was simply a case of an academic being obstinately pedantic to the point of eccentricity.

He agreed with Mr Pownall for the prosecution that he had received a jacket from Mr Day on 16 July 1963. Asked what colour it was, Mr Kayser did not remember. Shown Rooum's jacket and asked if he recognised it as the one he had received from Mr Day, Mr Kayser said he did not. Asked if he had examined that jacket, Mr Kayser stated that he did not know if it was that jacket or another one. Shown the receipt, Mr Kayser acknowledged that it was his and that the jacket appeared to correspond with the description he had written on that receipt. "Did you examine that jacket?" asked Mr Pownall.

"I do not know," replied Mr Kayser. "It might have been one like it and of the same colour."

"Did you receive that jacket from Mr Day?" persisted Mr Pownall, only to receive the reply, "I do not know."

Mr Justice Lawton's patience had now reached its limit, and he snapped, "Let us assume that you did."

Cautiously agreeing that he had examined a jacket which was similar to the one he had been handed, Mr Kayser told the court that he had paid particular attention to the contents of the pockets.

He was able to say "most definitely" that the pockets did not appear to have been recently cleaned out, and among the debris found in both pockets there was no sign of brick dust, "none whatsoever."

In detailing his examination, Mr Kayser said this: "I was very careful to turn the pockets out so that nothing would fall out. Then I have a stereoscopic microscope – you have one tube to each eye – and I went over every bit of it. I gave a quarter of an hour to each pocket. The magnification was about twelve times, which is ample for the sort of material I was looking at. I could see no brick dust, although I was expecting, from what I had heard, that I would find it. I could not find the slightest trace of it."

Asked by Mr Justice Lawton to explain the exchange principle of Locard's Law,[9] Mr Kayser gave the very clear example: if one were walking on the sand at the seaside one's shoes would leave an imprint in the sand, and also some sand would collect on one's shoes. Therefore, had a portion of brick been in Rooum's pocket, there would have been particles of brick dust present.

Unfortunately, Mr Kayser was inclined to wander in his testimony; he declared that he did many things which interested him, and when asked about the last time he had anything to do with domestic house bricks, he replied that it was a month previously at St Albans. However, this turned out to be to do with his views on Roman bricks. He told the court that he had given evidence in many courts, including in Calcutta, but it transpired that had been on behalf of the Gillette razor blade company. Both the judge and Mr Durand for the defence became quite short-tempered with Mr Kayser, who dreamily told them about the British Academy of Forensic Science, said that he had been interested in bricks from 1920 to 1933 and had foreseen the day when he might be engaged in a court case featuring bricks. "Was this the case?" asked Mr Durand, and received the reply, "This is the first case; this is the case that finally came along."

But dreamy academic or not, Mr Kayser was sure of one thing: there was not any brick dust in the pockets of Rooum's jacket.

Michael David Jesse Isaacs M.Sc., FRIC, who for the past seven years had been a senior scientific officer at the Metropolitan Police Forensic Science Laboratory, might not have travelled as far as Calcutta to give evidence in court, but he knew how to give evidence at the Old Bailey: briskly, accurately and professionally. He had carried out an examination of the portions of brick; in fact, Clinton Davis initially wanted the Forensic Science Laboratory

---

9. In fact, the judge was referring to Locard's Principle of Exchange.

to examine the contents of Rooum's pockets, something that the laboratory was only too happy to do – but when Davis discovered that as the officer in the case it would be Challenor who would have conveyed the clothing to the laboratory, he hastily withdrew his request.

Mr Isaacs examined the three portions of brick which had been attributed to Fear, John and Ronald Ryall and told the court that these portions fitted together to form part of a larger brick. The brick portions attributed to Ede and Rooum also fitted together; on one brick the letters 'MAR' could be seen, and on the other the 'S' fitted exactly into place to form part of the brick's brand name, 'MARSTON'. Asked if there was any doubt in his mind as to whether those pieces of brick fitted together, Mr Isaacs replied, "None whatsoever."

He could not say if the brick attributed to Hill formed part of the same brick relating to Ede and Rooum, but he did not discount the theory: "That is of a similar nature … in so far as you have got the same gradation to pinks, to light peach on the general body of the brick and it also has the same white inclusions formed from other minerals in the clay."

Mr Isaacs stated that the first set of brick pieces were different from the second, the first set being smoother. The word 'friable' was mentioned – Mr Isaacs explained it meant 'crumbly' and further said that if the piece of brick said to have been found in Rooum's possession had been in Rooum's pocket, he would have expected to have found minute brick fragments in the pocket.

It seems odd that Mr Durand for the defence did not clamp down on Mr Kayser's evidence; the continuity of Rooum's jacket had been deplorable, and Kayser himself had been unwilling to admit that it was Rooum's jacket he had examined. All Mr Durand had to say was, "You are not certain that the jacket you examined belonged to Mr Rooum, are you?" and it seems fairly certain that Mr Kayser would have replied, "No." Of course, Rooum could have been recalled to state categorically that it *was* his jacket, but would the word of a self-confessed anarchist have been accepted by the jury? Difficult to say. In addition, Mr Kayser had been allowed to ramble in his testimony to such an extent that he had obviously incurred the ire of counsel for both the prosecution and the defence, and of the trial judge, all of whom wanted rid of him. In dismissing him, they missed the opportunity to extract a vital piece of evidence which Mr Kayser had given when acting as a defence witness for Rooum at the Magistrates' Court: that had a brick segment of the size attributed to Rooum by Challenor been in Rooum's pocket, as well as leaving brick dust there, due to the size of the brick, the lining of the pocket would have been stretched and scratched – and no such markings were found. But that piece of evidence was not put before the jury.

Finally, Harry Pike – retired from the police and now a security officer – produced the notebooks of the three defendants. It was the practice, following an arrest, for police officers to make notes of that arrest in their official pocket books. This would be carried out at the police station – in police jargon, 'as soon after the arrest as practicable' – and the entry would be in abbreviated note form. A fuller account could then be written up later, but it was important to get those initial notes in writing whilst the memory of the incident was still fresh in the officer's mind. What follows is the pocket book entry by PC Battes:

> 9pm. 11/7/63, Davies Street. Saw them run from other officers down St Anselm's Place with bricks partly hidden in right hands. Followed back into Brook Street. Stopped. Asked "WeP" (weapon) "In case we get in bundle". Told arrest, caut. said, "They're only bricks, not weapons". Arr. Stat. 9.20pm. John Ryall, 1A Davies Mews, W1. Occupation Carpenter-apprentice, age 19. 15/4/44. CCC said "I had no weapon on me". On person one £1 note, 3d copper, one wallet containing corres. One roll Sellotape, one brick. Refused to sign.

And there was nothing extraordinary about that. But what the judge did notice – and drew counsel's attention to – was that the previous arrests (of Hill, Apostolou and Ede at 8.20 that evening) were shown entered into PC Battes' pocket book *after* the arrest of Ryall.

In addition, Pike read from the defendants' statements made for the Metropolitan Police Solicitors' Department in respect of the complaints which had been made against them; this concluded the case for the prosecution.

Therefore, it was now the defendants' turn to give evidence.

* * *

Oakey was first into the witness box. He told the court that he and Challenor had gone to Brook Street on the evening of 11 July and had met Battes there. Upon hearing the shout, "Get your stones ready, they're coming," he had heard Challenor say, "Go and get them" and he had arrested Ede; he had done so because he had seen his prisoner put his hand in his right pocket. Oakey said that he asked Ede, "Have you anything on you?" to which Ede replied,

"No." He then searched him and in Ede's right-hand pocket he found a segment of brick, which he placed in his own pocket and arrested Ede. He could see that Hill had been arrested by Challenor and Apostolou by Battes. Oakey denied any kind of conspiracy with the other officers to fit up the prisoners and similarly denied the use of force or bad language in arresting them.

He denied that Challenor had been shouting at the prisoners prior to Superintendent Burdett's entry into the charge room, but told the court that Challenor had "very bad hearing" and therefore, "You would have to speak louder to him than anyone else and it also meant that he tended to shout at you during conversation." During the journey from the male to the female charge room, Oakey denied that any kind of impropriety by anybody had taken place. He was unaware of the discussion between Challenor and Inspector Munns regarding charging the prisoners and said that Challenor had simply said they would go out to look for more demonstrators, which they did. Oakey agreed that he could have insisted that his prisoner be charged before going out again, but if he had, "Well, I would not have been – how I can put it is the difficulty – I would not have got on with Sergeant Challenor quite so well in the near future."

At about 8.45 he and Battes met PC Goldsmith at West End Central, and he joined them after they told him they were going to look for more demonstrators. At Davies Street, where there was a police cordon, Goldsmith had stopped to speak to one of the officers when he, Oakey, saw the four youths emerge from Davies Mews, then saw them break into a run and enter St Anselm's Place. They were holding bricks, and Goldsmith said, "Come on" and the three officers ran into Brook Street to the junction with Gilbert Street, where there was another cordon of police officers.

The four youths – the Ryalls, Derwin and Fear – had their hands by their sides as they walked towards them, said Oakey, and Goldsmith produced his warrant card, told the youths that they were police officers and asked them what was in their hands; the four each produced a piece of brick. John Ryall had said, "In case we get into a bundle" and Derwin, "We found them around the corner." Arrested, the youths were taken to a police tender and put into it; Oakey denied that any threats were made or bad language used. He denied seeing any bricks in an envelope in the corridor at West End Central. The pieces of brick were in Goldsmith's possession – at the police station Oakey saw Challenor and attached labels to the pieces of brick attributed to Rooum, Ede, Hill and Apostolou and wrote the names of the prisoners on the labels (Apostolou's in the name of 'Stylianou'). However, he would later say that it was possible that Challenor might have attributed the wrong bricks to the prisoners or muddled them up when affixing the labels and string; an honest mistake, nothing more.

Oakey denied that Challenor had said to him (and the other two defendants) at court on 8 August, "This is what I want you to say," because he had made a statement dated 7 August for the Solicitors' Department at New Scotland Yard, and Oakey said, "I cannot see any reason for that remark at all."

But when Oakey's pocket book was examined, like Battes' book, there were inconsistencies. For the arrest of Ede, the report ran as follows:

> On Thursday, 11/7, at 8.20pm, standing behind three youths, heard one say, "Get your stones ready, they're coming". When stopped, searched, arrested, another youth, Ronald George Ede said, "We were just going to have a bit of fun". Asked where he got the brick he said, "We found them near a building site". Told arrested, then CD, CCC "It's nothing to do with me".

Asked what followed, Oakey replied, "George John Hill, 161 Liverpool Buildings," and this was followed by 'DS Challenor, George Stylianou' and then '176 Battes' followed by Ronald George Ede and his address.

However, these entries were made in pencil – but following Ede's reply when charged later that evening ("It's nothing to do with me") there was another entry, this time in ink: 'Gilbert Street/ St Anselm's Place,' where the later arrest of the four youths had taken place; and apart from saying that the entry would have been made on 11 July, Oakey was not able to produce a satisfactory explanation as to why that entry should have been inserted between the charging of one of the first prisoners and the details of the others of that group.

There followed a somewhat bruising cross-examination by Mr Mathew for the prosecution. Oakey admitted that of the persons arrested for possessing offensive weapons that night only their eight prisoners were in possession of bricks. Furthermore, he stated that when he, Challenor and Battes were in Brook Street, they were approximately 200 yards from the entrance of Claridge's when they heard the cry, 'Get your stones ready, they're coming.' It must have seemed to the jury difficult indeed for anybody to have accurately thrown stones at Royalty who were the distance of two football pitches away.

However, as Mr Mathew pointed out, Oakey had never said in any of his statements that he had seen Ede put his hand in his pocket. Asked why, he replied, "I cannot answer that. I do not know why it is not in."

"May I suggest an answer?" asked Mr Mathew. "That you did not because it never happened?" Oakey replied, "That is untrue." Mr Mathew then said, "I suggest that the only time, the first and only time, this was ever mentioned by any of you three defendants was when Battes gave his evidence before the magistrate?" and received the reply: "No. I say here and now that is what happened on that night."

Mr Mathew mentioned that several witnesses – including a police officer – had given evidence that following Ede's arrest he had been marched off towards Bond Street without being searched. "Are they wrong?" he asked. "No," replied Oakey. "When I say I searched him, I did not search him thoroughly. I had found a brick and I did not look for any further weapons."

Oakey denied any suggestion of misconduct, or that he had said to Ede, "You cunts deserve all you get for booing the Queen". He further denied that Challenor's voice had been raised in anger in the charge room, prior to Superintendent Burdett's entry. "Sergeant Challenor's voice is a very hard one, it is not a soft one", said Oakey, adding, "He does tend to shout."Oakey agreed that he had heard evidence in court that a police tender was situated a few yards down Davies Mews and that it was nine o'clock when Challenor had deposited his prisoner Rooum in the vehicle, the same time that he, Battes and Goldsmith arrived at the cordon at the junction with Davies Street and Brook Street. But although he had said that he had seen the four youths emerging from Davies Mews, he had not heard Challenor shout, "Haven't you got a prisoner, yet? Cor, you're slow – nick 'em." Furthermore, he had not seen any of the youths speak to any of the police officers at the cordon or seen PC Stobbs direct them to the direction of St Anselm's Place.

The four youths had been walking towards St Anselm's Place and, as Oakey told the court, "I did not take any notice of them up to that point," nor had he noticed anything in their hands. But as they reached St Anselm's Place they broke into a sprint, and it was then – at a distance of 150 feet and just a second or two before they vanished round the corner – that Oakey noticed each had a piece of brick in his right hand. Asked if PC Brown, on the cordon, who had watched them walk away (with nothing in their hands) and had not seen them break into a run at all, was quite wrong, Oakey replied, "He must be." The same must have applied to PC Stobbs.

Because of a recent knee injury, Oakey was the last to arrive at the junction with Gilbert Street and did not hear any conversation between Goldsmith or Battes and any of the officers on the cordon. But according to Oakey there were the four youths walking straight towards the police cordon, openly holding bricks in their hands; and when asked by Mr Mathew if he could explain why the officers on the cordon failed to hear any of the conversation which he had recounted with the youths or why they had not seen the bricks, Oakey replied, "I cannot explain why they did not see anything or why they did not hear anything."

"Looking back on it now," said Mr Mathew, "does that observation you alleged Derwin made (he has told us he did not) make any sense: 'We picked them up round the corner'?"

"He must have picked them up from somewhere," replied Oakey.

"If he had them at all?" queried Mr Mathew, and Oakey replied, "He did have a brick."

Mr Justice Lawton had some questions of his own and he asked, "They came from the direction of Davies Mews?" and Oakey replied, "Yes."

"They then speak apparently of the cordon, if the jury accept the evidence of those police officers," continued the judge. "They then turn up the road, Davies Street, again if the jury accepts the evidence of the other police officers, they then turned into St Anselm's Place and they had the bricks before they got into St Anselm's Place?"

Since that was what Oakey had said, he replied, "So it appears."

"Did you see any pile of rubble from which they could pick up a brick?" asked the judge, and Oakey replied, "No, I did not see."

"Did you see anyone bend down to pick up a brick?" asked Mr Justice Lawton, and Oakey answered, "No."

Mr Mathew now pursued the matter of the labelling of the bricks. "As far as the fitting together of the Rooum and the Ede brick is concerned and the possibility of the Hill brick fitting as well, we have heard the evidence and correct me if I am wrong. What you say is you do not think there was but it is conceivable that there might have been a mix-up over the Rooum brick?" Oakey replied, "Yes – that was mentioned to Sergeant Challenor after the court case."

"After the court case in which Mr Kayser had come along and told the magistrate that the Rooum brick fitted the Ede brick?" asked Mr Mathew. "Sergeant Challenor did say something about the muddle of the bricks. I took the blame at the time and he said, 'Leave it down to me'."

"Is it the unhappy position, as I suggest it was that night, that you were misguided enough to do what that dishonest police officer told you?" was Mr Mathew's final question. "He is not dishonest and also he did not tell us to do anything improper," replied Oakey.

Mentioning that Challenor was not available to give evidence, Mr Durand in re-examination asked Oakey if he was sincere in his statement about 'that missing man', and Oakey replied, "Yes."

Referring to the Ryalls, Derwin and Fear, Mr Durand asked, "If they had gone on and no one had stopped them and there had been stone-throwing through the glass of Claridge's, do you think you would have been commended then, or would you have been blamed for not taking some action?"

"I would not have been blamed because no one would have known," replied Oakey, "but I would have felt inside that I was a fool."

"Wherever it may have been that they picked up their bricks, have you any doubt that the Ryalls, Derwin and Fear had bricks?" asked Mr Durand. It is quite possible that by now the jury had very serious doubts indeed whether those young men had had in their hands that evening nothing more sinister than tennis racquets, but they cannot have been encouraged by Oakey's oddly ambiguous answer, "They definitely *appeared* to have bricks in their hands." And if those smouldering doubts existed, there could well have been fuel added to the fire when Mr Justice Lawton suggested to Oakey – and he agreed – that had they thrown bricks at Claridge's, they would have had to throw them over the heads of police officers stationed on the opposite side of the road. Cracks were appearing in the case for the defence.

★ ★ ★

Frank Edward Battes entered the witness box to say that he had applied to become an aid to CID, probably in June 1963, had been appointed an aid in November of that year and that before 11 July 1963 he had not worked under the supervision of Harry Challenor.

Asked about the eight-page statement which he had made on 20 December 1963 dealing with the various allegations about him that were being investigated, and whether the statement was true, Battes rather obscurely replied, "I believe so, yes."

He described how on the evening of 11 July he was off duty, had put a raincoat on over his uniform and had walked down to Claridge's, "to see what was happening." He had met up by chance with Challenor and PC Oakey, and they stood chatting in Avery Row until the arrival of the royal cars, which were greeted with a mixture of cheers and booing. Seeing a group of youths, some carrying banners, others wearing 'Ban the Bomb' badges, Battes heard a shout from one of the group: "Get your stones ready, they're coming." Asked what happened next, Battes replied, "Sergeant Challenor said the thought that was in all of our minds: 'Stop those men'."

Battes stopped Apostolou and took him to a shop doorway, where he searched him and in the pocket of his dark blue seaman's jacket found a piece of brick. Apostolou, asked why he had it in his possession, "Just shrugged his shoulders in a sort of disdainful way."

In fact, after Apostolou was arrested he said nothing at all, and Battes put the brick into his own raincoat pocket. He described the crowd as "muttering and a little bit unruly", and as he took his prisoner into Bond Street, en route to West End Central, a body of demonstrators were approaching Brook Street from Bond Street. Battes told Apostolou, "Don't try and talk to them. Let's walk straight past," and Apostolou obeyed that instruction. Arriving at West End Central, Battes was aware that both Challenor and Oakey had also made arrests. In the charge room Apostolou provided his false particulars, and Battes accepted them as being correct.

Battes was also aware of a conversation between Challenor and Inspector Munns regarding the charging of the prisoners; Challenor told the inspector that there were others in the group with whom he wanted to speak, to see if they, too, were involved in the incident. Together with Oakey, Battes went to leave the police station, but in the corridor they met up with Goldsmith, to whom they explained what had happened and who joined them in the hunt for other demonstrators.

They arrived at the police cordon across Davies Street just after nine o'clock. Goldsmith was talking to one of the officers on the cordon when Battes stated that he saw four youths coming from the direction of Davies Mews. "My attention was not particularly drawn to them, then," he said. "In fact, I only just looked at them."

The youths moved up Davies Street, and when they reached St Anselm's Place they ran down that thoroughfare. "That is when I looked at them properly," Battes told the court, and he had noted that, "two were definitely carrying what I considered to be portions of brick and the other two, I thought they were. Two were definitely carrying these portions and the other two looked as though they were."

This was rather contradicted by a statement he had made in connection with this incident: "When I saw them first, they were immediately in front of Davies Mews in a loose group running to

St Anselm's Place." Battes tried to explain this contradiction by saying, "I saw them running from the centre of Davies Street when they were in a line with St Anselm's Place."

But in any event, Goldsmith called out, "Follow me," and the three officers ran round to Gilbert Street and saw the four youths walking towards them. Goldsmith asked what they had in their hands, each produced a portion of brick and they were arrested and put into a passing police tender. Battes stated that there had been no impropriety of any kind, and as to the alleged production of his truncheon, he said that he had not been in possession of one.

At the police station, Battes thought that Goldsmith had marked with pencil the two pieces of brick in respect of the two persons he had arrested. He described how Inspector Chidzoy had charged John Ryall, and he had made up his notes regarding Ryall's arrest then and there. After that, Inspector Munns was ready to charge Apostolou, after which Battes had made up his notes for that arrest – in reverse chronological order.

Regarding the comments allegedly made by Challenor on 8 August at court, Battes stated that he had not seen Challenor at court on that day: "The only person I did speak to was the defence solicitor."

Cross-examined by Mr Mathew, Battes agreed that it was a 'fortuitous coincidence' that arrests had been made, individually and collectively, with Challenor managing to find persons in possession of similar pieces of brick. Mentioning with his application to become an aid to CID, Mr Mathew suggested to Battes that since he was off duty he was keen to join in to show his willingness to be a hard-working police officer, to which he replied, "If anything untoward had happened"; and he agreed with Mr Mathew that something had.

Again, great play was made with Battes' statement to the court that he had seen Apostolou put his hand in his pocket when the cry 'Get your stones ready' went up, since it had not been mentioned in any of his statements. "It should have been there," said Battes.

Mr Mathew mentioned a number of witnesses who had already given evidence: Mr Ratman and Mrs Harrison, who both witnessed Apostolou's arrest and watched Battes search him in a shop doorway from a distance of six or seven paces. Both said that no brick was produced, but Battes insisted that he found the brick in Apostolou's pocket. He also insisted that he had simply taken hold of Apostolou's arm to take him from the crowd; Mr Mathew suggested that he had been more forceful than that, so forceful, in fact, that a Sergeant Reynolds grabbed hold of him and only released him after Battes told him that he, too, was a police officer, with the words, "It's all right, skip." But Battes stated that he had no recollection at all of that happening.

Battes insisted that the decision to go out again after he had deposited Apostolou at West End Central was on his own initiative, not because he had been told to do so by Challenor. "That you might find the other persons in that group in order to see whether they had bricks on them?" asked Mr Mathew. "And by this time, I thought that this sort of behaviour might have become widespread," retorted Battes, "and I considered it my duty to go out again."

He denied that he had heard Challenor shout out "Nick 'em" from the tender in Davies Mews, but agreed that very shortly afterwards the four arrests were carried out. Mr Mathew suggested there were inconsistencies in his evidence, saying that he had originally stated that the four youths had run up Davies Street from Davies Mews until they reached St Anselm's Place. Now, given the testimony of Police Constables Brown and Stobbs, Mr Mathew stated that he had altered his account to coincide with that of the uniform officers, saying that they had broken into a run only when they reached the junction with St Anselm's Place.

There were indeed inconsistencies in Battes' testimony, his deposition given at the Magistrates' Court and his statement, which he said was incorrect. He denied that he had been amplifying his evidence by saying that the youths had come out of Davies Mews and had immediately run up Davies Street. Battes initially denied speaking to any of the officers on the cordon at Gilbert Street, but when it was pointed out that evidence had been given that he had said, "We want those four people. Can you stop them, please?" Battes admitted that, "I could have said, 'Will you give us a hand?'" He denied hearing Goldsmith say that the four youths had been causing trouble at Claridge's and had been booing the Queen, but when Mr Justice Lawton said, "Do you agree that would have been untrue, if it was said?" Battes was obliged to answer, "Yes".

He said, in contradiction to the other witnesses, that the four were breathless as they walked down Gilbert Street; and after more searching cross-examination canvassing all the evidence he had given, in which Battes categorically denied any wrongdoing, he returned to the dock.

* * *

The last defendant, Keith Stanley Goldsmith, now entered the witness box. He made it quite clear that at no time had he been under Challenor's direction; on 11 July he had been posted to the 'C' Division 'Q' Car and had officially been off duty at five o'clock, but since there had been an attempted murder that afternoon he had been retained on duty, assisting Detective Inspector Taylor with searching an address in Finsbury Park. At approximately 8.45 he was about to leave the station when he was approached by Battes and Oakey, and he agreed to accompany them to find more demonstrators.

At the junction of Brook Street and Davies Street he saw the four youths and quite definitely heard Derwin – he was the tallest of the group – say, "Let's go round to Brook Street and we can get them over there." The youths started to move rather more quickly, before breaking into a run into St Anselm's Place – and, Goldsmith stated, he could see from a distance of ten to twelve yards that they were carrying pieces of brick. Shouting "Come on", he led the other defendants round to the junction of Gilbert Street. There he was engaged in a conversation with one of the uniform constables at the cordon, and as the four youths approached them along Gilbert Street, Goldsmith asked the officer, "Did you hear the booing?"

Goldsmith described the arrest and the confiscation of the brick segments and denied any wrongdoing. He mentioned that he had marked the bricks in possession of Derwin and Fear with their names in pencil in the tender, and later pencilled in the names of the Ryall brothers on the bricks which, he said, had been in their possession.

Cross-examined by Mr Mathew, Goldsmith was asked how he had arrived at Davies Street; he replied that he did not know, only that they had arrived in Brook Street via Avery Row. Mr Mathew pointed out that there were only two ways to arrive at Davies Street: by walking up South Molton Lane, then turning left into Davies Mews and left again into Davies Street – or by taking the more direct route, along Brook Street past Claridge's. However, Goldsmith insisted that he could not remember which route he took. And not only did he not hear Challenor shouting from the tender in Davies Mews, he had no recollection of even seeing the tender.

Regarding the remark attributed to Derwin ("We can get them over there") Mr Mathew said, "You must have been very close to those youths in order to have been able to hear that remark?" Goldsmith agreed, replying, "Yes, as I said, five or six feet."

"I thought you said five or six yards?" queried Mr Mathew, and Goldsmith qualified his answer: "I am sorry, five or six yards."

The waters became a little more muddied here, because Goldsmith stated that these words had been spoken by Derwin to his friends as he himself was talking to a police officer in the cordon; therefore that officer would have been in a position to have heard those words too – but he had not. In addition, Goldsmith told the court that the four youths had started to run along Davies Street when they were some fifteen to thirty feet from him, whereas the other two defendants had said that the youths had not started running until they had reached St Anselm's Place, 100 feet further on; he denied that he was in difficulties over this point, but was obliged to agree that he and Oakey could not both be right.

Referring to the cordon at Gilbert Street, Mr Mathew said, "Let me remind you of what that officer told us you said. You pointed out the youths to him and asked him to help the other officers because you said those youths had been causing trouble at Claridge's and booing the Queen. Did you say that?" Goldsmith replied, "No."

From now on Goldsmith's testimony went into free fall. He stated that he might have said words to the effect that some youths had been booing the Queen – then, that he really did not know if he had said anything of that nature. He had not been anywhere near Claridge's that night, he had not heard any booing, but the officer on the cordon might have told him that that had happened.

"These youths, coming down the road," said Mr Mathew, "you did not associate with trouble outside Claridge's or booing the Queen?" And he was quite right; Goldsmith could not have it both ways. He replied, "No."

"You probably ran up to the cordon and said, 'Quick, I want to stop those youths'. That was the upshot of you speaking to the cordon?" asked Mr Mathew, and Goldsmith replied, "Yes."

"Why did you not say to the officer, 'Help me. Stop those youths but be careful because they have got bricks?' " asked Mr Mathew. Goldsmith replied, "I may have done."

"You did not?"

"I cannot remember exactly what I did say."

"You may not be able to recollect now, but that officer can recollect and has told us what you said," said Mr Mathew. "You did not say anything about bricks at all, did you?" Goldsmith wretchedly replied, "I do not know."

In much of the cross-examination which followed, Goldsmith could not recall, did not hear what others had said or was unable to explain why none of the police officers in the cordon were unable to hear the incriminating comments made by the four youths. Asked if there was any conversation in the tender, Goldsmith replied, "No conversation whatsoever."

"You told us on Friday and indeed again in your written statement that in the tender with a pencil you wrote the names of the defendants upon those pieces of brick," said Mr Mathew, and Goldsmith replied, "Yes."

"How did you know the defendants' names?" asked Mr Mathew and was told, "I had asked them when I was walking towards the van."

However, this had been flatly contradicted by the officers from the cordon who had assisted in getting the prisoners into the tender.

Since there had been no conversation in the tender, both Mr Mathew and Mr Justice Lawton suggested that the agreement reached between the four youths to say that they had never been in possession of the bricks and to jointly refuse to sign for their property must have been made whilst they were in the police station, sitting in the passageway. Goldsmith replied, "Yes, there was an opportunity," but it did not, on the balance of probabilities, sound very convincing.

Goldsmith denied seeing any bricks in envelopes in the charge room that night, but then Mr Mathew asked him this: "When you were being cross-examined before the magistrates when the two Ryalls and Derwin were being tried, did you say in answer to a question put on behalf of one of those defendants, 'I searched the boys and found nothing of a contentious nature. There were quite a few bricks round the charge room." Do you remember saying that?"

"I cannot remember saying that," replied Goldsmith, "and I certainly did not see any others."

"I am referring to the note which the clerk took at the time," explained Mr Mathew. "It is not a deposition of yours, read over to you and signed by you; it is a note which apparently was taken by the clerk, and his recollection is that this was said, that you said there were quite a few bricks round the charge room. Do you remember saying anything like that to the magistrate?" Goldsmith replied, "No."

And that was that. There was some fairly ineffective re-examination by Mr Durand, the closing speeches for both the prosecution and the defence and the summing up of the evidence by the judge, during which he said, "When the charge alleges that these three defendants conspired together, by implication it means, too, that they conspired not only together but with Challenor to pervert the course of justice."

The jury then retired to deliver its verdict.

There was one matter which was not picked up by the prosecution or by the judge. Goldsmith had an entry in his pocket book at the material time which read: 'Information from a passer-by several men in crowd carrying stones and bricks. 8.30 p.m.'

Unfortunately, he had also provided a statement, as well as stating on oath, that he, Battes and Oakey had not left West End Central until 8.45 that evening.

"I saw Dave Oakey the night before," Len Smith, a Clubs Officer at West End Central told me. "He thought he was going to get off." Oakey was wrong. The jury, after considering the evidence for four hours, disbelieved them, and on 23 June 1964 they were all found guilty.

Mr Durand vainly attempted mitigation on their behalf, denouncing Challenor as 'a tyrant', but as the judge had said, "There comes a time when police officers, just as army officers, just as anybody else, when they are told to do something which is clearly wrong, have to say to those in authority above them, 'I can't do it. I won't do it'. If something of the kind happened here, that Challenor was giving instructions, it is no answer for them to say, 'I had orders from Challenor to do that which I did'."

Their lives, careers and reputations in tatters, the three aids stood up in the dock as the judge told them:

> Honest police officers are the buttress of society. But dishonest, perjured officers are like an infernal machine ticking away to the destruction of us all. As intelligent young men you must appreciate that a crime of this gravity must be punished, and the punishment must be such to show the revulsion of this court at your conduct and to warn any other police officer who might be misguided enough to do what you did of the dangers he is running ... I take into consideration your comparative youth; I take into consideration your good service and, above all, I take into consideration the fact that you were working, possibly under the direction, and certainly under the supervision of a detective sergeant who, I am satisfied, at the material time was mentally unbalanced.

Battes was sentenced to three years' imprisonment; Goldsmith and Oakey were each sentenced to four years' imprisonment (which in both cases was reduced on appeal to three years).

CHAPTER 15

The Search for the Truth

As the three former constables were led away to commence their sentences, the judge turned to one of the most senior officers present in the court, asked him to enter the witness box and said to him:

> Chief Superintendent Du Rose, I would be very grateful if you would bring to the attention of the commissioner my grave disturbance at the fact that Detective Sergeant Challenor was on duty at all on 11 July 1963. On the evidence which I have heard from the doctors when he was arraigned it seems likely that he had been mentally unbalanced for some time, and the evidence which I heard from Superintendent Burdett in this case has worried me a great deal. It seems to me the matter ought to be looked into further.

In fact, there was little that Du Rose could add to his report; it was topped and tailed, the sentences and the judge's comments were appended, it was submitted to the commissioner, and six days after the completion of the court proceedings it landed on the Home Secretary's desk; three days before that, Clinton Davis had written to the Yard's Solicitors Department alleging false imprisonment in respect of Francis and Bridgeman, two of the defendants in the failed conspiracy to pervert case.

On 2 July 1964 Henry Brooke MP, the Home Secretary, dealt with a barrage of questions in the Commons. Joyce Butler wanted a public enquiry set up and also wanted to know what investigations were being made to determine whether or not Challenor had accepted bribes; Tom Driberg (morbidly anti-police and a friend of the Kray twins) asked if all cases dealt with by Challenor would be re-opened; and Alice Bacon and Jo Grimond wanted a select committee set up, as did Reginald Paget (who was also vociferously anti-police).

The Home Secretary replied that in the case of King and Silver he had recommended free pardons, and that whilst Silver had already completed his sentence, King should be released immediately. John and Ronald Ryall and Colin Derwin, who were convicted on the evidence of the aids of possessing offensive weapons, were to receive free pardons and their fines and costs would be repaid to them. The cases of Pedrini, Ford, Cheeseman, Fraser and Oliva were to be referred to the Court of Appeal. (In fact, on 28 July, their convictions were quashed on the ground that there was fresh relevant evidence capable of belief and possibly carrying weight which, had it been before the jury at the trial of the five men, might have placed the jury in reasonable doubt and led to verdicts of not guilty; those still serving sentences were released.)

However, Reginald Paget,[10] never one to slip meekly into the shadows when there was an opportunity to give vent to his strident rhetoric, bellowed:

> Has the Right Honourable Gentleman considered that nine months ago, in September, he found that a considerable section of the prison population for which he is responsible were there because of the enterprise and the evidence of a man who had turned out to be a dangerous lunatic? Is he aware that he has kept a number of these men, whose innocence he now recognises by recommending a free pardon, in prison for nine months since then? Is he also aware that in this matter, he who refused a public enquiry is now the principal accused and that it is quite outrageous that he should attempt to appoint a public enquiry when nothing can meet this save a Select Committee of the House, and does he refuse to appoint one?

It was a wasted exercise; the Home Secretary replied that, "The Honourable and Learned Member's insinuations are quite disgraceful," and nobody took any further notice. Paget's bellicose outpourings were considered the norm, much in the same way that Challenor's pre-psychotic behaviour had been.

Not everyone whose details had been collated by the National Council for Civil Liberties was quite so fortunate. Wallace Gold had been arrested by Challenor on 1 November 1962 after he had searched his shop and found 347 stolen cigarette and pipe lighters on the premises. He pleaded guilty to the charge of receiving stolen goods at the County of London Sessions on 9 January 1963 and was sentenced to nine months' imprisonment. The thief from whom Gold had received the lighters was also sentenced on the same day. Gold made no allegations of impropriety at the time; later, he alleged to the NCCL that one of the lighters had been

---

10. And for further disgraceful examples of Paget's oratory, please see *Death on the Beat* (Wharncliffe, 2012).

planted. The Home Secretary decided that it had not and took no action in his case.

Similarly, Andreas Louciades, who was arrested on 17 August 1963 for attempted housebreaking and possession of housebreaking implements and was subsequently sentenced to concurrent terms of eighteen months' imprisonment at the County of London Sessions on 25 September 1963, alleged that he, too, was framed. He was one of three persons convicted for these offences. Louciades also alleged that Challenor was present at the arrest – he was not, and neither were two of the aids to CID whom he named, one being on annual leave, the other being off sick with an injured knee. He stated that he knew Challenor during the war when he (Challenor) was serving in the Military Police. This, of course, was untrue. He did know Challenor, but as a police officer, not from his war service. It is interesting to note that Louciades did not raise this matter of 'framing' with the Home Office; other prisoners, having heard his allegations, passed these matters second- or third-hand to Mrs Butler's ever-growing file at the NCCL. Henry Brooke could find no reasons for any action in his case.

Lastly, the Home Secretary appointed Norman Goodchild CBE, the Chief Constable of Wolverhampton Borough Police, to launch an enquiry (assisted by Detective Superintendent Harold Williams) into allegations of bribery in respect of Challenor. Goodchild had served with the Oxford City force for seventeen years before being promoted to Deputy Chief Constable of that force and was then appointed Chief Constable of Barrow-in-Furness. He had been Chief Constable of Wolverhampton from 1944 until 1966; for the last year of his service he would be Chief Constable of West Midlands Constabulary. He had a great deal of experience of sitting on national committees and enjoyed the respect of senior officials in the Home Office; hence this appointment.

It was to Goodchild that John Du Rose forwarded an anonymous letter, addressed to himself, which he had received on 27 November 1963. Challenor had been detained in Netherne Hospital one month previously, so Du Rose could not have interviewed him about the content; it was a rambling, illiterate missive, spattered with capital letters and exclamation marks to stress a point to the reader, of the kind that one would expect from someone with a paucity of education and immersed up to their armpits in Soho's crime scene. Briefly, the writer stated that Challenor had for months visited a number of clubs in the area, including L'Atelier at 9 Berwick Street, W1, to collect what he (Challenor) referred to as 'hush money' and also 'holiday money'. The writer also mentioned a man who, if the letter was to be believed, had been fitted up by

Challenor; but when this man complained of the fact to the NCCL, he had neglected to mention that he had offered to pay Challenor a bribe to 'take things easy'. If the offer was made, it is clear that Challenor neither accepted the bribe nor 'took things easy'.

In fact, nine months later, another anonymous letter – and because of the similarity of handwriting and the same misspellings, certainly from the same author – was sent to the Commissioner of Police, Sir Joseph Simpson, who received it on 28 August 1964. This letter stated that 'there seemed little doubt' that Detective Sergeant Ken Etheridge had accepted bribes from a club owner – also resident at 9 Berwick Street. There also seemed little doubt that if this was true, the writer was hardly relaying current information, because Etheridge had left West End Central three months previously to return to the Fraud Squad and later to receive promotion to detective inspector.

This letter, too, was forwarded to the Chief Constable of Wolverhampton by Du Rose, with a rather caustic note to the Assistant Commissioner (Crime), who stated that Goodchild was '"reviewing" the earlier cases and "enquiring" into any similar fresh allegations', the tone of which suggested that Du Rose was not completely enthusiastic regarding Goodchild's competence in carrying out the investigations. Du Rose's feelings were echoed by his assistant, Detective Inspector Ken Oxford, when he received the docket back eighteen months later; on 28 February 1966 he minuted a report with the cutting words, 'It is *presumed* this matter was dealt with by the Chief Constable in his confidential report to the Commissioner.'

It might well have been that having carried out such a thorough investigation, Du Rose was rather miffed that instead of being permitted to continue his enquiries to deal with allegations of bribery (or indeed, any other complaints of misconduct), an outsider – and one for whom, it appeared, he did not have a great deal of time – had been appointed. If that was the case, then Du Rose had a point. However, the appointment of Goodchild had been at the Home Secretary's instigation. But this was no more than a glitch in Du Rose's career; within one month he was promoted to deputy commander, to oversee both the Richardson and later the Kray investigations.

Meanwhile, the Chief Constable of Wolverhampton continued sombrely carrying out his investigation into allegations of Challenor's soliciting bribes. John Troon interpreted for Ernest Pink – he described the Chief Constable's assistant, Detective Superintendent Williams, as 'the hatchet man' – but Pink refused to implicate Challenor in any way. "I think he respected Harry," Troon told me.

★ ★ ★

On 18 August 1964 the Home Secretary appointed the Recorder of the Borough of Great Grimsby, Arthur Evan James QC, to hold a public enquiry under the provisions of Section 32 of the Police Act 1964, to determine the circumstances in which it had been possible for Challenor to continue on duty at a time when he appeared to have been affected by mental illness. It was a good choice. James was then forty-eight years of age and had been called to the bar in 1939, before serving in the Royal Corps of Signals during the Second World War and being demobilized with the rank of major. Appointed Queen's Counsel in 1960, at the time of what became known as the 'Challenor Enquiry' James had just concluded the highly publicized trial of the Great Train Robbers' at Aylesbury Assizes as the senior of the four prosecution barristers. He was therefore well used to the attacks by defendants and their barristers on the honesty of police officers.

One of Her Majesty's Inspectors of Constabulary, Commander William John Adlam Willis CBE, MVO, CGM, DL, RN (Retired), was also appointed to act as an assessor on the enquiry, and the secretary was to be Mr G. H. Baker DSC of the Home Office. The enquiry was held at 6 Burlington Gardens, W1, the evidence was presented by Hugh E. Park QC (later the Honourable Mr Justice Park) and by Mr M. L. M. Chavasse, both of whom had been instructed by the Treasury Solicitor, and proceedings got under way on 28 September 1964.

In all, 131 witnesses were interviewed during the enquiry, which concluded two months later on 26 November 1964. Thirteen barristers instructed by ten firms of solicitors appeared on behalf of the witnesses, although there was a great deal of disparity regarding the number of witnesses for whom the barristers appeared; sixteen were represented by two barristers, the same number who represented PC Ray Jones and also Harry Challenor. Mr James refused Legal Aid certificates for both the Metropolitan Police and the National Council for Civil Liberties. So when a witness gave evidence, he (or she) was likely to be cross-examined by any or all of the other barristers.

The witnesses could roughly be split into four groups:

1. Those who spoke the complete unvarnished truth.
2. Witnesses who, although they did not make a note of the proceedings at the time, did their best to be accurate, but at the time of the enquiry were forgetful or unsure.
3. Those who, because of their dislike of Challenor (and perhaps the police in general), embellished their account in an attempt to make it more credible; in other words, they 'over-egged the pudding'.

4. Lastly, those for whom lying was second nature: they lied to the police, the court, often to their instructing solicitors, sometimes to their colleagues; and now, they lied to the enquiry.

A number of the witnesses complained that, having given evidence already in court, they were now compelled to do so again, and this was unfair and oppressive. However, it should be pointed out that some of them, having concocted alibis prior to their court appearances, then lied their heads off in court and now experienced grave difficulties in remembering what lies they had initially told. In addition to that, they had provided statements to the police who were investigating allegations against Challenor, so matters were becoming more and more obfuscated. Most annoying of all, as many of them discovered, was that they were not giving evidence to a credulous jury; they were dealing with experienced lawyers heading the enquiry who were well able to determine what was relevant, what was true and what was not. One of the witnesses who received strenuous cross-examination was Sydney Padmore, who summed up his feelings as follows:

This is now six times that I have visited this place. I have been subject to cross-examination, worry, called names and stuff like that. I have even been asked to admit some of my personal business. This is affecting me tremendously, Sir. I can't sleep, I can't eat. This has really gone, I think very, very far, as far as I am concerned. It is very, very bad for me.

However, Mr James would find much of Padmore's evidence "far from convincing".

* * *

Mr James' findings, very briefly summarized, were as follows: that Challenor's symptoms of paranoid schizophrenia manifested themselves on 5 September 1963.

In the case of Silver and King, Mr James rejected the allegation that Challenor had planted the detonator. He felt that Silver's evidence, of Challenor's putting his hand into his raincoat pocket prior to slitting open the cushion containing the detonators, was "inaccurate and deliberately untrue", and furthermore, it was quite unsafe to accept King's evidence as to the alleged threats made to him by Challenor. It did not rule out the possibility that a third party – someone other than the police – had planted the detonators in the cushion, but, then again, that was not the issue.

With regard to Pink (who stated that he was frightened to give evidence to the enquiry, because he had been threatened by a police officer) Mr James stated, "I formed the impression, the strong impression, that Mr Pink was not frightened of any person or any matter." Mr James found that with regard to Pink, Brown, Francis or Bridgeman, neither Challenor nor any other police officer had planted the weapons on them. He did criticize the amount of time that the four men were in custody before being charged, and said that Challenor's rubbing his hands, saying "Lovely, lovely, lovely" and "More and more" may have been an indication of his mental deterioration, but that this would not have been apparent to those present.

In the cases of Braggins, Matthews, Ireland and Steel, Mr James ruled that although their arrest was unlawful and showed a lack of judgement on Challenor's part, no one could have said at the time that the arrest was prompted by mental illness. Regarding the complaint of Challenor's rudeness and obstruction by the legal executive, Irvine Shine, Mr James blamed the long hours which Challenor had been working for his raised voice and abruptness and decided that 'the complaints were without real substance and sprang from over-sensitivity on Mr Shine's part, in the circumstances in which he found himself'; therefore, no senior officer should be criticized for failing to spot the possible onset of mental illness.

Mr James now turned to the cases of Padmore, Hawkins, Browne and Broulio Dario Oliva. He did not believe that Mrs Hawkins had been assaulted or that Challenor was drunk. He did believe that she was involved with Padmore and Dario Oliva in the running of the Boulevard Club and rejected the allegations of both Padmore and Oliva that they were assaulted on 6 July. Mr James was assisted in reaching his conclusion by the evidence of Detective Inspector Ronald Burrows (then a detective sergeant at West End Central), who saw Padmore sitting in the typist's cubicle and went right up to him and looked at him full in the face to see who he was. He asked Police Constable Thomas Oliver Jones, an aid to CID, why Padmore was there, and upon being told that he was a prisoner being dealt with by Challenor, DI Burrows told him to take Padmore downstairs to hand him over to the gaoler. PC Jones did so and took a close look at him because of his size, since he was going to take him to the cells alone. Neither officer saw any sign of injury on Padmore. Mr James accepted that Challenor had spoken disrespectfully to Padmore on that occasion, that it was wrong that he and Oliva should have been placed in the cells without the station officer's knowledge and that they should not have been detained so long without being charged. Mr James felt that this had been due to Challenor's enthusiasm to find Miss Browne – this was confirmed by Turham Moustapha, the proprietor of the Venus Rooms Club, where Challenor had been making enquiries – and that this general behaviour could have been symptomatic of the mental illness which manifested itself in September.

Mr James accepted the evidence of Ralph Rodriguez that an agreement was reached between Padmore, Oliva and others to make allegations against Challenor to discredit him, and that after Padmore had taken a statement containing the false allegations to his solicitor, Stoller, it was a fresh statement, made at Stoller's dictation which – in Mr James' extremely tactful words – "contained embellishments, not of Mr Padmore's invention but which he was prepared to adopt".

Turning now to the evening of 11 July, Mr James felt that Challenor was abrupt, both to Padmore and Stoller, and was quite wrong in not permitting Stoller to speak privately with his client and not showing them the warrant for Padmore's arrest. Challenor was at fault for not charging Padmore at the earliest opportunity, although this would have made no difference to the amount of time Padmore spent in custody. There was no doubt in Mr James' mind that during that evening Challenor displayed a noisy, aggressive attitude and lost control of himself; that there were errors of judgment and breaches of discipline; and that Challenor struck Padmore.

It is interesting to mention at this juncture that Challenor, who, it must be said, was extremely selective in his memoirs as to what he could (and could not) remember, did recall hitting Padmore. Although he was unaware if it was on 6 or 11 July, he stated that Padmore had said to him, "Why should I talk to the son of a back-street whore?" Since his mother was working as a tea lady, Challenor took exception to her profession being thus erroneously described and punched him on the temple, knocking him down. There was no need for Padmore to make a scurrilous allegation of assault, said Challenor; had he been able to attend the enquiry, he would have readily admitted the attack. Yeah, right. At the time, Challenor's behaviour was attributed to tiredness and overwork, although seen retrospectively it was a symptom of the mental illness which was established in September.

On the same night occurred the 'Bricks Case' involving Rooum, Hill and Ede. On board the tender which conveyed Rooum to the police station were Police Constables Graham

George, Ralph Pearson, Richard John Plester, Roger Purrington and Melvin Raffle, who either thought there was nothing unusual in Challenor's behaviour or were surprised, in various degrees, by it. However, Police Constable Brian Burton, who was also on board the tender, told the enquiry that he thought that Challenor's conduct was "markedly abnormal in respect of his shouting to the crowd and other officers"; and taking everything into consideration, Mr James found that it was clear that on that night, "Detective Sergeant Challenor departed from the standards of behaviour to be expected of a police sergeant and did not keep a check on his ready wit and boisterous behaviour." Mr James accepted that Rooum had been subjected to 'some force' by Challenor – he rejected the assertion by Rooum that he was a victim of a great conspiracy by the police – and found that the same officer had 'boxed the ears' of Ede and Hill. When Ede complained to the enquiry that the incident had adversely affected his school work and sport, Mr James opinion was, "I am not satisfied that there was any substance in that suggestion". Whether or not Challenor was guilty of conspiracy to pervert the course of justice by planting bricks on the night of 11 July did not, said Mr James, come within the scope of this enquiry. However, during the enquiry, Detective Superintendent Townsend was asked to comment on this situation, assuming that it was true and that the three junior officers had followed his lead in the matter; and if this was the case, did it suggest a breakdown in discipline and morale at West End Central?

Townsend replied that whilst he accepted the jury's guilty verdict in respect of Oakey, Battes and Goldsmith, he was unable to accept the validity of that verdict. He was then asked:

Of course, on the other hand, if one accepts the decision of the jury then it does show there was something very wrong with morale at that police station, does it not?

To this, Townsend replied:

I do not think I can answer that, sir. If we accept something that I am not happy to accept, then I fail to see how I can say there was something wrong with morale. As the superintendent at West End Central, I would say that the morale at that station was as high as I have ever seen it, anywhere. I had the most loyal and efficient set of officers I have ever worked with. I do not think there is anything wrong with morale there.

Mr James ruled that the assaults upon Rooum and the two youths had been carried out by Challenor whilst he was in an excited and emotional state, due to long hours, overtiredness and strain.

The reason why the cases of Pedrini, Ford, Fraser, Joseph Oliva and Cheeseman were raised in the enquiry was because a suggestion was made at the Court of Appeal, when their convictions were quashed, that Challenor was mentally ill at the time of their arrest – a view which Mr James rejected – and that had certain evidence been placed before the jury at the original trial, it could have led to the defendants being acquitted. But because attacks upon the characters of a number of persons had been made – and these included allegations of assault and planting of offensive weapons, as well as accusations that Challenor had accepted bribes to show favour to persons in custody – Mr James decided to include this case within the remit of the enquiry.

In determining the events surrounding their arrests, Mr James relied not only on the testimony given by the witnesses but also on their demeanour. As a result, Mr James dismissed the allegations of planting weapons – this included the bottle containing turpentine found in Oliva's car – and assault.

Victor Berrill – Wilfred Gardiner's former doorman – had given evidence at the Appeal Court hearing in this case one month previously, when he said:

> I knew the day before the bottle was found on Oliva that it was going to be found. Gardiner told me. He told me, rubbing his hands, 'There's going to be a gun, a bomb and tools.' He made it very clear they were going to be 'planted'. It had cost him a lot of money to get them put away but he didn't care if he had to pay forty policemen to come to the Old Bailey to swear their lives away. Those were Gardiner's own words.

This evidence appeared to have slipped Berrill's memory at the time of the James Enquiry one month later, and he had to be reminded of it; he stated that the words were not absolutely accurate but were roughly what Gardiner had said; and, furthermore, they might have been said on a different occasion than the one referred to in the statement. Although he admitted that his memory might be deficient, he did recall that Ford was going to be arrested "with a bomb wrapped in a towel and tools or knives or other things found in his car".

Understandably, Gardiner denied these assertions and in return stated that Berrill had told him that Pedrini had said he intended to burn Gardiner's club down, but had decided against this course of action because people lived above the club.

Mr James' most scathing remarks were reserved firstly for Joseph Oliva ("I reached the conclusion that he had no regard for the truth and the taking of an oath to tell the truth meant nothing to him") and then for Fraser ("I found to be a witness of utter unreliability in that he revealed himself to be a person prepared to invent and to swear to the truth of a pack of lies when it served his interests or those of his friends").

There is an interesting footnote to the Fraser episode: following Mr James' hard words, Fraser went on to higher things. Two years later, he was arrested as part of the Richardson torture trial; again, he was acquitted, of demanding money with menaces. He pleaded guilty to assaulting the blackmail victim and because he had spent a year in custody, was given a sentence which permitted his immediate release. His uncle, Francis 'Mad Frankie' Fraser, who appeared in the same trial, was not so fortunate and was sentenced to ten years' imprisonment.

However, before Don Gibson gave evidence to the James Enquiry, he had a notice served on him by Detective Inspector Oxford which stated that if it was found that he had erred in his duty in any way, the police would not pay his legal costs. He was, of course, completely exonerated, as were the other police officers who gave evidence to the enquiry.

At the time of Fraser's arrest in 1962, his wife and the wives of Don Gibson and Wilfred Gardiner were all expecting their first children. In 1976, Gibson – by then, a detective chief inspector – was making enquiries in a South London pub, and serving behind the bar was Jimmy Fraser. The two men shook hands, there was no animosity, and over a drink each asked after the other's daughter. It was the last time Gibson saw him. Fraser was later arrested for forging Bank of England notes in an office off the Charing Cross Road, and he was killed in an accident whilst holidaying in Florida in 2004.

★ ★ ★

With regard to the allegations that Challenor had accepted bribes, Mr James heard evidence from Victor Berrill, who stated that on at least twenty occasions, both prior to Pedrini, Ford and Co's arrest and afterwards, Challenor had visited the Phoenix Club, the inference being that he was accepting money from Gardiner. In fact, Berrill and two other men – Messrs Emmerson and Goff, two of Gardiner's former employees – had made statements to solicitors acting for John Ford in February 1964 or thereabouts. The addendum of 'thereabouts' was necessary because none of these statements were signed or dated. What was more, neither Emmerson nor Goff could be found to give evidence to the enquiry; nevertheless, sections of these unsigned, unattested statements were read to the enquiry. The upshot was that Emmerson had said, 'he (Challenor) would say, "Is Bill (Gardiner) in?" – then would go downstairs to his office.' As for Goff, he stated, 'On several occasions, Bill called to the cashier to enquire if there was any money in the (money) bag. I knew he meant money for Challenor. I don't know how much money Gardiner used to pay Challenor.' (Goff had shared a cell in Wormwood Scrubs with John Spiller, who had accompanied Ford to West End Central and had allegedly been slapped by Challenor for his pains. Gardiner, too, had been a guest of Her Majesty at the time.)

Berrill stated, 'Every Thursday, Sergeant Challenor, whom I recognised, used to come to the Phoenix Club to get his money ... The money had to be in notes. Gardiner was paying Challenor a long time after Ford and the others were sent to prison. Gardiner told me he was paying Challenor only because of Ford.'

But all of this was conjecture – Berrill was obliged to admit that he had never seen Challenor actually accept money from Gardiner, who in turn denied the allegation and told the enquiry that Challenor only came to the club on official business.

Now here matters become exceedingly unclear, and it is probably the fault of the James Report rather than that of any other person seeking to confuse the situation. In 1962, 23 September fell on a Sunday. It was on this date that John Cheeseman (whose son Alan had been remanded in custody) met Charles Ford (whose son John had similarly been remanded), and at the White Hart public house they met William Alfred Banner, who between 1923 and 1955 had collected fifteen convictions. The reason for the meeting was, as Mr Cheeseman told the enquiry, to find someone – in other words, a police officer – who could get matters 'straightened out', or in more prosaic terms, be bribed. Banner – he was known in police circles to be a 'fixer' – was given £5 for expenses and said he was going to find 'someone' for them the following day.

The following day was, of course, Monday 24 September, but it is referred to in the James Report as Monday 23 September – hence the confusion. It was during the afternoon of that day that Cheeseman and Ford allegedly met Detective Sergeant James Diamond from Bow Street police station who was the 'someone' who was going to 'straighten out' matters. That evening, Cheeseman stated that he met Challenor in the Premier Club, Old Compton Street; he went alone, because Ford had had too much to drink. The club was a disreputable drinking establishment and a rather shabby one, a meeting place for police officers (Ernie Millen, the head of the Flying Squad, was said to be a member), crooks (including 'Red-faced' Tommy Plumley, a notorious fixer and go-between for the Kray twins) and solicitors, where business (monkey or otherwise) could be transacted. Challenor told him it would cost £50 for favour to be shown to his son; this, said Cheeseman, was uttered in the presence of witnesses, allegedly including Banner, Diamond, Miss Margaret Laville, a managing clerk of Lewis and Shaw (Solicitors) of 61 Cary Street and her friend William Hemming, a barrister and former police officer. Their presence at this meeting was later denied by all four. Mentioning Oliva, Challenor told Cheeseman, "I've been out and got the bastard I want and what I've stuck on him, he'll never fucking get out of it." Furthermore, Challenor provided Cheeseman with the name and address of the solicitors Lewis and Shaw and told him to go there the following day. In fact, this company did represent Cheeseman's son at the trial, and William Hemming was briefed to act as Alan Cheeseman's barrister. On 25 September Ford's father Charles went to see Margaret Laville, together with Banner, to ask her to represent his son as well. Banner asked her if it would be all right for him to see Challenor, and she replied, "I can trust him with my life." This, Miss Laville later strenuously denied. However, as far as Ford was concerned, this meant that Challenor was capable of being bribed. According to Cheeseman, that evening, the £50 in £5 notes was handed over to Challenor in the presence of Charles Ford and Banner. However, no mention of the bribery allegations was made at the trial, or to police officers who made enquiries later. John Cheeseman would later say that following the handing over of the £50, bail was not opposed. "My son was granted bail," said Cheeseman. "He was the only one." But this was not the case. In fact, four days later, on 29 September, Challenor successfully opposed a bail application in respect of both Ford and Cheeseman at Marlborough Street Magistrates' Court, and they were remanded in custody. It was only on 10 October that Cheeseman was granted bail – against strong opposition from Challenor.

There was also strong opposition from those who were named as being present during these alleged bribery transactions. Miss Laville and Mr Hemming had of course denied any knowledge; Diamond – he retired from the Police Force in February 1964 – knew Banner as someone who had provided him with information in the past and he knew Challenor from seeing him at Bow Street Magistrates' Court in the normal course of his duties; but he stated that although he (Diamond) was a member of the Premier Club, Challenor was not, he had never seen him in the club and his CID diary proved that on the evening of 24 September he was conducting his police enquiries elsewhere. Furthermore, the only time he had seen Cheeseman senior was at the James Enquiry – two years after their alleged meeting.

Banner denied that Ford and Cheeseman had sought his assistance, or that he had seen them at the Premier Club; he said that he did not know and had not spoken to Challenor, and in consequence had not been present either to hear Challenor make his demand or when the money was allegedly passed over; in fact he had not accepted money from Ford or anybody else. And to put the cherry on top of the cake, Banner also denied being a police informant.

Francis Oliva now hopped on the bandwagon. He stated that Cheeseman had introduced him to Banner in order to obtain bail for his son; Banner, he said, had initially told him it would cost £60 but later reported back that Challenor, fearing a police trap, wanted nothing to do with the scheme. All of which was rather confusing; and, large sections of it, highly dubious.

In addition, Margaret Laville stated that she knew Challenor well and did not regard him as being a person who would take a bribe. She was corroborated in her belief by her friend William Hemming, who held Challenor "in high regard as a police officer". Detective Superintendent Townsend (also a member of the Premier Club) told the enquiry that he had never had occasion to believe that Challenor had accepted bribes for showing favours. In fact, he mentioned that there was every justification for Challenor to have met John Cheeseman for the purpose of gathering information, as was revealed in Challenor's CID diary. An entry for 22 October 1962 read:

> 8pm. Interviewed Mr Cheeseman senior for information re betting shop bombs. To Coach and Horses public house and purchased refreshment for an informant in respect of seeking information. Left 8.40.

This was emphatically denied by Cheeseman, who described the entry as "ridiculous", but his testimony of paying a bribe to Challenor, and that of Charles Ford and William Banner, was dismissed by Mr James.

Nevertheless, did Challenor accept bribes? James Fraser stated that £100 had been paid to Challenor in order for him to be dropped out of the conspiracy to demand money by menaces charge. This was utter nonsense. Fraser had been charged with that offence, and it was a jury who acquitted him, the same jury who convicted him on the offensive weapon charge. Jimmy Humphreys later said he paid Challenor £25 a time, on two occasions. Of course, this is possible, but perhaps because many people would have known that they associated together, Humphreys may well have been putting up a smokescreen before it could be alleged that he was Challenor's snout. A decade later, when Commander Ken Drury of the Flying Squad suggested just that, following revelations that he and Humphreys had spent a holiday together in Cyprus with their wives, Humphreys blew the whistle and the downfall of the CID commenced. After all, at the time when these allegations were being aired Challenor was not in a position to repudiate the assertion, and in those days an informant's true identity was known only to the detective running him.

But in rejecting assertions that Challenor took bribes, Mr James was helped in coming to this conclusion by Detective Superintendent Williams, who had been assisting the Chief Constable of Wolverhampton in the independent enquiry into bribery allegations. Williams informed the James Enquiry that a painstaking examination had been conducted into Challenor's financial affairs with the full cooperation of Doris Challenor. Bank deposits and withdrawals were scrupulously checked, but there was no evidence whatsoever of receipts of money which were anything but legitimate to supplement his weekly wage of £22 8s 6d, nor was there evidence of savings which had been concealed. In fact, the house at Sutton revealed that the Challenors lived simply, even frugally.

In the meantime, Norman Goodchild pressed on with his investigations, which would eventually be forwarded to the Commissioner of the Metropolitan Police in fifteen sections. What these reports contained was considered to be more than a little sensitive; they now repose in the National Archives at Kew, where they have been ordered to remain closed for 95 years, until 1 January 2061.

* * *

Thus the enquiry was wound up, and the evaluation of the evidence and the writing of the report commenced. It would take eight months to complete, and when it was published many people decried it, saying it was a whitewash. It was not. It was the result of a great many witnesses being subjected to often severe cross-examination and the most rigorous assessment of two months of evidence. A number of people, for a variety of reasons, wanted to see a severe castigation of the Metropolitan Police in general and officers from West End Central in particular. The reason why this did not happen was simply because the evidence was not there.

John Du Rose's enquiry was no less rigorous, and despite the claim that when the police investigated themselves in those far-off days, the inevitable result was a whitewash, that assertion regarding Du Rose is laughable. He was a top detective, he was determined to get to the bottom of the matter and he did. Had he wanted to produce a cover-up, he would have accepted PC Ray Jones' initial 'I wasn't there, I didn't see anything' statement as fact. He did not – he kept probing until he got to the end of the matter. And when Jones stated that he had heard gossip that Challenor had planted a detonator, he investigated that too. Challenor he was unable to interview; Peter Jay, who had been present when the detonators were found in King and Silver's possession, he could.

As Peter Jay told me, "When I was interviewed by Du Rose and Detective Inspector Ken Oxford, I was shown a photograph of two detonators and I was asked, 'Were these the detonators you found?' I replied, 'They appear to be similar' but what was written down was, 'They appear identical.' I disputed this and said I wanted my original words written down. 'It's not important', said Du Rose, but I replied, 'It is to me'."

The interview had been going on for hours, and Jay requested a break for lunch; instead, he was given a corned beef sandwich and a cup of tea. "I shall say that was an inducement!" said Jay, before walking out of the room. The gossip that had circulated regarding Challenor's planting the detonators (and which had reached the ears of PC Ray Jones) was just that – gossip. There was no way in which Challenor could have planted the detonators in the cushion.

This was reflected later in the words of Mr James, who stated that he preferred the evidence given by Jay; he was one of many officers who were praised by the enquiry for the accuracy of their evidence. During the next twenty years Jay rose through the ranks and retired with the rank of detective chief inspector.

* * *

When the James Enquiry's report was submitted to the Home Secretary on 16 July 1965, it was not Henry Brooke who received it. Following the Conservatives' election defeat he had left office on 16 October 1964, not before time according to many. His actions had caused controversy on several occasions, not least his failure to provide adequate security for the Greek royal visit, and he was generally regarded as one of the worst Home Secretaries of the twentieth century. His successor was Sir Frank Soskice, and on

5 August 1965 he made a statement to the House. Having read the report, the Home Secretary mentioned that he had conferred with the Attorney General, since there was a possibility that if Challenor was well enough he could be brought from hospital to stand his trial. If this were to be the case, he did not want to publish the report if it would prejudice any forthcoming trial. Nevertheless, he stated firmly, it really was a matter for the Attorney General to determine whether or not the original charges which Challenor had faced should be reinstated or whether there should be further charges. In order to assist the decision making, the Home Secretary had already requested further medical opinions on Challenor's condition.

Henry Brooke (now a backbencher) rather plaintively mentioned that since he and the Commissioner of the Metropolitan Police had been subject of criticism, would the Home Secretary confirm that the report completely disposed of these charges? The Home Secretary, who had already confirmed this, coolly replied, "I have already said so."

Given his trenchant anti-police views, Tom Driberg MP rather astonishingly said:

Quite apart from the question of prejudice, is it not rather hard on Mr Challenor himself that there should be this threat of a possible trial hanging over him for some months? Could this not actually impede his complete recovery? Would my Right Honourable and Learned Friend and the learned Attorney General consider that there must surely be a strong presumption that, if Mr Challenor was unfit to plead when he was charged, he was also mentally disturbed when he did the very terrible things that he did do?

These were matters, the Home Secretary assured his Right Honourable Friend, that would be taken into account; and whilst he wanted the James Report published as soon as possible, he would also consider publishing an interim report, or a summary, but only if this course of action was absolutely necessary. It was not necessary; the James report was published by Her Majesty's Stationery Office that month and was on sale to members of the general public at eleven shillings per copy.

At a Commons sitting on 4 November 1965 Sir Frank Soskice told the House that having thoroughly considered the report he fully accepted the conclusions reached by Mr James – by now, Mr Justice James – and was satisfied that no further enquiry was necessary. This was not to everybody's liking, especially Mrs Joyce

Butler, who asked, "Will he please arrange for a full debate in the House on the whole subject, which has been treated very casually so far," and then amazingly added, "and also arrange for the release of the three officers who appear to have been made scapegoats in the Challenor case?"

The question of a debate was, said the Home Secretary, a matter for the Leader of the House, but with regard to the three imprisoned officers, he felt that Challenor's influence on them had been taken into consideration by the trial judge when passing sentence. Although it was a difficult decision, which had been 'carefully and anxiously' considered, the Home Secretary did not feel justified in recommending the exercise of the Royal Prerogative.

★ ★ ★

It is therefore an interesting anomaly that whilst the Royal Prerogative was not extended in favour of the three aids to CID, it was, several years later in the case of the Soho pimp, Jimmy Humphreys. Serving an eight-year sentence for his part in slashing his wife's former lover, Humphreys grassed up every police officer with whom he had had dealings, and was released after serving just two years of his sentence, in recognition of his services in exposing the corrupt practices of which he had been the prime mover and instigator. Of the seventy-four officers named by Humphreys, just thirteen were jailed. Following his release, Humphreys vacated his luxury Soho apartment but was able to return to his twenty-eight-room Kent farmhouse.

There is, no doubt some kind of moral justification to be found for the clemency proffered to Humphreys, if one digs deep enough.

CHAPTER 16

The Later Years –
Happiness and Desolation

Harry Challenor remained at Netherne Hospital for three years. He received electric shock treatment, was prescribed tranquillizers and drifted in and out of a fantasy world in which the SAS featured prominently and old memories revisited him. It has been suggested that within a week, 'Harry was running the place. He'd say to his minder, "Come on, me old darling, we're going down the pub",' but this story is almost certainly apocryphal. He was very sick indeed, and it was only later that he received visitors, including Peter Jay and Ken Rexstrew. And when Thomas Proudfoot, his fellow constable from Mitcham, returned an inmate who had absented himself from the hospital, whom should he see but Challenor sitting in a recliner chair on a balcony, reading a book. "Hello, me old darling," called out Challenor, recalled Proudfoot. "We had a chat whilst one of the nurses fetched us a cup of tea. That was the last time I saw him. I got on very well with Harold and was pleased to have known him."

"Doris was a wonderful lady who dealt with Harry wonderfully," Coral Rexstrew told me. "She went to see Harry every day, without fail. Sometimes Ken (Mrs Rexstrew's husband) was able to drive her there, but if not she would walk, even if it was snowing. She never missed a day."

It was eventually considered reasonably safe to discharge Challenor from Netherne, but this was by no means the end of his problems. When the stress of everyday living became too much for him, he was periodically admitted to Belmont Hospital in Homeland Drive, Sutton, a 313-bed institution dedicated to the study and treatment of neurosis. The hospital closed in 1975; thereafter, he attended the Chiltern Wing of the Sutton Hospital, Cotswold Road, Sutton, which deals with patients suffering from mental health problems that, because of their seriousness or complexity, cannot be treated within primary care.

He tried employment; he secured jobs at a couple of metal-fabricating companies – no pun intended! – which lasted several years, and then became a clerk at a firm of Norbury solicitors, with less success. When he went to Brixton Prison in the latter capacity to take a defence statement from a remand prisoner, Challenor remarked to a prison officer, "I used to come here as CID, then I came as a prisoner myself and now I'm here for the defence. That's what you call bloody good all-round experience!" This did not endear him to the prisoner, who demanded another solicitor.

These periods of employment were interspersed with admissions as an inpatient to Sutton Hospital, before he found work as an iron moulder in the self-same foundry where he had worked after demobilization from the army, and where his father-in-law was still employed.

The fact that Challenor had tried to integrate himself back into society prompted Arthur Lewis MP to use this to his advantage when he demanded in the Commons to know from the Attorney General why he would not institute criminal proceedings, "in view of the fact that ex-Sergeant Challenor is now fully recovered and has for some considerable time been back in full employment." The Attorney General pointed out that the Law Officers had decided in 1965 that no proceedings should be taken against Challenor; this caused Mr Lewis to roar:

> I am now approaching forty years in public life. Is the Attorney General aware that I have learnt that, in cases such as this, the Establishment is only too willing and able to twist the law when it suits it?

Replying that he was not prepared to alter the decision because he thought it was a correct one, the Attorney politely refrained from mentioning that he was also aware that the Right Honourable Gentleman may have had a hidden agenda. Arthur Lewis had been fined £5 with £10 costs at Bow Street Magistrates' Court for obstructing a police officer in the execution of his duty, following strike disturbances outside the Savoy Hotel in 1947.

★ ★ ★

Following his release from Netherne Hospital (he jokingly referred to it as 'my country home' and the 'funny farm'), Challenor travelled to Italy on a motoring trip with Doris and their son Andrew. The trip was very enjoyable, he was reunited with those remaining members of the Eliseio family who had not emigrated to Australia and the holiday passed off without incident. Then in 1980 came an invitation from members of the Resistance to a reunion, through the SAS Regimental Association, for former members of 'Operation Wallace'. This, too, went smoothly, almost certainly because Doris and Challenor's mother accompanied him.

And during a later visit to Granrupt-les-Bains, Challenor – who was regarded as a hero by the population of the area – was awarded the Resistance *Médaille d'argent de la Légion Vosgienne*. It was there that during German reprisals two priests had been executed and over 200 occupants of the village had been sent to concentration camps, where 116 of them had perished. Other recipients of the medal were Captain Brian Stonehouse MBE (not a member of the SAS but an intrepid agent of SOE's 'F' Section who survived incarceration in three concentration camps) and Major Roy Farran.

It was on a later trip to France with Farran that Challenor accepted his former squadron commander's invitation to extend their trip to Italy. It was a huge mistake. For some inexplicable reason he flushed his tranquillizers down the toilet, and the excursion degenerated into a nightmare, with Challenor swimming out to sea, attempting to climb to the moon, wrecking the furniture in a hotel and wrestling with the owner's dog. He and Farran were then kicked out of one hotel after another before events culminated in Challenor diving off the top board into a hotel's swimming pool, stark naked. The flight home saw Challenor wrapping his jacket around his head, since he believed that people were trying to read his thoughts. Upon his return, Doris immediately telephoned Sutton Hospital, which just as immediately accepted him for a six-week stay.

In the spring of 1988 the Challenors moved from Sutton to a bungalow at Minster Avenue, Bude, in Cornwall. It was a tranquil setting and one that suited Harry Challenor perfectly. He was now of state retirement age, and it is highly likely that this was the happiest time of his life. The rather odd reason for moving to the area was because his father-in-law had been a member of the Duke of Cornwall's Light Infantry during the First World War and he liked the inhabitants of Cornwall very much; it must be assumed that Challenor liked them as well. Challenor had a black Labrador named 'Ebby' (probably a diminutive for 'Ebony'), a black cat named 'Timothy' and two geese – 'Bert' and 'Gert' – which he kept in the garden (a ploy used by the ancient Romans, and at least one SAS officer in Ireland, to act as guardians against intruders). A parrot, which had been fed on a diet of fried eggs and Guinness, did not make the transition from Sutton to Bude. It was whilst he was there that he happened to meet Frank Rushworth, whom he had known as a Clubs Officer at West End Central and who, having retired four years previously, was living a few miles away. Rushworth had to remind him of their former trade or calling, since Challenor believed that they had served together in the SAS. "His book had just come out and he'd been on the radio," Rushworth told me, "and we played golf together." Recalling their service at West End

Central almost thirty years previously, Rushworth stated, "The villains were terrified of him!"

The launch of Harry Challenor's memoirs had taken place in London's West End. Rex and Coral Rexstrew attended, as did members of Challenor's family, including his elderly mother. The Rexstrews had also stayed with the Challenors at their home in Bude. "He had a wonderful garden of which he was very proud, which overlooked both the sea and the countryside," Coral Rexstrew told me. "We went to various pubs in Bude with him, where he was very popular."

Challenor was also friendly with Gordon Pugh, a neighbour who lived four doors away. Pugh had returned to Bude six months prior to the Challenors' arrival, having served in the Royal Navy as a submariner. This was quite sufficient for Pugh to be included in Challenor's small circle of friends, since he held the Navy in very high esteem – his close police associates Etheridge and Dilley had both served in the Royal Navy, and Rexstrew had been in the Merchant Navy – and the two neighbours were soon engrossed in tales of Challenor's wartime adventures during Operation Marigold on the submarine *Safari*.

"The first time I saw him, he was gardening," recalled Pugh. "He was always seen wearing a flat cap and smoking a pipe or taking snuff (which Doris – who was referred to as 'Dot' – hated), and wearing a tweed or check jacket. She called him 'Peter', and I believe it was an Italian family who called him 'Pietro' during his escape from a POW camp during World War Two; his army friends called him 'Tanky' and for everybody else it would be 'Harry'."

Speaking of Doris, Pugh told me, "She was a very kind person, who saw nothing bad in anyone and would help anyone, but she put up with a lot from Harry. He suffered from mental health problems (I think it was manic depression) and every couple of weeks or months Doris would detect that he needed to take a lithium tablet[11] to get his feet back on the ground. He called them 'bombs' – he hated taking them, as they made him feel ill."

But during his upbeat times Challenor was the best of company. "Harry's great loves were gardening and golf and he would spend all day at both – he was very fit and strong for his age. He played with a retired group of locals at Bude Golf Club whom he referred to as 'The Crazy Gang'," Pugh told me. "Harry would always talk about his past, how tough his upbringing was, he had no qualms

---

11. A mood-balancing drug for people suffering from illnesses such as manic depression.

talking about his wartime experiences and I loved to sit and listen. The war was a place where a lot of people perished but not only did he survive, he thrived. He would talk about his police life but not as much; it was a bit sketchy and had no recollection of the 'brick incident'. He was a perfect gent around women but would curse and swear when just men were in attendance. During Christmas gatherings at his bungalow he would be the centre of attention with his stories, and we, his neighbours, all loved it."

It was certainly true that Challenor enjoyed being the centre of attention; he had told fanciful stories to the inmates of Leavesden Hospital before the war and organised a bawdy play entitled *A Night in Sadie's Joint* for the wartime SAS which degenerated into a brawl, complete with black eyes and a broken jaw. During his stay at Netherne he told fantastic stories to one of the more credulous inmates, and later, at Pullen Foundries Ltd, he devised a paper for the workers entitled *Operation – Preserve Sanity*. He also wrote a short novel, a skit on his time in the SAS, entitled *Without Dark Glasses*. It is not known if he ever offered it to a publishing house; but if he did, it was never published.

★ ★ ★

After forty-eight years of marriage, Doris, his mainstay, died of cancer. Gordon Pugh visited her in Stratton Hospital, Bude just before she passed away on 18 October 1992 after a very short illness. She was cremated at the North Devon Crematorium, Old Torrington Road, Barnstable – one of Challenor's sisters and some neighbours attended the service – and her ashes were removed by the funeral directors and handed to Challenor; it is believed that the ashes were strewn in the garden at Minster Avenue. He had been utterly devoted to her – and very dependent on her – and now he simply did not know what to do. He was completely lost without her. How he must have rued the time when he had stormed out of the bungalow, telling Doris he was leaving her – only to return, downcast, the following day, to find a smiling Doris patiently waiting for him. But no longer.

His friend from the SAS, Russell King, a very kindly man and a philanthropist, then living in Barnstaple, Devon, went walking with Harry and his dog Ebby for four or five hours a day, just letting him talk, before finally sitting down with him for a beer.

Challenor was invited to the Bradbury Lines,[12] the Regimental Headquarters of the SAS in Hereford, to give a talk about his

---

12. Known as the Stirling Lines since 30 September 2000.

exploits behind the lines in wartime Italy. One of the sergeants plied him with beer until eventually Challenor collapsed and had to be carried to his room. The following morning, breakfast was served in the Officers' Mess. When he eventually entered the Mess, Challenor spotted an attractive young woman who was the girlfriend of one of the officers and made an indecent proposal to her that was so explicitly jaw-dropping that an eyewitness told me, "I didn't know where to look!" Challenor later received a letter from the Regimental Headquarters which he assumed would be full of praise for his talk; instead, couched in chilly terms, it informed him that he would no longer be welcome in the Officers' Mess!

It was during this period that there was a profound disagreement with his married son Andrew, who had separated from his wife; Challenor told him, "I never want to see you ever again!" – and as far as it is known, he never did. He changed his will, and his daughter-in-law became his beneficiary and next-of-kin; the new will was witnessed by Gordon Pugh.

"Harry went off the rails," recalled Pugh. "Doris had kept him in check and now that influence had gone, he became very unkempt and very drunk at the golf club. He was banned and sent to the club's greenhouse (not a very prudent move!) due to his offensive language. He didn't take his medication; one morning I found him face-down in his own vomit, having drunk a bottle of whisky. He told me he had been dancing with Ebby to the soundtrack of *South Pacific*." The two geese, Bert and Gert, wandered around the house, making a very predictable and odoriferous mess; when Pugh asked Challenor why the back door was not kept shut, he replied, "That would fucking offend them!"

Challenor's mental condition, always precarious, degenerated fast; he had stopped taking his medication and, according to Pugh, "He became very scary, shouting late at night." He also recalled approximately two tons of horse manure being deposited on Challenor's driveway and Challenor talking to the steaming mound, telling it 'how wonderful and beautiful it was'. Unfortunately, he had failed to remove his car from the driveway prior to delivery of the manure, so until it was spread around the garden Challenor was housebound. He also mentioned to Pugh that when he was at his most delusional he believed that he was on the cross next to Jesus, who told him, 'I'm sending you down to save the world as it needs to be a bastard who does it.'

His religious fantasies apart, matters culminated one evening when Challenor knocked on a neighbour's door and told the occupants of the house that he wanted to shoot everyone. Enough was enough. The police and a doctor were called, and Challenor was persuaded to voluntarily enter what was then St Lawrence's Psychiatric Hospital, Boundary Road, Bodmin (known since 2002 as Bodmin Hospital) – Harry referred to it as 'The Nut House' – where he spent some time before he sold his house. The new owner took over in February 1994, and now, just approaching his seventy-second birthday, Challenor settled half of the money from the sale on his daughter-in-law and moved into a care home, Kingswood Grange, in Lower Kingswood, Surrey, which was supported by the charity 'Combat Stress'. He had the remainder of the money from the sale of the bungalow to finance his stay, plus his state pension, his police and army pensions and a widower's pension, since Doris had worked for Marks & Spencer.

Ken Rexstrew had retired from the Metropolitan Police in 1975; his new employment took him all over the world but he steadfastly and loyally visited Challenor, bringing with him pipe tobacco from airport duty-free shops. On one such occasion Challenor was sitting on a bench watching the traffic go by when quite suddenly he told Rexstrew, "I don't want anyone to visit me any more." Rexstrew was understandably very upset – it is highly likely that such an apparently unkind comment was symptomatic of Challenor's illness – but he obeyed his old friend's strictures and never visited him again.

* * *

When Kingswood Grange closed in June 1999, Challenor was one of twenty-three patients who moved into Amberley Lodge in Downlands Road, Purley, Surrey, a home providing nursing, dementia and respite care, where he occupied one of the sixty rooms. The secretary, Rekha Gangadeen, told me, "He was my favourite patient," and one of the nursing staff, Janet Janes (who referred to him as 'Tanky'), told me that he was "a lovely man."

In the last few years of his life Harry Challenor's health rapidly deteriorated, and he died on 28 August 2008, aged eighty-six, from a chest infection and bronchopneumonia; he was cremated at the North East Surrey Crematorium on 8 September 2008. The coffin was draped with a Union Jack. The service was due to take place at two o'clock but the vicar did not arrive until three, and Coral Rexstrew, who attended with her daughter-in-law, had to miss the service, since they had to collect the children from school. Mrs Rexstrew saw Challenor's daughter-in-law Lesley at the crematorium but told me, "It was poorly attended"; Ken Rexstrew, although terminally ill, insisted that he attend the service and spoke to Lesley Challenor afterwards. The funeral directors,

W. A. Truelove, had their account paid 'privately'. Amongst the mourners were three members of the SAS, including Jamie Lowther-Pinkerton MVO, MBE, the former Commanding Officer of 'G' Squadron, who at the time of writing is the personal secretary to Prince Harry of Wales and the Duke and Duchess of Cambridge. In accordance with his instructions, Harry Challenor's ashes were scattered into the Atlantic near his old home in Bude.

His impressive row of medals – the Military Medal, the 1939–1945 Star, the Africa Star with 1st Army clasp, the Italy Star, the France-Germany Star, the War Medal, the General Service Medal with Palestine 1945–48 clasp and the *Médaille d'argent de la Légion Vosgienne* – had been donated by Challenor to the Duke of Cornwall's Light Infantry Museum, The Keep, Bodmin, on 19 August 1991. At the same time he also donated to the museum the First World War medals of his late father-in-law, Private 13487 William James Broome: the 1914–18 Star, the British War Medal and the Light Infantry Victory Medal – known as 'Pip, Squeak and Wilfred'. "He often came to the museum," recalled Major Hugo White. "He was a sad, often incoherent individual. He just wanted to talk." Two odd matters arose from this donation. On 5 September 1994 Harry Challenor borrowed his French decoration from the museum; it was never returned. And the second (and very strange) matter was that he left quite explicit directions that the medals were never to be handed over to the SAS Regimental Association.

CHAPTER 17

Aftermath

At Challenor's removal from the West End, the gangsters, thugs, pimps and strong-arm men of Soho could scarcely believe their good fortune. Although they had been prepared to make a capital outlay of £1,000 (£16,000 by today's standards) to rid themselves of the pestilential Challenor, a skinny little anarchist, who was unknown to them, had done it for them free of charge; the resultant publicity had tarnished the police in the West End of London, and it would be a reckless copper indeed who now took a stand against the Soho gangs. In fact, they could behave as they pleased – and they did. They issued huge payments to the small but influential corps of venal police officers, and their businesses flourished. It would take another ten years before there was a clampdown, in the form of the new Commissioner, Sir Robert Mark GBE, QPM, but this was not without its downside. In endeavouring to stop corruption and see crooked coppers imprisoned or at the very least kicked out of office, Mark took the very blinkered – and inaccurate – view that all CID officers were corrupt and set about undermining their power. He achieved limited success in his first goal, although corruption was not (and never will be) completely eliminated. With the second of his objectives Mark scored a spectacular success. Infiltrating the ranks of the CID with uniform officers – few of whom had any experience of investigative police work – meant that the reputation of New Scotland Yard, which the entire world had looked up to for high standards of criminal detection, started a long and slippery downward path before it came to rest with a bump; it became an organisation riddled with apathy, political correctness, health and safety and a lack of leadership. For the remaining police officers who wanted to get out and serve the public it was a catastrophe. The same applied to the general public, who paid their salaries.

The National Council for Civil Liberties was on a roll. Martin Ennals, the organisation's Secretary-General, went on to better things; his place was taken by Clifford Anthony Smythe. Imprisoned in 1958 for three months for being a 'conscientious objector' and refusing alternative civilian service, Smythe was sent to prison three years later for one month for refusing to be bound over to keep the peace, following a sit-down by the Committee of One

Hundred. Now, as leader of the NCCL – he was referred to as a 'radical anarcho-pacifist', rather a contradiction in terms – Smythe widened the scope of the organisation to encompass the plight of gypsies, ethnic minorities and prisoners. The group also took up the subject of children's sexuality. This included incest, in the belief that 'public discussion on the subject has often been ill-informed and irrational' and that 'the advent of reliable contraceptives and safer abortion weakens this argument'. In addition, the NCCL believed that the age of consent should be abolished, adding, 'Childhood sexual experiences willingly engaged in with an adult result in no identifiable damage ... the real need is a change in the attitude which assumes that all cases of paedophilia result in lasting damage'. Unsurprisingly, the Paedophile Information Exchange (PIE), a pro-paedophile activist group, became affiliated to the NCCL, although for some unaccountable reason it was later excluded from the organisation. Doubtless, PIE must have felt that their human rights had been breached.

So now, thanks to the NCCL (in 1989 it changed its name to 'Liberty'), everyone is aware of what that organisation perceives to be their 'rights'. All walks of life are now bound with legislation to such an extent that the ordinary man or woman in the street seems powerless to say or do anything about any subject which flies in the face of common sense, offends morality or the security of this country, without fear of censure or prosecution. Yes, the general public have good cause to be grateful to the NCCL.

★ ★ ★

Marlborough Street Magistrates' Court, the scene of so many dramatic court appearances by the personnel of West End Central, is no more. Since 1981 it has been the Courthouse Doubletree, owned by Hilton Regent Street, a five-star hotel with 112 rooms and suites, a private cinema, five conference rooms, a gym, sauna and indoor swimming pool. No. 1 Court, where a trembling Harry Challenor had to be helped from the dock on his very last appearance, now houses the oriental-themed Silk Restaurant.

Following Challenor's departure there were changes at West End Central. Dave Dixon recalls approximately half a dozen new CID officers being transferred there under the supervision of the late Detective Inspector John Morrison. "There was a big backlog of aids waiting to be 'made' [appointed detective constables]," recalled Dick Docking. "Some went to 'C4' at 'CO' (Criminal Records Office at Scotland Yard) hoping that they'd come out as DCs on Division, but not many did."

In fact, the Challenor case saw the end of the aids system. Temporary detective constables (TDCs) were introduced into the Metropolitan Police to replace the aids; no longer were they regarded as police constables in plain clothes and therefore permitted to claim overtime. Now, as soon as they were appointed they were considered members of the CID and as such were able only to claim the niggardly CID allowances – and were expected to work for as long as necessary, just as the CID had always been. It also meant that they had to pass the ten-week junior CID course prior to being selected as detective constables. (This was one of the recommendations made in the James Report.) But otherwise, it was a case of 'a rose by any other name'; the TDCs went out in pairs and roamed the streets looking for likely 'bodies', and they were supposed to be closely supervised by the rank and file CID, although this was not always the case. They could expect to be thus employed for two to three years before selection boards were available, and if at any time they were not considered suitable, for any number of reasons, they would be sent back to uniform. But part of the Challenor legacy had been indelibly stamped on the new system: when any arrest for possession of an offensive weapon was challenged at court, a strict, unequivocal directive in *General Orders*, the police officers' bible, stipulated that legal representation *must* be requested.

In fact, there were more changes in the Metropolitan Police than just at West End Central. It would, of course, be quite wrong to suggest that the demise of Challenor and the three aids to CID, which brought a slump in morale, contributed to 1964 being (then) the worst year during the twentieth century for crime. However, it would be right to say that during the night-duty operations Challenor and his aids effected a tremendously significant decrease in crime, and the only reason it was not even greater was because there were simply not enough hours in the day. Challenor did not stop crime in Soho; but it was his presence which terrified the hoodlums, slowed down their criminal activities and made them far more cautious. Now, with Challenor gone from Soho, the Drugs Squad at Scotland Yard had to be augmented. They had investigated 152 offences in 1962; the following year, the number of cases rocketed to 1,074, the Obscene Publications Squad's workload rose to 307, and the disastrous crime figures overall led to the formation of the Regional Crime Squad. Coincidence? Maybe.

* * *

Goldsmith, Battes and Oakey were released from prison in 1966. Opinions vary considerably as to where they went and what they did, but suffice it to say, they vanished into anonymity, hopefully to live long, productive lives and to regain some of the happiness that had been snatched from them – admittedly, wholly or partly as a result of their own actions.

Detective Superintendent Ron Townsend was transferred on 10 February 1964, having served less than eighteen months at West End Central. He was posted to 3 District Headquarters and there he remained until his retirement two and a half years later, having served over thirty years.

And Detective Chief Inspector Harry Pike, having survived a nightmare four months at West End Central acting as Harry Challenor's nursemaid, retired on 5 December 1963. He had served twenty-six years with the police when he left aged forty-seven.

The Commissioner, Sir Joseph Simpson KBE, like the Home Secretary, came in for fierce criticism. In office since 1958, Sir Joseph was the first commissioner to have joined as a constable, in 1931. He had been a good leader, who introduced new crime-fighting initiatives and organised some much needed reforms in the police. So in the wake of the Challenor enquiry Sir Joseph should have sent out a firm message to the public that such malpractices would not be tolerated – but unfortunately he was not the most articulate of commissioners. The vocal, left-wing groups brayed their delight at his silence – and proclaimed that the enquiries had been whitewashes, which they quite conspicuously were not.

Harold Macmillan had already tendered his resignation as Prime Minister on 18 October 1963, due to ill health. The unrelenting pressure that had been brought to bear during his time in office had left its mark. The Profumo Affair had permanently damaged the credibility of his government, the Denning Report (like the James Enquiry) had been branded a whitewash and Macmillan felt that he had been hounded out of office due to a minority of backbenchers. And at about the same time the Assistant Commissioner (Crime), Sir Richard Jackson CBE, similarly resigned; his place was taken by Sir Ranulph 'Rasher' Bacon KPM. Prior to that appointment, Bacon had been Assistant Commissioner 'A' Department, having spent all of his previous service in uniform. Perhaps it was a portent of things to come.

Challenor – rather like James Bond – was regarded as 'a blunt instrument' to subjugate crime and criminals, and that was exactly what he did. Following his fall from grace, newspapers suggested that he had carried out 600 arrests during his career; and even allowing for press hyperbole, that number is not excessive, since it amounts to one prisoner a week on average. Which raises this point: if it is accepted that during his career Challenor did carry out that number of arrests, it was a very small percentage indeed who alleged impropriety. Of course, the fact that a small minority had suffered miscarriages of justice was bad enough and completely unjustifiable; but remember, the bulk of the allegations came flooding in *after* the charge against Rooum had been dismissed. Had there been other cases, given the enormous publicity which was generated before the enquiry – plus of course the eagerness which the National Council for Civil Liberties would undoubtedly have exhibited to take them on board – it would be reasonable to assume that they would have surfaced as well. But they didn't.

CHAPTER 18

Harry Challenor: Saint or Sinner?

O pinions varied about Harry Challenor. To the general public his name was mainly synonymous with a copper who was mad and who beat and fitted people up.

Mary Grigg, the assistant secretary of the NCCL, wrote a book, *The Challenor Case* (Penguin Books, 1965), which drew fierce criticism from A.A. Muir, the Chief Constable of Durham. 'This is a bad book, badly written, badly put together and it is a bad thing that it should be published with the apparent object of promoting the chuckleheaded pursuit of anarchy which seems to be the guiding principle of the National Council for Civil Liberties', he thundered. Mr Muir went on to say, 'In the author's eyes, all Challenor's victims are as pure as driven snow. If they have no previous convictions, they are obviously innocent. If they have previous convictions, they are victimised because of these convictions.' Mind you, there were many who must have thought that the chief constable had a point.

In the world of fiction, former police officer Bernard Toms wrote a novel, *The Strange Affair*, in 1966, which two years later was turned into a film directed by David Greene. In it, Michael York played PC Strange, who became involved with a girl (saucily named Frederika) played by Susan George and a mad detective sergeant portrayed by Jeremy Kemp. Strange went off to prison for corrupt practices and the sergeant was sent to a mental hospital. (This film had no connection with Robert Siodmak's psychological film-noir thriller, *The Strange Affair of Uncle Harry*.) The playwright Joe Orton lost little time in bringing to the stage his two-act play *Loot*, which was premiered on 1 February 1965. "Most people think *Loot* is a fantasy" said Orton, "but Scotland Yard knows it's true." In it, the brutal Inspector Truscott was allegedly based on Challenor, as was Inspector Potter, played by the actor Nigel Davenport the following year in Clive Exton's television drama, *The Boneyard*.

When the notorious safe-breaker and prison escapee Alfie Hinds successfully sued Harry Challenor's old boss Bert Sparks for libel in 1964, Sparks was seen to bury his face in his hands, and one of Hinds' supporters in the High Court's public gallery gleefully shouted out, "Watch out – he's doing a Challenor!" Like many of Challenor's prisoners, Hinds, who had denied blowing a safe at

Maples department store and claimed that he had been fitted up, was almost certainly guilty.

Derek Webster, who was a police constable on 'A' Division in 1966, recalled there being a demonstration practically every weekend, with the presence of the glitterati of demonstrators – Tariq Ali, Vanessa Redgrave et al. – and remembered officers still jocularly using the phrase, 'The biggest brick for the biggest boy!'

So how was the 'Challenor Case' viewed by the police themselves? Firstly, the greatest sympathy was universally extended to the three aids to CID who went to prison. Leonard 'Nipper' Read QPM arrived at West End Central as a detective chief inspector three years after Challenor's downfall, but as he told me in 2012:

> Nevertheless, it was still brought up in conversation when opinion was almost equally divided. On the one hand, his supporters felt that Harry had been shabbily treated and more could have been done to help him, although what form this could have taken, I can't imagine. Such people emphasised his war record and the success he had achieved when running the aids squad and felt, generally, that he was a great character. On the other hand, his dissenters thought he had brought considerable disgrace upon the service and bearing in mind his attitude and behaviour, more attention should have been paid to his supervision. These people always drew attention to the fact that some good budding detectives were ruined because of the influence exerted by Challenor, whilst he escaped almost unscathed … his behaviour was such that he ignored any attempt to insert supervision and his seniors looked only at his spectacular results with the aids squad.

Dick Docking said:

> He might be described as a 'man of his time' which fitted well with his role during the war and his experiences of it, but the war was over. Possibly, many thought that crime – and criminals who were engaged in it – meant that in some cases, it was still 'a war' that could be dealt with in the same manner, but things were changing and although it wasn't quite so 'politically correct' as now, certain methods of fighting crime were not really acceptable. The role and duties of a police officer have been changed by the politicians but in my view the principles laid down by Peel still remain the same and therefore we have to adapt and use whatever resources might be available to satisfy the justice system. It used to be said that

'the end justifies the means', but what happened to Harry Challenor proved the opposite for perhaps it permitted some who were not innocent to escape justice, and we had to adopt a more cerebral approach than the heavy-handed one which might have existed before.

Opinions were split as to Challenor's sanity. Some thought him certifiably mad, and one of these was Fred Burgum, who knew him as an aid to CID during the 1950s. "He was as mad as a March hare," he told me. Others – admittedly a small minority – thought him completely sane. However, Harry Challenor was not one of them. "I accept that I'm mad," he once said. "I don't say 'mentally ill'; that's a bloody silly expression. I'm mad and I get on with it". There is the possibility that because of his traumatic experiences during the war Challenor was a victim of post-traumatic stress disorder (PTSD); sufferers from this have often experienced an unstable family background and may have been severely punished during childhood. Whilst symptoms may emerge within a month of witnessing a traumatic incident, a small minority of sufferers might have their symptoms delayed for months or even years. A victim may have a state of mind known as 'hyperarousal', which manifests itself in being constantly aware of threats and can be accompanied by irritability, angry outbursts and difficulty in concentrating. A sufferer can also experience long periods when these symptoms are less noticeable; this is referred to as 'symptom remission'. However, these periods are often followed by an exacerbation of symptoms. Alcohol abuse can also feature. All of the above could have fitted the bill for Harry Challenor. But this was 1964, and the term PTSD was not formally recognised until 1980.

Others still believed that he was not as psychotic as he was made out to be. Dick Docking told me, "I don't think he was as bonkers as all that. He knew how to play his cards and he had a lot of people supporting him." This was a popular theory, and it suggests that influential people contrived to bring about the verdict of unfit to plead; although if this was indeed the case, it is difficult to say who provided this assistance. His senior officers? With the connivance of a number of doctors and psychiatrists? This is nonsense; their actions were authenticated before the enquiry even commenced. Challenor was a freemason – could there have been sinister links with freemasonry, which included the judiciary? One popular hypothesis was that his contemporaries from the SAS had engineered the verdict. But how, and to what end? Why would – and more importantly, how *could* – members of an élite army unit, completely divorced from law enforcement, judicial processes or psychiatry, wish to intervene? This, too, is nonsense.

The truth is much more prosaic and in line with the official version. Nothing was done, because there was nothing *to* be done – Harry Challenor was found unfit to plead because he was certifiably insane, and the three young police officers went to prison because they had been found guilty of a serious criminal offence. It was as straightforward as that.

Did Challenor have many friends? There were very few, it seems. Ken Rexstrew, maybe one or two others. "I liked Harold and he seemed to like me," Peter Elston told me. "However, we weren't friends. I don't think he had any friends; he was a loner." However, he was enormously respected. Some officers regarded Challenor as something of a saint; one (unnamed) detective chief inspector said, "Society didn't deserve a man like Challenor. He did his utmost for them and they sent him to a mad-house." And as Don Gibson told me:

> I had the honour and privilege of serving with 'Uncle Harry' at 'CD'. The villains walked the streets in fear of meeting Harry – it set their little hearts beating with terror, and we young aids glorified in being associated with Harry and his arrests.

Speaking metaphorically, Des Prendergast told me:

> To put it bluntly, he was turned loose in the West End and given a licence to kill. When things went wrong, he was encouraged to greater excesses, until finally the wheels came off big time. Then he was dropped like a hot potato and was given no support by those in authority.

And before I spent a considerable time speaking to Peter Jay regarding his memories of Harry Challenor, he issued a cautionary word, saying:

> A word of warning, though – I have nothing but admiration and sorrow for him. He was a war hero, a dedicated police officer and sadly he had a personality disorder that we did not recognise and identify. We thought he was an eccentric, never realising he was actually very ill.

Peter Jay's sentiments were echoed by an unnamed officer, who stated:

I felt desperately sorry for him. The bricks business was a sad state of affairs; Harry adored the aids who he worked with. The Guv'nors gave him too much work – but then, Harry was a workaholic. He was told to go to the West End and clear up the club scene; the villains were just running riot. He was a good, grafting sergeant; interviews didn't last long before he got a confession. Harry was desperately fit; he used to walk home at night – I saw him do it. He went back to his old SAS training to de-stress himself. I have to say that of all the CID officers I ever met, Harry was the one who influenced me the most. He was a great guy, a phenomenal copper and a very brave man.

During the trial of Oliva and others, Judge Maude had said, "No doubt the business of catching the wicked cannot be done with kid gloves," and these sentiments were agreed with by many, including John Simmonds:

One has to be aware that Soho was a jungle and the 'natives' had taken control. There were gangs of criminals who had taken control of the streets, there was a high degree of police corruption and the honest cop was virtually powerless. Harry was not to my knowledge financially corrupt, he was fearless and set about cleaning up Soho. The only way was to be brutal and deal with the villains in a way they could not fight; he took out the bad guys but not according to the Marquis of Queensberry rules. Despite that, the villains understood him and feared him; given time, he would have cleaned Soho up, and I am sure his motto would have been 'all's fair in love and war'. He was a fighting soldier and he saw a war on the streets of Soho and went into battle. If he had done this in Italy or Germany during the war, he would most likely have been given a bar to his well-deserved medal!

Putting matters succinctly, an officer who did not wish to be identified told me, "He did more to clean up Soho than anybody before him." That unidentified officer was right.

Norman 'Nobby' Birch told me, "Harry, being the man he was, was a 'hands-on' copper and not exactly a 'paper tiger'. I personally was proud to have known him, particularly with his military background in mind." Arthur Porter agreed with those sentiments. "There is no doubt his wartime experiences put him under a great deal of stress," he told me. "He was quite a likeable guy. I think some of the CID Guv'nors encouraged him to act the way he did, but it got out of hand."

And to a degree, Challenor agreed with those remarks about his wartime experiences. "When a man is obliged to spend months behind enemy lines and is taught to take a pleasure in killing," he once told a friend, "it is bound to leave some mark on his personality." This, of course, is indisputably true, and it may also be stamped on that person's physiognomy. In 1970 Police Constable Laurie Young was attached to West End Central's Clubs Office and he was with a colleague drinking in The Crown and Two Chairmen, a pub in Dean Street, Soho. He saw a bulky man talking to some other customers. "Know him?" asked Young's companion. Young didn't. "That's Harry Challenor," said the officer; Young had heard of Challenor, naturally, but this was the first time he had seen him. "He looked like an ageing hit-man," Young told me – and many would have thought this to be a fairly accurate description.

Then again, John Legge told me, "Harry was a character, a good thief-taker whose heart was in the right place." The way that things were in the West End of the 1960s was given an interesting perspective by Ken Neville-Davies, who was a probationary police constable at West End Central at that time:

I saw the world of Central London as being made up of the 'Good Guys', the respectable, hard-working, law-abiding, taxpaying citizens. Society had a fair number of 'Bad Guys', more often referred to as 'Villains', who were the opposite. It was the job of the police to protect the Good Guys from the Bad Guys. It was a bit of a game with rules that were never written down, but generally understood by all the players. A villain caught bang to rights goes before the Bench and pleads guilty, was the way it should have been done. The villain, the police and the Bench all know the score. However, there were occasions when the evidence was not as clear cut, the villain was still a villain and it was the role of the police 'to keep him in order'. The plea may have been guilty or not guilty; nevertheless, the Bench came to a decision and I am sure that they understood the rules, too. The police were the knights in shining armour protecting the Good Guys from the Bad Guys.

There were some very big Bad Guys operating in London at the time and a Big Strong White Knight was needed to protect the Good Guys. Enter Harry, the Champion with a proven history of winning. I cannot believe that the Guv'nors did not know how he operated. If I remember rightly, he did win initially but then went beyond the rules. I think then, that I saw him as a hero.

Let the last word go to David Woodland, who told me:

> Harry had a real hatred of thieves and was renowned throughout
> the Met for his occasionally somewhat unorthodox methods –
> with Harry, it wasn't a job, it was a mission, a one-man crusade
> to clean up Soho, and he was genuinely feared by criminals.
> Unfortunately, he was given his head, and the general consensus
> of all who had worked with him was that he was allowed to go
> unchecked when more should have been done to control his
> excessive enthusiasm. For this, his immediate senior officers
> should have been held responsible when it became increasingly
> obvious he needed medical treatment.

So Harry Challenor was a 'Marmite' character: either loved or
loathed. But although a huge amount of controversy about him was
promulgated – and to be fair, whenever the name of 'Challenor' is
mentioned, always will be – we must consider the official version of
his character, as laid down by the Metropolitan Police.

Harry Challenor was a police pensioner. Having served thirteen
years and two days, he had been awarded a supplemental annual
pension of £234 2s 7d, index-linked. It was paid to him religiously
every month, for almost exactly forty-four years. Unlike the three
aids to CID, who had gone to prison and who received no pension
whatsoever, Harry Challenor had never attended a discipline
board, nor had he been convicted of any offence or sacked. As
far as the pension department was concerned, Challenor was
simply a sick man, who had been pensioned off suffering from
paranoid psychosis. The only clue was contained in his Certificate
of Service, which, in the case of most officers, unless something
catastrophic had occurred, was normally marked 'Exemplary'.
But in Challenor's case the Commander 'A' Department had
authorised that the certificate be 'Open' – it merely showed that
Harold Gordon Challenor MM had served with the Metropolitan
Police from 24 September 1951 until 25 September 1964, and that
was all, with no reference to his conduct.

* * *

Like Julius Caesar, Harry Challenor 'bestrode the narrow world
like a Colossus'; and when he spoke, law-breakers trembled.

As Challenor once said, "Fighting crime in Soho was like trying
to swim against a tide of sewage. For every villain put behind bars,
there were always two more to take their place". It is possible
that Challenor saw himself as something of a philanthropist. Just

prior to his death, he was asked about his alleged use of 'verbals' – attributing incriminating admissions to prisoners upon their arrest. "I was only helping them to tell the truth!" he indignantly replied. For his neighbour Gordon Pugh the most fondly remembered Harry Challenor quote was, "I only ever lied under oath." But at the time of these utterances, it must be remembered, Harry Challenor was very mad indeed.

During the course of researching this book I encountered a number of stories about Challenor's conduct involving guns, gelignite and housebreaking implements which I decided not to include, firstly because they could not be authenticated, and secondly because it was highly likely that they were the result of 'Chinese whispers'. The truth – especially in the case of someone like Harry Challenor – could be stretched to such an extent that some of the stories surrounding him could be likened to the old army joke: the order, 'Send reinforcements – we're going to advance' is passed down the line, but by the time it reaches its final recipient, the message has become, 'Send three-and-fourpence; we're going to a dance'. So it was with Challenor; many of the stories became so distorted they were nonsensical. In this, Challenor was not alone; over forty years ago a story was circulated about me, to the effect that at the end of a week's attendance at the North East London Quarter Sessions, the senior judge Peter Mason QC, MC sent for me, showed me a flick-knife and said, "Now, look here, Mr Kirby; this is the third time this week I've seen this flick-knife in three separate cases and it's got to stop! Still, keep up the good work and come and have a glass of sherry." It was a silly story and one which was quite conspicuously untrue in all of its component parts: firstly, the only conversations I had with Peter Mason were within the confines of court. And secondly, although I dealt with large numbers of offensive weapon cases – beer glasses, bottles (both broken and intact), knuckledusters, coshes, chair legs (with and without six-inch nails protruding from them), open razors, a studded belt, an African spearhead, a homemade contraption involving nuts and bolts on the end of a chain rather like a medieval mace and a variety of knives (lock, pen, kitchen, Stanley and hunting) – I cannot readily recall a flick-knife being among them.

And yet the person who promulgated this daft story told it in such an authoritative, compelling fashion that it was accepted as being true at the time; and it would not surprise me to hear that there are people even now who still believe it. It goes back to what I said at the beginning of this book: was everything alleged about Challenor true – or was there a hidden agenda?

★ ★ ★

If the criminal element, the scum who now effectively run the streets, should read this book, they will laugh out loud with relief that they have never encountered anyone like Harry Challenor.

Present-day senior police officers will read this book – they will probably deny it, later – and at certain sections of it they will gasp and their eyes will grow as round as saucers, rather like small children who have been told a frightening fairy story out of the pages of Andersen or Grimm. And when they finish the book, they will expel audible sighs of relief that their careers have been cocooned in a police world of political correctness and diversity; a world where they have been taught that to use an expression as offensive as 'Father Christmas' is a double-whammy, because it is regarded both as an affront to non-Christians and a controversial gender issue. They will never have faced an angry man in their lives; their biggest concern in their ivory towers of make-believe police-land will be deciding how best to discipline the constable who has recklessly used the phrase 'as sure as eggs is eggs', since this expression would be sure to offend non-fertile women.

To reassure the nervous, puffy-faced senior police officers who will wonder if there is there anyone even remotely like Harry Challenor in today's Metropolitan Police or if there will be in the foreseeable future, I can assert with considerable confidence – there is not, nor will there ever be.

Whether or not that is a good or a bad state of affairs – you must be the judge.

Bibliography

CHALLENOR, Harold & DRAPER, Alfred, *Tanky Challenor – SAS and the Met*, Leo Cooper, 1990

CHALLENOR, Ex-SAS, Sergeant H. (Tanky), MM, *Without Dark Glasses*, Unpublished typescript, date unknown

COOPER, Johnny, *One of the Originals*, Pan, 1991

COX, Barry, SHIRLEY, John & SHORT, Martin, *The Fall of Scotland Yard*, Penguin, 1977

DARMAN, Peter, *A-Z of the SAS*, BCA, 1992

DARMAN, Peter, *Weapons & Equipment of the SAS*, BCA, 1993

DURNFORD-SLATER John, *Commando*, William Kimber, 1953

FARRAN, Roy, *Winged Dagger*, Collins, 1948

FIDO, Martin & SKINNER, Keith, *The Official Encyclopedia of Scotland Yard*, Virgin, 1999

FORBES, Ian, *Squadman*, W. H. Allen, 1973

GRIGGS, Mary, *The Challenor Case*, Penguin, 1965

HATHERILL, George, *A Detective's Story*, Andre Deutsch, 1971

JACKSON, Sir Richard, *Occupied with Crime*, Harrap, 1967

JAMES, Mr A. E., *Report of Enquiry, Cmnd. 2735*, HMSO, 1965

KELLAND, Gilbert, *Crime in London*, Bodley Head, 1986

KEMP, Anthony, *The SAS at War: 1941–1945*, John Murray, 1991

KIRBY, Dick, *The Guv'nors*, Wharncliffe, 2010

KIRBY, Dick, *The Sweeney*, Wharncliffe, 2011

KIRBY, Dick, *Scotland Yard's Ghost Squad*, Wharncliffe, 2011

KIRBY, Dick, *Death on the Beat*, Wharncliffe, 2012

LADD, James D., *Commandos and Rangers of World War II*, A David & Charles Military Book, 1978

LADD, James D., *SAS Operations*, Robert Hale, 1991

LANGLEY, Mike, *Anders Lassen VC, MC of the SAS*, New English Library, 1988

LAURIE, Peter, *Scotland Yard*, Bodley Head, 1970

MARK, Sir Robert, *In the Office of Constable*, Collins, 1978

MORTON, James, *Gangland, Vol. 1*, Little, Brown, 1993

MORTON, James, *Bent Coppers*, Little, Brown, 1993

MORTON, James & PARKER, Gerry, *Gangland Bosses*, Time Warner, 2005

MORTON, James, *Gangland Soho*, Piatkus, 2008

MURPHY, Robert, *Smash and Grab*, Faber & Faber, 1993

READ, Leonard and MORTON, James, *Nipper*, Macdonald & Co, 1991

ROBEY, Edward, *The Jester and the Court*, Kimber & Co, 1976

SLIPPER, Jack, *Slipper of the Yard*, Sidgwick & Jackson, 1981

SPARKS, Herbert, *The Iron Man*, John Long, 1964

STEVENS, John, *Not for the Faint-Hearted*, Weidenfeld & Nicolson, 2005

STRAWSON, John, *A History of the SAS Regiment*, Guild Publishing, 1985

SWINDEN, D., KENNISON, A. & MOSS, A. *More Behind the Blue Lamp*, Coppermill Press, 2011

THOMAS, Donald, *Villains' Paradise*, John Murray, 2005

THOMPSON, Julian, *War Behind Enemy Lines*, Sidgwick & Jackson, 1998

THORP, Arthur, *Calling Scotland Yard*, Allan Wingate, 1954

WARNER, Philip, *The Special Air Service*, William Kimber, 1971

Index